D1396718

338.973
R6625 Romasco
        The politics of recovery

                                870662

DATE DUE

FEB 29 '00			
DEC 21 '00			

THE POLITICS OF RECOVERY

The Politics of Recovery

Roosevelt's New Deal

Albert U. Romasco

New York   Oxford
OXFORD UNIVERSITY PRESS
1983

Library of Congress Cataloging in Publication Data

Romasco, Albert U.
   The politics of recovery.

   Includes index.
      1. United States—Economic policy—1933–1945.
   2. United States—Politics and government—1933–1945.
   3. Depressions—1929—United States.   4. Roosevelt,
   Franklin D. (Franklin Delano), 1882–1945.   I. Title.
   HC106.3.R578   1983   338.973   82-14499
   ISBN 0-19-503248-9

Printing (last digit): 9 8 7 6 5 4 3 2 1

Printed in the United States of America

For
Walter Johnson,
Teacher-Scholar,
and a rare spirit to boot

Preface

America's greatest economic depression—its most severe and
longest—lasted a decade, from 1931 to 1941. These years
spanned Herbert Hoover's first and last presidency, and the
first two of Franklin D. Roosevelt's four administrations.
Chronologically, at least, the Great Depression might properly
be called the Hoover–Roosevelt years. My purpose here is with
President Roosevelt's conduct on the dismal presidential stage
vacated by the defeated Hoover.

Roosevelt brought vibrant life, vitality, and an uncommon
human touch to the nation's most visible podium. The defeated
and the nay-sayers were brushed aside at Washington, and a
swarm of enthusiasts joined with Roosevelt to concoct a dynamic and spirit-lifting mélange of initiatives, legislative acts,
and federal agencies. This outburst was called the New Deal. It
is nearly fifty years now since Roosevelt was inaugurated as
President; and after a few days' grace, he inaugurated the New
Deal. In retrospect, the entire sweep of the New Deal, if it is
visualized as an object on the American historical landscape,
appears as a mammoth waterfall cascading with an endless din
and viewed with an enduring fascination.

My intention is not to swallow this waterfall, nor to drown
in it. I have chosen instead to contemplate what strikes me as
the core of President Roosevelt's leadership in his confronta-

tion with the nation's economic collapse and the economic policies he chose, or acquiesced in, to restore the nation to a prosperous state. The Great Depression, after all, was a devastating economic crisis, and its intended antidote was an economic program, or so it would seem. Reality, which might be thought of here as a small but vital part of a big waterfall, is not often what seems to be. This book is not called the economics of recovery; it is the *politics* of recovery. My object is to pursue the difference and perhaps cast in a clear light part of the landmark that was Roosevelt's New Deal.

I have been aided greatly in my work on this study by friends and colleagues, fellow historians, archivists, and librarians. I am particularly indebted to Vincent Carosso, whose knowledge of twentieth-century America runs as deep as his generosity in sharing his insights and research with me. His comments on the entire manuscript provided me with an invaluable sounding board. Paul Baker and Irwin Unger read an earlier, incomplete version (minus chapters IV, XI, and XII), and offered extensive comments. The early version was also read with meticulous care by Ellis Hawley of the University of Iowa, and Bernard Sternsher of Bowling Green State University. I am grateful for their detailed reactions and suggestions which served to guide me in writing the remaining chapters and the final revision. Tessa De Carlo subjected the manuscript to a careful and skilled copy editing. Much of the manuscript was written at the Highlander Research and Education Center at New Market, Tennessee, where I had the benefit of sharing political discussions with Myles Horton, Mike Clark, and John Gaventa. My research visits to the Franklin D. Roosevelt Library at Hyde Park extended from the directorship of Dr. Elizabeth Drewry to that of Dr. William R. Emerson. I am especially grateful to Joseph Marshall and Robert Parks for their patient assistance.

The manuscript divisions of Butler Library at Columbia University and the Federal Reserve Bank of New York permitted me to quote from the papers of George L. Harrison. I also wish to thank the staffs of the New York Public Library, economics division; the Library of Congress, manuscripts division; and the Bobst Library at New York University.

This study would have been inconceivable without the existence of the extremely rich literature which Roosevelt scholars have produced. The footnotes attest my deep obligation and reliance on them.

For my wife, Anne Lockwood Romasco, and our children, Calem and Senta, this book has been like a third child in the house, and I thank them for their kind consideration of it. As the first to leave home, we all wish it fair weather and good speed.

New York   A.U.R
October 1982

Contents

THE POLITICS OF RECOVERY

ONE

The Political Face of FDR

THE PARALYSIS THAT SETTLED over the American economy during 1930–31 turned out to be far more severe and prolonged than anyone had expected. The crisis in fact persisted throughout the entire decade, its solution eluding the prescriptions of Republican and Democratic politicians alike. Neither Herbert Clark Hoover nor Franklin Delano Roosevelt, nor the parties they led, was able to devise a generally successful economic recovery program, although the political consequences of their common failure differed dramatically. Economically the central consideration of these years was clearly the existence of protracted depression itself, while politically the foremost preoccupation was always the urgent necessity for action to promote recovery measures that would first restore national prosperity and then sustain it. Although economists increasingly spoke of the nation's intractable economic malaise as a deep depression, they continued to disagree among themselves in their analyses of both its causes and, more important, its cure. This absence of consensus among economic analysts was more than matched by the widespread disagreement among politicians regarding the proper policies needed to end economic stagnation. Yet politicians, functioning as they must in the exposed political arena, could not afford the luxury of detached theoretical speculation; temperamentally and professionally they required a

3

program of visible action that promised quick, tangible results. This recognition of the urgent political necessity for movement was most clearly evident in the political behavior of the dominant personality of the New Deal depression years—President Franklin D. Roosevelt.

Roosevelt's most notable public characteristic was his political finesse, his command of a wide variety of political techniques which he skillfully deployed and utilized to the full. In this, his natural element, he was an acknowledged master player. He has been variously described as "the champion campaigner" and "the master politician," but perhaps the most astute characterization of the essential man was Jesse Jones's comment that Roosevelt was "a total politician."[1] Jones did not intend this as a compliment, but his observation suggests the basic core of the Roosevelt persona as well as the fundamental nature of his leadership.

Roosevelt tended to define himself—something he seldom did—in deceptively simple ways. He was, he said, a Christian and a Democrat.[2] This seemingly forthright statement concealed far more than it exposed of the inner man. Roosevelt's contemporaries were left as perplexed as were latter-day historians in their search for a distinct personal philosophy to explain what made the man run. Taken at face value, his self-description offered broad, open generalities and an alarming paucity of specific content. Here was a nearly perfect cover for a political leader, an inscrutable shield against too-close scrutiny. Matched against Roosevelt's virtuoso performance during the New Deal years, his statement of belief explained nothing. Roosevelt was perceived as an extraordinarily complex personality: the array of traits cited ranged from Justice Holmes's dictum of "a first class temperament" to such qualities as charm, openness, deviousness, and demagoguery.[3] Still, during the 1932 campaign Walter Lippmann had expressed a widely shared view when he judged Roosevelt merely a shallow young man anxious to be president.[4] Such critics were confounded by the activist Roosevelt in the White House, by the momentum and scope of the First Hundred Days, by the magical lifting of the pall over the public mood and the call into being of a new spirit of hope.

4

The dramatic impact of the New Deal did not occur by chance. The national transformation was led and controlled by an unusually gifted political leader with finely attuned political perceptions—a prime specimen of Aristotle's political animal. Roosevelt, I would suggest, can best be understood as a complete, thoroughgoing political being, a man who saw his world through cultural lenses that were politically tinted and who, consequently, understood and dealt with both people and issues from a consistent, political frame of reference. When Roosevelt is viewed in this fashion, as a total politician, then his confusing shifts in tactics and policy, the contradictory twists, turns, and gyrations from one ideological position to another, even combining them indiscriminately, begin to assume a pattern of meaning.

Ideologically Roosevelt and the New Deal were a no-man's-land. Roosevelt's leadership and the New Deal had nothing to do with logic or consistency. Instead Roosevelt used his position of power to carry out what was essentially an exercise in political eclecticism; he drew freely from a wide and contradictory variety of ideological programs both home-grown and imported, and more often than not he used them simultaneously.[5] The resulting confusion was monumental and enduring: it provoked intense uncertainty and resentment among many contemporaries, especially in financial and business circles, and it inspired several generations of historians to search out some form of intellectual order and rational progression amid this ideological and programmatic outburst. From this enterprising search emerged several rationalized reconstructions of the New Deal's endemic disorder, attempts to tidy up the marvelous disarray into some comprehensible, rational, intellectual order: the First and the Second New Deal, New Nationalism into New Freedom, the shift from the left to the right, or vice versa.[6] One unfortunate consequence of these formulations was that they muted the characteristically freewheeling nature of Roosevelt's leadership; another was that they blurred the important fact that the New Deal was ideologically, if anything, a hybrid. More significantly, by obscuring the essential political eclecticism of Roosevelt's program they left largely unexplored the intriguing problem of why such heterodox methods were so peculiarly Rooseveltian, as well as the specific personal political uses Roosevelt made of this approach in the exercise of power.

A score of Roosevelt's intimates and advisers have recorded their recollections of Roosevelt's personality traits, his manner of dealing with people, and his methods of conducting public business. Collectively these accounts provide a valuable description of the president's style of work.[7] What emerges is the portrait of a genial, affable man with a ready smile, pleasant and outgoing and anxious to put his callers at ease. Roosevelt was clearly an accomplished and avid conversationalist, but in his talks with the varied host that trooped in and out of the Oval Office he had far more in mind than merely passing the time of day. For Roosevelt's principal means of learning was not through books but through discourse and conversation. His earlier talkfests with the members of his Brain Trust were only a more concentrated and systematic example of his habitual manner of acquiring a store of knowledge that might prove of use. As he listened to the ideas, the plans, and the panaceas of his visitors he nodded encouragingly, in apparent agreement. This particular mannerism, which subtly enticed his callers to speak freely, was deceptive in that it mistakenly convinced most that the nodding head signaled Roosevelt's agreement. But while Roosevelt thus avidly absorbed ideas, he thoroughly concealed how and when he intended to use them. He fully intended to retain personal command of the decision-making process. He kept his own counsel as he planned his political strategies; despite his openness to people and ideas, he selected and fashioned the information they provided to fit his own uses. Roosevelt, in short, typically bent these extensive, wide-ranging contacts to a political purpose.

And indeed, Roosevelt needed all the grist that he could gather for his mill, for what was at stake was nothing less than establishing and then maintaining his political leadership. Because of Roosevelt's initial dramatic success in winning enthusiastic public approval for whatever he decided to do, and his later ability to broaden his base of support, one is inclined to forget that had he instead faltered, there were potentially powerful rivals waiting in the wings with their own ideas and programs. The most obvious rival for power was the Congress it-self. During the interregnum following Hoover's defeat, Congress had thrashed about in hopeless, futile disorder, inca-pable of enacting even a portion of a recovery program. But this impasse was in large part the by-product of the tug of wills between President Hoover and President-elect Roosevelt over a number of issues which had in common the question of politi-cal responsibility—a responsibility Roosevelt stubbornly refused to accept until he came into office and power.[8] The ensuing deadlock on Capitol Hill did not, however, signify that this was a know-nothing Congress, bereft of ideas. In fact, Congress was seething with schemes and proposals for recovery, the most prominent of which was inflation in its many guises. Thus be-fore the special session of the Seventy-third Congress con-vened, it was at least an open question whether Roosevelt or Congress would seize command and shape the recovery pro-gram. And clearly whoever formulated the recovery policies would also be the locus of national power.

The prospect of a reckless Congress enacting an outright inflation-based recovery program terrified the business-financial community. It was primarily fear of this possibility that induced this powerful group to side initially with Roosevelt, looking to him to restrain if not control the Democratic Congress. Al-though the image of businessmen and bankers had been badly tarnished by the time of Roosevelt's inauguration, the low es-teem in which the public held them scarcely affected the real bases of their economic and political power. These stood nearly intact and, if politically unified, could represent either the most formidable support for or the most damaging opposition to Roosevelt's leadership. The configuration of that outcome hung upon Roosevelt's behavior and actual policies. Could he fore-stall or minimize what business leaders conceived to be threats to their interests and position? Recall that at this time ominous murmurings of revolution and dictatorship were being heard; the possibility of concerted movement by the financial-business-industrial class toward greater political control could not be dis-counted, and certainly was not discounted by Roosevelt him-self.[9]

Here then, in Congress and in the nation's business leadership, were two potential rivals to Roosevelt for control of the levers of power. There were others as well. American farmers had already long endured a sustained agony which had commenced considerably before the onset of the New Deal. Signs of rebellion were apparent in the farm belt, with plans for farm strikes and talk of marching on Washington. Roosevelt was particularly sensitive to agricultural discontent, and he had a politician's healthy respect for farmers' efficiently organized power, both within the Congress, through the farm bloc, and beyond Congress, in the activities of the national farm organizations. Roosevelt and his closest advisers gave the demands of the agricultural interests first priority. In fact, they took the position that general economic recovery hinged upon the prior recovery of the agricultural sector.[10]

Agrarian distress, which stretched back to the price collapse of 1920–21 and had become even more dire by 1933, was at least matched if not surpassed by the plight of the urban industrial masses after three years of unrelieved depression. But this, the nation's majority group, was badly handicapped by its relatively weak organized power. Organized labor, represented by the American Federation of Labor, had always constituted a miniscule portion of the country's workers. The AFL's membership had been further eroded by the counteroffensive of organized business in the post–World War I years, which used such devices as the "American plan," welfare capitalism, and red-baiting.[11] Three years of the Great Depression reduced its membership even further. Beyond the enfeebled American Federation of Labor, the vast majority of workers remained unorganized and, therefore, politically impotent. Since the workers' political visibility was scarcely impressive, they suffered from Roosevelt's initial indifference and neglect. It was more because of labor's low profile than Roosevelt's agrarian bias that industrial workers received scant consideration during the early New Deal. Roosevelt often spoke in these days of the danger of "marching farmers"; he did not mention marching workers.

In politics, as in love, the principle "out of sight, out of mind" applies. This was evident not only in the case of the politically invisible industrial workers, but in that of other neglected groups as well: consumers, tenant farmers, domestics, and the aged. When dynamic individual leaders of the politically outcast groups emerged nationally in 1934, they lifted their constituencies into the political arena and thus commanded Roosevelt's attention. The challenge posed by Senator Huey Long, Father Charles Coughlin, and Doctor Francis Townsend—and the mass misery they dramatized—demanded a rearrangement of priorities. In 1935 Roosevelt moved to neutralize the threat of these mass movements by what he regarded as politically acceptable measures. The operative principle here was to devise precisely the necessary concessions required to extinguish these incipient movements and cast them back into the political limbo whence they came. Had Huey Long lived, he would not have deprived Roosevelt of reelection in 1936, as Roosevelt and his advisers feared; but Long might very well have kept "the bottom third" politically visible and alive, and gotten for them more than the short rations they received.[12]

Recent critics of the New Deal have made much of the evident discrepancy between Roosevelt's noble, ringing words, his large, generous promises, and the meager results.[13] There is much truth in this, and one cannot deny the obvious disparity between what many understood to be the promise of the New Deal and its actual achievements and consequences. But if we mean to understand Roosevelt, it is necessary to tie this observation to the ever-dominant political motivation of his behavior. What, after all, was Roosevelt's purpose when he verbally lashed "the money changers" and "the economic Royalists," or when he castigated Hoover as fiscally irresponsible and proposed drastic government economy to achieve a balanced budget, or when he described movingly the plight of "the forgotten man" and pledged powerful aid for "the bottom third" of the nation? Two possible answers immediately suggest themselves: that Roosevelt did not mean what he said, or that he spoke sincerely but was unable to deliver politically on his promises. A third, more plausible reply would concede that Roosevelt meant what he said at the time he said it. That is, he was speaking, as he always did, politically, within the context of that time, to achieve specific, calculated effects: to encourage,

9

or warn, or appease or counterbalance the swirling, contending group interests he was determined to master and to control.

Perhaps a few illustrations will clarify the distinction implied here regarding truth, untruth, and political truth. Roosevelt, for example, could and did attack Wall Street, always a popular ritual, while he saved the private banking system of the country; he could rebuke selfish vested interests while he suspended the antitrust laws and permitted businessmen to fix prices and limit production. For that matter, he could continue to urge the virtue of a balanced budget while unbalancing it in an unprecedented manner, because even conservatives understood the political danger of allowing people to starve. If Roosevelt was hostile to business, then he seems to have confronted it with a little stick—and a big carrot. However one regards any president's version of political truth, justified subjectively as a necessary technique of leadership or part of the mechanism of public control, there remains in it an irreducible element of political expediency. It may well be that the political craft inevitably includes expediency among its essential tools. If that is indeed the case, then Roosevelt was a master craftsman. What is undeniable, I think, is that beneath the genial exterior, Roosevelt was always the tough, resourceful practitioner of power politics.

American politics was once pungently described by Harold Lasswell as the art of "who gets what, when, and how."[14] A corollary to this aphorism, more immediately related to the present subject, is that a politician can be defined as the artist who gives what, when, to whom. Art aside, the fact that government grants favors is certainly no new revelation. The difference, however, between Roosevelt's New Deal and prior administrations is both quantitative and qualitative. More and bigger favors were granted to more groups than ever before. But political patronage should never be confused with indiscriminate largesse; it is what social workers otherwise call discriminate giving. The Reconstruction Finance Corporation, for instance, although created by the Hoover administration, was transformed in the Roosevelt years into the world's most powerful bank. It dealt in billions and its major clients were banks, railroads, insurance companies, and, to a lesser extent, states, cities, corporations, and individuals. The RFC was merely one of a new host of government agencies servicing bankers, businessmen, industrialists, farmers, home owners, depositors—in fact, nearly anyone classified as either a property owner or the owner of capital. For those outside these charmed circles—the great mass of the nation's wage earners—the New Deal created a different species of patronage agency: one that dispensed minimum relief and minimal Social Security. The principal function of these institutions, as Frances Piven and Richard Cloward have demonstrated, was, to use their words, "regulating the poor." [15] Thus the common purpose running through all the New Deal's vast and elaborate patronage apparatus was to exercise effective political control and direction from the top, no matter how insistently it might be proclaimed by Roosevelt partisans to be "grass-roots democracy." [16]

Great wars have much in common with catastrophic national disasters, such as the Great Depression, beyond the destructive effects they both have upon individuals and the social fabric. In such times of intense turmoil and crisis, the slow and often deceptive process of acquiring self-knowledge is immeasurably speeded up, as cultivated surface conventions are stripped away. Individuals unadorned are revealed starkly to themselves and to their fellow beings. Not only strengths and weaknesses, but the best and the worst are thus exposed to view. What applies to individuals applies equally well to the larger society, its institutions and the complex of abstract processes through which it functions. In a democratic polity, operating within a free-enterprise, capitalistic system, these periods of stress provide us all with an unmatched illumination of the essential techniques, values, and principles which characterize its political process. The protective coloration of more normal, more affluent times is less distracting then, the barriers obstructing reality more easily penetrated.

This study, in its broadest sense, is concerned with the American political process and the nature and function of political leadership in a democratic society. It attempts to deal with these matters realistically—concentrating more on behavior than on words—to show them in the forced light of a prolonged, severe economic crisis: the New Deal years of the Great Depression. The central, commanding character in this account is Franklin D. Roosevelt—the dominating influence in that vital space where economics and politics intersect to determine public policy. The approach chosen to view these topics is not a comprehensive, chronological narrative of all that is comprehended by the New Deal. What is undertaken here is a more restrictive and selective focusing on the most crucial issue of these years: economic recovery. This, then, is an analysis of the politics of recovery. It concerns itself only secondarily with the important relief and reform components of the New Deal, that is, only to the extent that it is necessary to help us to understand further and more clearly the nature of New Deal politics and Roosevelt's leadership. In terms of institutions, the major preoccupation is with the Roosevelt administration itself, the Congress, and the business community. But since none of these groups functioned as a monolithic entity, the treatment is of the interplay, or the politics, among them as well as *within* them.

TWO

Anticipations of the New Deal

A DEEP DISQUIET existed among business organizations and their spokesmen as they awaited Roosevelt, for there were ominous signs of what businessmen could only regard as an impending public madness. Rumors of some undefined form of inflation were rampant in the land. Businessmen, who were ultrasensitive to this issue, feared their inability to forestall disaster after three years of depression. Fully aware of their own impaired prestige, they cast about anxiously for a sound and safe man to advocate their cause and protect them and their own.[1] The private sector, as represented by the nation's corporate-financial elite, seemed listless and sapped of vitality, incapable of providing the leadership to move the stalled economic machine off dead center. The counsel of the economically orthodox, whatever merit it might have had in more benign days, had by now entirely lost its credibility among a people dead tired of a depression that refused to resolve itself naturally, in accord with what some were pleased to call economic law. Indeed, it was past time for the government to step in to show the way out. But the government, as of March 4, 1933, was first and foremost Franklin D. Roosevelt, and for the business community especially, Roosevelt and the intended content of the promised New Deal were largely unknown factors, a matter for anxious speculation.

Throughout the preconvention and presidential campaign, there had been an insistent public demand for leadership, for forceful action, that often verged on the hysterical. Among seasoned political commentators, the usual tolerance for the politician's typical ploys reached a low ebb. They too yearned for exceptional leadership in this time of national crisis, and that required, they insisted, plain, unequivocal talk—the suspension of politics as usual. Roosevelt replied, in effect, that before he could lead as they wished, or govern, he had first to be elected.[2] That meant winning the nomination and the election in the usual tried and tested political ways. So Roosevelt regaled the nation with a masterful display of exceptionally adroit political footwork, joyfully dancing on both sides of every fence.

It has sometimes been asserted, particularly by the Brain Trusters and by some of his speech-writers, that Roosevelt arrived at the White House with a planned, coherent set of policies—a preformed New Deal ready to be implemented. They were men who took speeches seriously, and they insisted that, taking the preinaugural addresses as a whole, one could find there most, if not all, of what came in time to be the New Deal.[3] This large claim for Roosevelt's forethought and consistency (or that of his advisers) would have confounded contemporary Roosevelt-watchers. They had scrutinized those speeches with unusual attention in search of clues to what Roosevelt intended, and had concluded that they were tied together only by Roosevelt's desire to win. Nor were they amused by the political spectacle of Roosevelt's brilliant quarterbacking, now to the left, then off to the right or down the middle. Like most informed political analysts, they had scant respect for Roosevelt's leadership ability.[4] But if they were wildly wrong in their estimate of the man, they were essentially correct about the New Deal. When Roosevelt did arrive at 1600 Pennsylvania Avenue, he carried with him an imposing baggage of ideas from which he might pick and choose. But as to which of them he would actually choose to use, and how and when, that would depend primarily upon events he was yet to confront. Roosevelt at this time, just as later, scrupulously kept all of his options open. One consequences of Roosevelt's style was that it left businessmen, whose affairs required stability and predictability, in a state of suspended anticipation about the New Deal. They were reduced to guesswork about Roosevelt's recovery program. One obvious course open to them, one which they exploited energetically, was to affirm publicly their own economic credo in the hope that Roosevelt was listening and that he would attend to their proffered advice.

The American economy was already well established and mature by the 1930s, an intricate, complex industrial system which operated on a global scale. Clearly the nation's economic life was so vast, so diverse that it would be naive to expect that all businessmen thought alike on economic and political matters. Yet to comprehend the range of opinions held by businessmen, it is useful to start with a model of core beliefs—that is, broadly held ideas, attitudes, and assumptions. Once this climate of opinion is established, it will provide a useful reference point for recognizing the numerous variants in economic thought among business groups and, more important, the consequent diversity in their political behavior. The materials for such a model are abundant, since the business community was not at all hesitant about stating and repeating for emphasis its economic and political convictions. Both before and after Roosevelt's inauguration, business groups, economic forecasters, and business spokesmen were prolific in their commentary on Roosevelt and New Deal policies, on what was occurring, and, perhaps most revealing of all, on what they hoped and longed for as well as feared.

The political economy espoused almost as a matter of course by many spokesmen of the business community was grounded on a set of notions which can best be characterized as orthodox internationalism—a complex intermingling of the tenets of orthodox economic thought with the assumption that these required a world stage for their most efficient and profitable operation. Many businessmen, more than others in the 1930s, recognized the intricate web of connecting links between their own economy and that of other nations. The Great Depression was a worldwide phenomenon, and businessmen, who perceived it as such, judged governmental policies within the context of this larger perspective. At a time when economic nationalism was a strong current everywhere, and long before the crisis leading to World War II turned American public opinion and government policy away from going it alone, businessmen repeatedly stated and defended the essentials of an international recovery program. Economic recovery, if it were to be sound (and the qualifier "sound" was invariable), had to conform to certain specific political and economic postulates that remained deeply rooted in business thought.

"If I were dictator and could write my own ticket," Hoover's secretary of the treasury confided to two intimates in December 1932, "the first two goals which I would reach for would be the balancing of the budget of the United States Government and the return to the gold standard by Great Britain." Ogden Mills merely expressed here more forcefully and bluntly what many other business spokesmen firmly believed as well: a balanced federal budget and the return of all nations to the traditional gold standard were the two most crucial prerequisites for a sound and lasting economic recovery. These objectives were especially important now that Roosevelt was president-elect. Domestically, Mills predicted, "it is likely that a good many foolish experiments will be tried in the course of the next year or so. With the credit of the Federal Government firmly established and a balanced budget, we can stand quite a bit of experimentation. But," he concluded gloomily, "superimpose experimentation affecting the public finances on an unbalanced budget and you will so bring the credit of the National Government into question as to create a situation more dangerous than the one we faced a year ago."[5]

Mills's pessimistic private warning about the likelihood that Roosevelt would indulge in economic vagaries indicated that the speculation that Roosevelt was considering monetary and fiscal experiments rested on more than rumor. The subsequent breakdown of negotiations between Roosevelt and Senator Carter Glass, the conservative Virginian who finally rejected the proffered post of secretary of the treasury, was even more conclusive evidence of Roosevelt's unwillingness to make firm commitments to placate conservative elements, particularly if this closed off his options.[6] The anticipation that Roosevelt would break loose from orthodoxy was thus shared by others, but they, unlike Mills, expressed their concern more circumspectly in a public dialogue that aimed to set and hold the New Deal upon the proper track.

The most conspicuous public advocates of orthodox internationalism were the multinational financial and industrial organizations. For example, the International Chamber of Commerce, representing financial and industrial interests in forty-seven nations, urged an internationally agreed-upon recovery program that would resolve those issues which it viewed as choking world trade and, consequently, effectively frustrating all piecemeal, individual attempts at national recovery. It exhorted the commercial nations, in particular the United States as the world's chief creditor, to utilize the proposed World Economic Conference, scheduled to be held in London in June 1933, to undo much of the economic and political mischief which stemmed from the disruptive aftermath of World War I. The prescription offered was basically a negative undertaking—that is, the emphasis was upon *removing* existing obstacles to world recovery. The outstanding problems included some persistent, thorny holdovers from the 1920s: foreign war debts and reparations, chronic monetary instability, and an array of restrictions on foreign trade. The International Chamber's remedial program specified prompt debt settlement, the restoration of the gold standard, and a return to the free flow of goods in international trade.[7]

The American wing of the International Chamber reinforced the analysis of the parent body with its own report, a detailed international program for economic recovery. The report, proposed and supported by a blue-chip group of American financiers and industrialists, called upon all nations to start at the beginning by balancing their own budgets, largely through stringent governmental economy and increased taxation. Then at the World Economic Conference, upon which so much of the internationalists' hopes hinged, the principal commercial nations should reestablish the gold standard, fixing definite ratios among all national currencies. Of equal urgency was the necessity of abolishing all exchange controls—those numerous artificial devices used by some fifty nations in their frantic efforts to gain a trade advantage or to achieve the elusive goal of national self-sufficiency.[8]

A similar internationally oriented perspective characterized the pronouncements of the Bank for International Settlements. This organization, with its succession of American presidents, was regarded as "the major international voice for restoring the gold standard." In its third annual report, for 1933, it denounced those nations that were deliberately depreciating their currencies as a matter of national policy. The BIS's program emphasized the worldwide adoption of the gold bullion standard, the redistribution of the world's gold reserves, and the need for politically stable governments. It deplored economic nationalism, or what it described as "efforts at national self-sufficiency." This expedient, it declared, had only brought further deflation and stagnation. "The world," it concluded, "is at a crossroads and must shortly choose whether further to stake its course along the lines of closed national economies with reduced standards of living or to revert to the international economy. . . ."[9]

Closer to home, within the United States proper, the National Foreign Trade Council reiterated much of the message of the international economic organizations. Its seventeen-point program for reviving world trade—an objective it regarded as synonymous with world economic recovery—specified a government commitment to foster foreign trade, a prompt settlement of the pervasive foreign-exchange-restrictions tangle, and the adoption by all nations of reciprocal trade agreements. Domestically, it castigated the expedient of fiat money as an unmitigated national disaster and opposed isolationist policies such as the "Buy American" campaign. When a dispute developed over the wording of the final draft of its program, the council brought in Fred I. Kent, exchange controller at the Federal Reserve Bank of New York, to reconcile the plan with what were thought to be the preferences of the Roosevelt administration.[10]

The viewpoint of these organizations was in no sense exclusively American. Shared by internationalists elsewhere, it was in fact a commonplace among business spokesmen in Europe, especially those of Great Britain. Sir Walter Layton, editor of the London *Economist,* speaking to the British Chamber of Commerce, declared that "the *sine qua non*" for world recovery was political stability, since stable governments were essential if trade barriers were to be cut down, a development which in turn would permit the world economy to resume its normal functioning. Drastic tariff reductions were imperative—he specified a 50 percent cut to ensure success. He also insisted that the new gold standard must be so designed as to prescribe an automatic adjustment of domestic price levels to reestablish equilibrium, instead of allowing trade imbalances to be corrected by continued uncontrolled gold movements. The new gold standard, in short, must be made to function in actuality as the traditional gold standard was supposed to perform theoretically: that is, to provide an objective signal to financial authorities to implement changes in economic policy aimed at bringing the domestic economy in line with the dictates of the international gold standard. Under such a system, of course, much that was central to the early New Deal would have been expressly precluded. Purely domestic considerations, such as the objective of restoring the 1926 price level, would have been subordinated to international priorities and agreements.[11]

Among the most articulate and cogent expositions of orthodox internationalism were those offered by highly respected professional economists and analysts—the business counterparts of the political seer Walter Lippmann—such as Benjamin M. Anderson, Jr., and Colonel Leonard P. Ayres. Both men wrote and spoke regularly on all aspects of political economy, relating theory to practice in their close scrutiny and analysis of Roosevelt's economic leadership and the course of the New Deal. Anderson, an economist for the Chase National Bank, expressed his views fully in that institution's monthly report on political and economic developments, while Ayres, vice-president of the Cleveland Trust Company, put out a similar detailed critique in his bank's monthly *Bulletin.*

Anderson was a leading defender of the corpus of orthodox

economics, or what he ironically termed "the so-called old economics." For Anderson, the old economics was universal in its applicability, timeless in its validity, and infinitely profound in comparison with the shallowness and downright perversity of "the new economics." Under the latter category he included most of the economic theories used to rationalize so many New Deal experiments, among them economic planning, monetary inflation, price-level manipulation, the quantity theory of money, and economic stabilization schemes. The common element in all these programs was that each represented in varying degree an artificial, *political* interference in the economy to achieve one or another desired objective. With the attainment of the specified objective, the road to recovery would presumably open wide. In regard to all these theories, Anderson was a man of little faith; he remained an eloquent spokesman for the continued utility of orthodox economics. The specific content of that way of thought requires some attention, since it constituted the very bedrock of orthodox internationalism.[12]

Much of the commentary on orthodox internationalism by its adherents was advanced defensively, in support of a body of ideas that seemed to them under siege in the 1930s. The attack stemmed in part from the national reaction against an internationalism critically associated—in the 1930s at least—with America's allegedly ill-advised participation in World War I, while another major source of criticism was the frequent tendency of many to assume a cause-and-effect relationship between economic orthodoxy and the debacle which had plunged the high-riding New Era through the Great Crash of the stock exchange and into the Great Depression. Understandably, then, Anderson and others of like mind were at pains to vindicate their economic philosophy from the least suggestion of culpability for these disasters. In their minds, the only problem with orthodox economics was that its tenets had been honored more in the breach than the observance. It was the imperfection of man, not the failure of theory, that accounted for the economic collapse. Economics was not so much a dismal science as a persistently misunderstood, misapplied one.

Anderson justified the past performance of the old economics, in large part, by contending that the policymakers had the unfortunate but all too familiar failing of disregarding the rigorous *restraints* demanded by orthodoxy throughout the 1920s. "I think," he affirmed, "it can safely be said that there has been no failure of the old economics in this postwar period, because so little of what the old economics advocates had been done." In defiance of sound doctrine, tariffs, which were already "unduly high," were made higher still; trade barriers proliferated; excessively cheap money and credit policies fostered a speculative mania which was bound in time to burst, with severe repercussions; and the dampening effect of international debts on world trade could not be removed by repayment in goods and services because most nations, including the large creditors, were preoccupied with showing an export surplus with each and every one of their trading partners.

Anderson's catalogue of economic transgressions was merely a preliminary to the more essential task of restating correct theory and the sound policy that ought to have been followed by enlightened nations. This primer on the essentials of orthodoxy can be summarily stated. At the beginning and end of neoclassical economics there was some paraphrase of Say's Law and the logical ramifications derived from it. This central proposition stated, in brief, that the productive process itself generated the necessary purchasing power to absorb the entire output of an economy. Or, to quote Anderson's own exposition of this law and its significance:

> The old economics taught that there is no such thing as a general overproduction. It taught that the power to consume grows out of the power to produce, that consumption grows out of production. . . . The old economics saw purchasing power growing out of production, and it held that a good equilibrium among the various elements of production meant large aggregate purchasing power, which would take care of large aggregate production.[13]

Thus the proper starting point for economic recovery was to increase production—then and only then would all other desirable things follow in good measure and time, such as increased wages and higher prices.

This reasoning and the economic program it dictated were implicitly based upon the existence of an open international field of business operations where all nations, schooled in common principles, followed similar, compatible policies. But the nations of the world had, in recent years, backed far off from the ideal of a functional international economy of mutual benefit. Instead, economic nationalism had gained ascendancy as the expedient way to national economic recovery. The imminent danger was that this parochial ideology would soon win full command of the field. To avert this possibility, the orthodox internationalists needed some political means to bring about a change in the world's economic course. Many of them, including Anderson, saw their chance, or at least a glimmering of it, in the proposed World Economic Conference. "I am convinced," Anderson declared optimistically, "that, if the London Conference is successful in getting these trade barriers down, there will come a great rise in commodity prices throughout the world." Opening the road to recovery was thus possible only if emergent economic nationalism was decisively turned aside by a persuasive reaffirmation of orthodox internationalism. Sound principles, once publicly disseminated, would ensure correct policy.

The underlying purpose of influencing current political practice by the continual affirmation of established economic theory can be seen in much of the contemporary commentary on Roosevelt and the emerging New Deal. Many analysts were not primarily concerned with making factual reports on actual events; their accounts were more in the nature of ideological exhortations, distinguishing safe and sound policies from misguided, fanciful ones. This was a subtle way of educating the public, and particularly the public's elected representatives, in orthodox thought and practice. In this vein, for example, Anderson remarked, "It is important that we should recognize that the vast powers which our Congress is giving the President, in legislation adopted or pending, do, in fact, represent political compromise rather than consistent economic planning, and that the simultaneous exercise of all these powers would get us into hopeless chaos." Then came the veiled advice: "The President does not need to do all the things he has authority to do, and there is every reason for believing that he intends to do only those things which he believes to be necessary to get the business machinery working." Or, as Fred I. Kent, using the same didactic tactic, stated more baldly:

> Unfortunately in the United States the pressure of hardship has developed a demand for changes in our monetary system that our lawmakers cannot ignore. . . . The fact, however, that our lawmakers have had such an insistent and tremendous pressure put upon them to undertake inflation in some form or another has made it necessary for the protection of the people and the protection of our lawmakers for the President of the United States to have the full power to regulate questions having to do with our money placed in his hands. Thus lodged with the President, who has several times declared himself as being in favor of sound money, this power can be held without exercise while opportunity is given for industry to proceed toward recovery and develop a momentum that will result in general re-employment. By this process of legislation our people are protected from themselves. . . .[14]

This suggestion that Roosevelt was actively soliciting dangerous powers from Congress only to preclude their actual use provoked Senator Elmer Thomas of Oklahoma, one of the main proponents of inflationary policies, to demand Kent's resignation from his post as exchange controller at the New York Federal Reserve Bank.[15]

A more common tactic used to influence public policy was for business spokesmen to announce that the deflationary spiral had spent itself, that the economy had turned the corner, that recovery was already underway—all due to natural recovery forces. This was merely another way of saying that all artificial, political recovery measures were superfluous. Colonel Ayres, for instance, insisted that world recovery had commenced abroad just a year prior to Roosevelt's inauguration, and that after the American economy reached its lowest point in March 1933, recovery began here as well. The lesson this taught, according to Ayres, was that

> the great depression has forced enough of the essential readjustments to be made, and has resulted in creating sufficiently serious shortages of essential goods, so that industry, trade,

and transportation are expanding. In this country they are doing so with a vigor never before equalled. This recovery does not now need the additional stimulation of artificial credit expansion, great public works financed by huge Governmental deficits, bonuses paid to farmers, or the Federal promotion of irrigation and power projects. Business revival once well under way thrives best on a program characterized by a minimum of interference. What this country needs most just now is to be saved from its rescuers.[16]

Colonel Ayres was hardly unique in his conviction that most, if not all, of the New Deal should immediately be put into cold storage and forgotten. The Guaranty Trust Company of New York, responding to signs of recovery in July 1933, announced:

There is ample ground for the belief that the advance in business activity is due largely to natural factors in the economic situation and is capable of proceeding on a sound and normal basis without any dangerous efforts at artificial stimulation by currency manipulation, subsidies to special groups, or other forms of governmental interference.[17]

These judgments reveal the tenacious hold that orthodox economic thought retained on the minds of business leaders and spokesmen, as well as the persistent tendency among them to judge the economic policies of the Roosevelt administration in terms of a well-established, consistent body of axiomatic truth. They also demonstrate, perhaps more significantly, that businessmen harbored a deep and profound distrust of governmental initiatives. Typically, they spoke of government action as "interference," especially if the new venture encroached on the fields of economic and social policymaking. And all such initiatives promptly received the epithet "artificial." Theoretically, at least, there was a strong bias against a powerful federal establishment, a bias which extended to both the Congress and the presidency when either branch of government poached on the sacred preserve of the marketplace. It was inevitable that such a constricted conception of federal prerogatives and power would repeatedly collide with Roosevelt's large conception of his office.

Admittedly, we have been concerned here with a *model* of

expressed beliefs. Perhaps it might be better, for the moment, to think of this value system as a creed—that is, a complex of idealized convictions ritualistically voiced. The usefulness of such a creed, at least for our present purpose, is that it provides a readily identifiable reference point for measuring the varied distances from it that men's behavior took them. However, this creed, or model, has not been constructed for the purpose of fashioning a moral yardstick to show the inconsistency between affirmation and action among businessmen. Its justification is that it establishes a distinct marker on the business community's topographical map for differentiating the varieties of political behavior contained within it. The model helps us recognize the greater or lesser deviations that occurred from a well articulated system of values. Its primary utility, in other words, is to help in identifying what might be termed the deviant political behavior of the differing segments of the business community.

Orthodox internationalism was only one of many views among businessmen during the New Deal years. Many businessmen shared the prevalent attitude that economic recovery policies had to be devised within the domestic American context and not by international agreements affecting the world economy. In their view the first priority was to straighten out matters at home, and this required far more of a free hand than was permitted by negotiating international economic policies. However, even among the domestically oriented, the order of preference in choosing the objectives to be pursued further differentiated businessmen. Some became vocal exponents of monetary manipulation, while others were among the foremost advocates of structural reform of major segments of American business life. The underlying element among them, separating them sharply from the orthodox internationalists, was their common embrace of economic nationalism.

Economic nationalists, both within the business community and beyond it, in other circles, were politically ascendant during the years 1933 to 1935. As a consequence, President Roosevelt was initially much occupied with them and their demands. However, from 1935 to 1939 the balance shifted. The fear of economic and social chaos lessened while the prospect of a permanent institutionalization of the New Deal alarmed increasing numbers of businessmen. In this context, advocates of the ideology of orthodox internationalism took on new assurance and vitality. As they called many of the wayward back to the fold, including the Chamber of Commerce of the United States and the National Association of Manufacturers, conservative businessmen confronted Roosevelt with a new, broader challenge to his efforts to manage economic recovery.

THREE

The Politics of Maneuver

ROOSEVELT'S FIRST CONGRESS, the Seventy-third, was and remains one of the most celebrated Congresses in American history—celebrated for its unprecedented prolificness, some would say its profligacy, in managing to mold the chaotic outburst of ideas and schemes released at the special session on March 9, 1933, into concrete legislative enactments. It was equally celebrated for the intense criticism it generated, the abuse that was heaped upon it by distraught partisans of the American System and the old order, who felt that their idealization of traditional America was being recklessly subverted, thoughtlessly cast aside.

Ironically, however, the Seventy-third Congress has not been celebrated for what, after all, was its most notable achievement: the crucial role it played as Roosevelt's indispensable partner in the making of the initial New Deal. Without this Congress and the particular makeup which distinguished it, there would have been no New Deal, at least as we know it. Indeed, to state the issue in positive terms, the nature of the early New Deal was decisively influenced by the ongoing cooperation, rivalry, and spirit of bargain and compromise which characterized the relationship between Roosevelt and the members of this collectivity called the Seventy-third Congress. Roosevelt and his advisers did not present this Congress with a packaged New Deal. The New Deal evolved, and its evolution was the product of a protracted process—one distinguished by intricate maneuvering that not only produced a recovery program but established for the moment Roosevelt's tenuous political ascendancy over a volatile, often unpredictable Congress.

Among the more damaging criticisms hurled at this Congress by contemporaries was the repeated accusation that it had abdicated its proper legislative function, that it was little more than a rubber stamp for the Roosevelt administration. Roosevelt and his Brain Trusters, according to this view, had usurped the constitutional jurisdiction of the legislative branch by the new procedure of writing their own bills and presenting them to a Congress which dutifully certified them as legislative acts. In fact, the New Deal legislators were depicted as a miserable lot of camp followers who had wantonly conferred upon Roosevelt sweeping, dictatorial powers, especially in the realm of economic policy. But even here, where the sacred ground of free enterprise was deeply penetrated, there was no unanimity of response among the business community.

Predictably, the adherents of orthodox internationalism denounced this dramatic expansion of federal authority and executive responsibility with unqualified condemnation. No set of circumstances, not even the admittedly turbulent conditions of the domestic crisis, could justify to them the dangerous concentration of power in the hands of any one man. Others, less resolute in the faith, or perhaps more realistic, rationalized their acquiescence in the sudden enlargement of federal authority by contending that Roosevelt was far too wise and experienced a man to use the new powers lavished upon him. Still others saw the aggrandizement of the presidency as an unavoidable excess of the moment, the lesser of two evils—that is, a necessary maneuver to forestall the determined inflationists in Congress from enacting wild inflationary legislation and enforcing its implementation by mandatory provisions.

Thus a central issue that developed in the special session, and was to persist, was the proper way of defining the newly granted presidential powers: should they be made mandatory, or permissive and discretionary? This problem preoccupied not only the Congress but the business world especially. For the

members of Congress, one highly relevant aspect of the calcu-
lation was: did Roosevelt respond better to a nudge or a shove?
For businessmen, the issue was posed differently: could Roosevelt be trusted to hold vast, unchecked power without using
it, or if he were pressured to utilize it, would he make it innocuous? In either case, the outcome depended upon Roosevelt
himself, and on which direction he decided, or could be pushed,
to go. Conservatives hoped that Roosevelt might be persuaded
to hold a steady course, one that kept international priorities
and domestic restraints always in view, while other, bolder spir-
its urged him to veer to windward and travel fast with the impatient, hurrying crowd of inflationists.

The special session of Congress gathered for the first time
on March 9, 1933, and before it adjourned, on June 15, it had
launched the New Deal on what was soon recognized as peril-
ous waters. During this extraordinary session—the justly re-
nowned First Hundred Days—Roosevelt and the Congress
hammered out a broad program ambitiously aimed at achieving the combined effects of relief, recovery, and reform. Beyond these conventional designations, however, many of the
multipurpose acts were essentially distinguishable parts of a
single, gigantic preservation operation. The overall program
served, both in the short and long run, to shore up and preserve the basic institutions of a free-enterprise, capitalistic system by using extensive governmental support.

Among the major measures passed in this short span of time
were the Emergency Banking Act (signed on March 9) and the
Glass-Steagall Banking Act of 1933 (June 16), which respectively saved and then strengthened the nation's private banking
system; the Agricultural Adjustment Act (May 12), which supported farmers by attempting to raise agricultural prices by
controlling production, while in Title II, the Emergency Farm
Mortgage Act, it provided for the refinancing of farm mortgages with low-cost government credit; the Home Owners' Loan
Act (June 13); and the National Industrial Recovery, Farm
Credit, and Railroad Coordination Acts, all signed by Roosevelt
on June 16 and aimed at rehabilitating these economic sectors
and group interests with direct government aid. Beyond these,

there was the Federal Emergency Relief Act (May 12) and the Civilian Conservation Corps (March 29), providing, respectively, direct assistance and work relief to the unemployed; and the so-called Beer Act (March 22) and the Securities Act (May 27), which sought to restore vitality to two demoralized enterprises.[1]

This remarkably broad rescue effort was the end product of a congressional session that functioned somewhat in the mode of a spontaneous political happening. It featured complicated political compromises arranged by determined members who saw their opportunity to realize in law many projects which they had previously advanced unsuccessfully against conservative Republican opposition. With Roosevelt now in power, the old barriers seemed to soften. It is important, consequently, to know exactly what was traded off for what, since understanding this compromise process helps to identify the most energetic and strongest groups in the New Deal coalition. But it is also essential to pause a moment over those plans that lost out in the bargaining process, because they dramatize the unequal attention given those groups on the periphery of the New Deal, the less powerful or the badly led.

The complete collapse of the nation's banking system coincided exactly with Roosevelt's coming to power. The spectacle of commercial America with all its banks shut down symbolized the demonstrated failure of the old order not only to restore the nation's business prosperity but even to preserve its own vital institutions. The debacle also provided Roosevelt with a somber, dramatic setting for inaugurating the new order. Roosevelt, at this moment, held unlimited credit with the people and the Congress to try out and experiment with whatever was new about the New Deal, or whatever was old about it for that matter, as long as it promised some hope of good results. And Roosevelt possessed the will and self-confidence to exploit the opportunity presented him.

Banks and banking clearly were not Roosevelt's choice as his first order of business. They were given priority by inescapable events. Once in office, with authority and responsibility solely his, Roosevelt moved quickly to implement a bank rescue plan which he had previously refused to cosponsor with President Hoover. By invoking the authority of the Trading with the Enemy Act, a holdover from World War I days, Roosevelt officially closed the banks. This was merely a preliminary step to reopening all those banks certified to be sound, a procedure whose details were worked out by the new secretary of the treasury, Will Woodin, and Raymond Moley, the organizer of the Brain Trust, in collaboration with such Hoover lieutenants as Ogden Mills, the departing secretary of the treasury; Arthur Ballantine, undersecretary of the treasury; Francis G. Awalt, acting comptroller; and Walter Wyatt, general counsel of the Federal Reserve Board.[2]

The bipartisan bank plan had still to be legitimized by formal legislation, and this provided the immediate occasion for Roosevelt's decision not to await the regular session, scheduled to convene on January 1, 1934, but to call Congress at once to an emergency meeting. His original intention was to have the Congress meet for a few days to dispose of the banking problem and then recess. This would have permitted Roosevelt and his advisers more time to work out a full legislative program.

Instead, a major portion of the New Deal was enacted in the ensuing Hundred Days. The unplanned nature of Roosevelt's decision can be seen in an interchange of correspondence he had with John A. Simpson. Simpson, president of the National Farmers' Union, was angry over the failure of the House to accept his "cost of production" amendment to the Agricultural Adjustment Bill then being resolved in joint conference. He therefore reminded Roosevelt of their meeting on March 6, which included representatives of the Grange and the Farm Bureau. Simpson, who was scheduled to begin a series of meetings throughout the farm regions on March 7, assured Roosevelt that he would cancel his tour if the president planned to include farm legislation in the special session. "You told me," he recalled, "that the Congress would only be in session three or four days—just long enough to take care of the bank situation. Then they would recess for about three weeks."[3] In reply, Roosevelt wrote, "I hope you will realize that on Monday, March 6th, I acted in entirely good faith in telling you that probably

Congress would be in session only three or four days. Things moved so fast, as you know, that during the next two days it became obvious that other matters had to be taken up to meet the financial and economic crisis." [4]

Henry Wallace, who corroborated Roosevelt's reply, added a further reminder to Roosevelt of those hectic days: "It was, I believe, the evening of March 8 that Professor Tugwell and I talked with you about the possibility of something being done in the way of farm legislation. You suggested that we might call in the farm leaders." But by then Simpson had left Washington, and Wallace was unable to reach him by phone. Consequently, in place of Simpson, Wallace invited Congressman W. P. Lambertson of Kansas, the vice-president of the Farmers' Union, to attend the important meeting of farm leaders on March 10. [5]

This impromptu decision by Roosevelt and his advisers to extend the special session almost on the spur of the moment is an indication of the high priority the farm problem held in the Roosevelt administration from the very outset; it also reveals Roosevelt's supreme self-confidence, his readiness to play it by ear even in such a crucially important venture as the beginning of his legislative program. It provides as well a revealing insight into the unexpected ways in which the New Deal actually evolved by pushing through the crevices opened by chance.

The joint bank plan was transmitted to Congress as the Emergency Banking Bill; its near-instant enactment was a token of the pervading sense of national crisis and desperation. Congress was willing and eager in this initial encounter to suspend its rules and traditions to do something, anything, to get the nation's economic life unstuck and moving. The bill was presented by Democratic leaders without the customary committee hearings and reports, and it was voted on by members who had not even seen a printed copy. The House passed it in a record forty minutes; the Senate, always the more leisurely body, approved it that evening. [6]

Despite its evident merits as a reconstruction measure, the Emergency Banking Act involved results that did not appear to fit a recovery program. For this first bold step of the New Deal was an acknowledged deflationary move in its immediate consequences, since it effectively tied up $7 billion in deposits in those banks which were not considered sound enough to reopen. Eventually, however, some 95 percent of the funds in liquidated banks were released to depositors through the work of one of the many affiliates of the Reconstruction Finance Corporation, but that operation took time and was not completed until long after the immediate crisis.

Hard on the heels of this first deflationary act followed another, the Economy Bill, which sought to realize Roosevelt's campaign promise to balance the federal budget by initiating drastic cuts in expenditures. Specifically, Roosevelt proposed to slash the salaries of government employees by 25 percent, and to make a similar deep cut in the benefits paid to veterans and their dependents. This deflationary proposal was not greeted with the same broad approval as the banking plan. While businessmen were certainly lyrical in their praise of Roosevelt's fiscal orthodoxy and his courage in taking on the powerful veterans' lobby, there were clear signs of discontent in Congress. The congressional debate provoked, in fact, the initial signs of resistance and opposition to the conservative course Roosevelt apparently had chosen to follow, an attack led by such redoubtable champions of the forgotten man as Representative Wright Patman of Texas and Senator Huey Long of Louisiana. Despite this crack in Democratic solidarity, the opposition was surmounted and the bill became law on March 20.

In the meantime Roosevelt had turned his attention to his first priority, the farm problem. On March 16 he called upon Congress to unite behind the new version of the domestic allotment plan which M. L. Wilson of Montana State College had devised and which the president and Henry Wallace had accepted. Roosevelt had been unusually forthright in publicly endorsing this plan during the presidential campaign, even though few beyond the farm organization leaders understood what he was talking about.[7] The introduction of the administration's farm bill, touching as it did on the diverse interests of the farm spokesmen in Congress, presented Roosevelt and his congressional managers with a number of complex political problems.

33

The advocates of inflation, for example, saw an opportunity to reverse the deflationary trend of legislation by attaching a variety of drastic inflationary amendments to the farm bill. They moved with alacrity to seize that opportunity. Roosevelt tried at first to divert the minds of the legislators from heavy thoughts of inflation to the more convivial subject of beer by suddenly sending the Beer Bill over to Capitol Hill. The bill readily passed but the diversionary tactic failed, and the beginning of the long struggle between Roosevelt and the inflationists entered its initial, earnest phase.

In the Seventy-third Congress, Roosevelt was confronted with both the advantages and disadvantages which an overwhelming Democratic majority offered. The Senate tally was 59 to 37, while in the House the Democratic margin was even more lopsided, at 312 to 123.[8] The advantages of such large majorities are apparent. Roosevelt certainly had the votes, theoretically, to carry whatever measures he and his fellow Democrats might agree upon as necessary and good. The probability that the Democratic leaders in Congress would deliver the votes to Roosevelt seemed excellent. Roosevelt clearly had a number of things going for him beyond his own political talents—above all, the very fact of the persisting, deepening depression itself, which severely shook customary restraints and made men more receptive to new programs. In addition, there was the natural desire of Democratic partisans to help a Democratic president succeed, especially after the party's long years in the wilderness.

The disadvantages of one-sided party dominance in Congress, while more remote, were nonetheless real. One must start with the misconception that is fostered by the very use of the name "Democratic party." It would be more precise to speak of the Democratic parties, for the party label was a convenient umbrella covering a congeries of large and small factions representing different regions, diverse and conflicting interests, and the entire political spectrum from left to right. All these unwieldy components were held together under one designation, mainly by the uncertain glue of tradition and party loyalty. In actual fact, the Democratic party was a coalition party, and coalitions are never distinguished by coherence, unity, or discipline. The latent danger for Roosevelt here was that one or more of the party's factions, made bold by the top-heavy majority, might unite in support of alternative measures, or even devise an entire program of their own, leaving Roosevelt a leader without a following. Effective opposition to Roosevelt's leadership was, therefore, much more likely within the overblown Democratic party itself than in the official opposition Republican party, which the election had left decimated in strength and demoralized in spirit.

Roosevelt was well aware of the strong appeal that inflation exerted among members of Congress as the certain cure to the depression long before he confronted the issue directly in the special session. To ensure against any doubt on this score, Senator Elmer Thomas of Oklahoma, one of the most tireless, irrepressible inflationists around, took the precaution of reminding Roosevelt of his version of the inflationists' analysis shortly after the presidential election. "For some time," he wrote Louis McHenry Howe, Roosevelt's alter ego,

> I have been convinced that the major issue before not only the United States but the World, is the money question. We have arrived at a point now where a decision must be reached. Apparently there are two roads to travel—one a continuation of the three-year deflation process, wherein prices have fallen, security values have vanished, credit has been restricted; and a continuation of this policy will force further unemployment, further deflation and, eventually, wholesale repudiation.
>
> On the other hand we can follow the policy adopted in other countries, by increasing the volume of money in circulation, thereby restoring dollar values in commodities and securities. No one in responsible position favors a policy of uncontrolled inflation, but I am thoroughly convinced that sufficient money should be forced into circulation to bring the buying power of the dollar back to where it was when the vast majority of our $200,000,000,000 of massed debts were contracted.[9]

Thomas cited the advantage Italy, France, and Great Britain had gained by devaluing their currencies, and he pointed

35

out that the United States, with $4.5 billion of the world's $11 billion of monetary gold, was "dominating the financial policy, not only for this country, but for the world." The United States, in short, was largely responsible for the continued high buying power of gold. Consequently, foreign and domestic debtors, who had borrowed on a dollar worth 65 cents, were now confronted with a dollar worth three times that value. "I am demanding," he continued, "that additional money be forced into circulation so that money will become more plentiful, thereby cheaper, and as money falls in buying power, commodity prices and security values of all kinds will rise in proportion." Thomas argued that the cause of the Great Depression was deflation, its cure was inflation, and the proper place to start the recovery mechanism was by expanding the money supply. Roosevelt's recent election victory, he added pointedly, was "in effect . . . a declaration of revolution against the existing depression, and of course against the causes and policies which brought about such depression. A continuation of existing policies will lead the new administration on to the rocks." Senator Thomas's forthright advice was marked, top and bottom, with the handwritten caution, "Careful," "Careful"—an eloquent response.[10]

John Simpson, who minced even fewer words in advocating inflation than had Senator Thomas, his fellow Oklahoman, reminded Roosevelt of what he took to be the president's prior commitment to an inflationary program. "I recall, with pleasure," he wrote on April 3, 1933, "that you called me over the telephone during the National Democratic Convention in Chicago. I remember you told me, when I complained of the money plank that had been adopted by the Convention, that you would interpret it liberally and by liberally you said you meant we must have a dollar with less purchasing power." But the legislation of the New Deal to date, Simpson pointed out, was all deflationary in its effects. The American dollar still stood as one with an "extortionate purchasing power" that brought "destruction and repudiation" instead of permitting the people to repay their debts. The money problem clearly remained unresolved, and Simpson bluntly insisted that the time for the president to make good on his earlier commitment was now. "The money question," he stated, is the biggest and most important problem you will have to solve. All other measures will fail until such time as our monetary system has been intelligently revised.

You can not balance the budget. You can not make farm relief legislation work. You can not save the banks, the railroads, the insurance companies and other commercial and industrial enterprises with a dollar that buys four bushels of wheat from a Kansas farmer, ten bushels of corn from a Nebraska farmer or twenty pounds of cotton from a Texas farmer.[11]

Later, in June, Simpson congratulated Roosevelt on his decision to take the country off the gold standard as well as for his request for authority to cancel the gold clause in contracts. But while acknowledging that there was "some improvement in the farm situation," he added significantly, "I am also convinced that the thought of inflation is ninety per cent of the cause of this improvement. However, it is my firm belief that unless there is real inflation, instead of just fear of it, improvement will cease and we may even lose the advances we have made."[12]

These champions of the inflationary cause stated their case to Roosevelt with unusual bluntness, but they nonetheless represented the majority sentiment for some form of inflation which prevailed among farmers and members of Congress. Beyond this base, the inflationists gained further support and respectability by the lobbying work of a minority business group, the Committee for the Nation to Rebuild Prices and Purchasing Power, which initially claimed a membership of three hundred industrial leaders. Although it spoke for a dissident view in the business community, the Committee for the Nation was a vocal educational and propagandistic instrument for spreading the gospel of inflation. Its chairman, James H. Rand, Jr., head of Remington Rand, was a regular correspondent of Roosevelt's, keeping him informed of the committee's support of the whole gamut of inflationary proposals circulating within the government and throughout the nation. The committee provided Roosevelt with a running barrage of analyses, resolutions, and demands promoting such expansionary monetary measures as the abandonment of the gold standard, the Thomas Amendment to the farm bill, the Warren-Pierson gold experiment for raising commodity prices, the revived interest in the Goldsborough bills for stabilizing prices, and the commodity dollar plan that derived from Professor Irving Fisher's ideas, as well as other inflationary proposals designed to raise the commodity price level by monetary means.

The introduction of the administration's farm bill acted on the advocates of an inflation-based recovery program like a fire bell. As one critical senator remarked, "It's not a bill, it's a dream, a hope."[13] Still, it was the dreamers, not the critics, who commanded the stage. In public statements, in speeches, and in debate on the floor of Congress, the inflationists spoke out in vehement defense of their particular pet schemes for immediate recovery.

Senator Elmer Thomas proposed that the secretary of the treasury be authorized to issue what he called "prosperity notes" (better known to others as greenbacks), in amounts sufficient to raise the commodity price index to an average of the years 1921–28.[14] Senator William Borah (R–Idaho) expressed the widely held conviction, especially of the farm spokesmen, that effective farm relief and inflation were inseparable. "They come together logically," he informed the Senate,

> they are one and the same proposition. We must raise the prices of commodities or the farm measure will fail, and the only way to do that is by some means of inflation. All schemes of rehabilitating agriculture rest on raising the prices of commodities, and I ask you how you are to do that except by some well-thought-out and controlled form of inflation?[15]

Unless there was a decided improvement in prices, Borah predicted, Roosevelt's farm program would fail as surely as Hoover's Farm Marketing Act, and such a failure would be fatal to the administration's popularity.[16]

Senator Tom Connally (D–Tex.), in a speech that might have been given by any of the leaders of the national farm organizations, declared:

> Debts contracted when wheat and cotton and other commodities were worth two or three times their present value cannot be paid on the present basis of the gold dollar.
> Mortgages on farms and homes cannot be discharged on

dollars of present value. Unless the value of the dollar is decreased, foreclosures and bankruptcy will liquidate not only individual indebtedness but many banks, insurance companies, and mortgage companies.[17]

Connally denied that issuing greenbacks would increase the price level as long as the new money remained redeemable in gold. A more direct way of rising prices and ending the depression was to devalue the dollar by changing its gold content. He proposed to get to the base of the matter by reducing the gold content of the dollar by one-third. While conceding that this was "drastic action," he justified it by citing "the critical emergency" of the country, "the general welfare" of millions of debtors faced with ruin, and the need to recapture the nation's export trade from foreign countries who enjoyed the benefits of having already devalued their currencies.

In the House the inflation fever ran even higher. The Speaker, Henry T. Rainey of Illinois, announced publicly that support for an inflationary recovery program was very strong among the members, and he added, "Personally, I am a sixteen-to-oner, an old-fashioned Bryan silver man."[18] Later, in a speech at Rochester, New York, he predicted that legislated inflation was surely coming. Rainey then volunteered his own explicit endorsement of inflation by declaring, "There must be legislation for the debtor classes. They must be made able to pay what they owe and we've got to relieve them. We've got a revolution on in this country from Pennsylvania to Utah by farmers who will not allow foreclosure sales." Then, in a xenophobic aside, he exposed one of the many faces of economic nationalism by stating, "The United States is the victim of foreign nations who have out-generaled this country by their going off the gold standard, selling their goods to us for our gold dollars, then hoarding this gold in our banks by earmarking it."[19] The conviction that the United States was paying the piper for the economic revival of other nations by adhering to the traditional gold standard, and thereby sacrificing its own prospects for recovery, was a recurrent theme among politicians bent upon inflation.

The scramble to enact inflationary proposals took different

forms in the Senate and the House. In the Senate, the competing schemes were shaken down to four major plans, all advanced as amendments to the farm bill. In addition to Senator Thomas's direct expansion of the currency by the outright printing of unsecured greenbacks, Senators Lynn Frazier, Huey Long, and Burton Wheeler each sponsored his own preferred method to reverse the deflationary process, to lighten the load on the nation's debtors, and to raise commodity prices. Frazier (R–N.D.) proposed to concentrate directly on the farm mortgage problem as the most critical priority; his plan called for refinancing the entire farm mortgage indebtedness of $8.5 billion at the low interest of 1½ percent by issuing low-rate government bonds. The controversial inflationary component here was the proviso that should the bonds fail to sell, the government would issue paper money instead. That is, the likely outcome of this plan was an indirect $8.5 billion increase in the nation's stock of money, secured by nothing more tangible than the government's promise to pay. Long's amendment would allow the government to purchase silver at its current market value, paying the producers for it with silver certificates that would then circulate with all the privileges of legal tender. Senator Burton K. Wheeler (D–Colo.) championed the most popular program of all—the emotionally charged grand old cause of bimetallism, the remonetization of silver at 16 to 1.[20]

In the House, the surge toward an inflationary recovery program took the more disturbing form of a party split: the revolt of an inflationary bloc of Democrats, led by Wright Patman and Martin Dies of Texas, Terry Carpenter and Edgar Howard of Nebraska, and John Hoeppel of California, against the party leadership. The immediate cause of the split was the insurgents' dissatisfaction with the leaders' failure to bring forward any sort of inflationary program. Patman, the most active and vocal insurgent, was known as the father of the "Pay the Bonus Now" movement. His strategy was to combine the many different species of inflationists with the sympathizers of the veterans around the issue of an immediate cash payment of the bonus, an insurance annuity scheduled for payment in 1945. The inflationary aspect of this proposal was that it would have provided hard-pressed World War I veterans with desperately needed purchasing power and, incidentally, added approximately $2.5 billion to the circulating medium. It was imperative, however, for the success of this and other inflationary measures that the insurgents retain their ability to circumvent the party leaders' control of the flow of bills from the committees to the floor. Under the existing rule of petition, only 145 signatures were required to discharge a bill from committee and bring it to the floor for debate and a vote. Speaker of the House Rainey and the House majority leader, Joseph W. Byrns of Tennessee, now moved to close off this possibility as well as to tighten party control generally by proposing to restore the old Longworth rule, which required a majority, or 218 signatures, to discharge a bill from a committee.[21]

On April 18, fifty-nine Democrats met in a rump caucus to organize a resistance to the proposed change in the rule, which would require a two-thirds vote to carry. The caucus adopted a barbed resolution, presented by Patman, that declared:

> Resolved that we commend President Roosevelt for his efforts to restore the country to a prosperous condition; that we express our confidence in his leadership, ability and sincerity; that we pledge our allegiance to his program; that we especially commend his efforts for driving the big, powerful bankers from the United States Capital and depriving them of the special privileges enjoyed in the past against the general welfare.[22]

This slap at the big bankers was no incidental rhetorical flourish. Those in earnest about the money problem have invariably held a jaundiced view of Wall Street, and they have not hesitated to condemn the baleful influence exerted by the big banks. Patman and his followers were no exception. While Terry Carpenter, who had a bill proposing bimetallism in the House, attacked Will Woodin as a friend of Wall Street, Patman was busy behind the scenes preparing a more direct assault.

On March 16, Patman presented to Edward W. Pou of North Carolina, chairman of the Rules Committee, a copy of a resolution Patman wanted cleared for House action. He was proposing the creation of a select committee "to conduct a thorough investigation of the monetary, banking, and currency systems of the United States for the purpose of securing information for use as a basis for legislation to correct the defects and weaknesses of such systems." This committee was clothed with broad authority, including the power to subpoena witnesses, gain access to all pertinent bank books and documents, and obtain the full cooperation of all government officials. It was to report its findings and make recommendations during the first regular session of the Seventy-third Congress.[23]

Pou in turn immediately consulted Roosevelt, enclosing a copy of the proposed resolution. "It has occurred to me," he wrote, "that the resolution presents a question of policy of such importance that action upon the same should be determined by yourself." Then, in a revealing indication of Roosevelt's influence with the party leaders, that was also a measure of the barriers that faced any maverick, Pou continued, "Within the next few days a Steering Committee, created by the Democratic Caucus, will be ready to function. I told Mr. Patman that the resolution should certainly have the approval of the Steering Committee, and I feel that I am safe in saying the Steering Committee will be only too glad to cooperate with you. Indeed, I am sure any suggestion from you will receive the prompt approval of the Steering Committee."[24]

Roosevelt, confronted with what the House majority leader described as a "bad" situation, was advised to use the "big stick" to avoid the danger of an uncontrolled party, the complete blockage of the administration's legislative program, and, above all, an independent House-sponsored inflation program.[25] Henry Steagall of Illinois, chairman of the Committee on Banking and Currency, in whose committee major legislation was stalled, including the Federal Emergency Relief Bill, the Farm Mortgage measure, and the Glass-Steagall Banking Bill, was unwilling to be rushed by Rainey and Byrns in reporting out these measures. Steagall, insisting that the proposed bank bill include a provision for a 100 percent bank deposit guarantee, badly wanted—as did so many of his colleagues—some inflation. "I think," he announced, "there is a general feeling that there ought to be some form of expansion of the currency and I am in favor of it, and I hope we will have some inflation before this session adjourns." It was essential, he added, to agree upon "some plan under which the people can get a little easy money to do business with."[26]

It was these indications of a groundswell in the House for an inflationary program that propelled Rainey and Pou to close out one avenue leading to it by making the discharge rule more stringent. "Not in years," the *New York Times* reported, "has such a well organized propaganda been in operation as is now being used to press the passage of currency inflation." "The opinion is general," it concluded, "that under the rule as now in force, it is more than a probability that legislation, the passage of which might embarrass the administration, could be brought out of committee and to the floor, causing an open fight which might disrupt the party organization. This cannot be accomplished if the old Longworth rule is restored."[27]

These seething, as yet uncoordinated impulses in the Senate and the House posed two serious challenges to Roosevelt: the possibility that the Democrats would break loose from the tenuous control that he and the congressional leaders exerted, and the chance that, seized by an unchecked fervor, they might move rapidly beyond the president's cautious attitude toward inflation. Roosevelt responded energetically with a number of initiatives designed to assert his political control and to confine what Senator Joseph T. Robinson, the Senate majority leader, called "the delicate subject" of inflation to the safer confines of "reflation" or "controlled inflation."[28]

Roosevelt's efforts to circumvent direct inflation included meeting with the rebellious House inflation leaders; summoning the members of the Federal Reserve Board to Washington in an attempt to pressure the bankers to liberalize their credit policy and to increase the money in circulation; an ambiguous reference to an international gathering to discuss bimetallism; and the announcement of an administration plan variously described as involving "controlled expansion" or "indirect inflation." Roosevelt's alternative turned out to be a proposal for a large public works program, an approach to recovery popular in Congress but one that he had spoken distainfully of during the recent campaign.

Roosevelt's most direct and effective maneuver, however, was his dramatic announcement, on April 19, of an embargo on gold exports, thereby taking the United States off the gold standard. Here was unambiguous evidence that Roosevelt was shifting toward inflation, although it was not clear just precisely what his version of controlled inflation would entail. Since Roosevelt was pushed to this decision by mounting political pressure, it was reasonable to assume that he would attempt to hold to a cautious, limited policy of monetary expansion. Nonetheless, Roosevelt's action in cutting the dollar adrift from gold won him a badly needed respite. It gave him additional time to arrange a political compromise with the surging inflationary forces which were on the verge of uniting to enact their own recovery program.

Two days earlier, on April 17, the Senate defeated the Wheeler silver amendment by the narrow vote of 43 to 33 (23 Democrats and 20 Republicans opposed; 25 Democrats, 7 Republicans, and 1 Farmer-Laborite in favor). An indication of the rapid growth of inflationary sentiment is provided by comparing this vote with an earlier one, on January 24, when this same amendment was handily defeated in the Seventy-second Congress, 56 to 18. Actually, the ten-vote margin against bimetallism was deceptive, because certain Democratic senators who were publicly committed to inflation voted "nay" only after Senator Robinson explicitly announced that the president was opposed to the amendment.[29] The *New York Times* reported that "Senators . . . reiterated what they had said before, that if the advocates of various schemes could reconcile their differences they would find themselves in a majority."[30] In fact, the Senate inflationists were a majority restrained temporarily by loyalty to the president and the anticipation that Roosevelt would negotiate the issue with them.

The giveaway that a compromise was imminent came when Senator Thomas moved that the administration be given a "breathing spell" by the temporary withdrawal of all inflationary amendments to the farm bill. This cease-fire came at the express request of the White House. The Senate, in effect, would first wait and see what Roosevelt had to offer by way of inflation.

Roosevelt's decision to abandon the gold standard pleased the inflationists but merely whetted their appetite for more. Amid the general bipartisan approval expressed in the Senate, the doubting voice of Senator Tom Connally was most prophetic of things to come. He insisted that more had to be done to raise commodity prices, that eventually the gold content of the dollar must be reduced.

Prominent banking leaders, on the other hand, endorsed the decision with loud praise. J. P. Morgan "welcomed" the move, and added:

> It has become evident that the effort to maintain the exchange value of the dollar at a premium as against depreciated foreign currencies was having a deflationary effect upon already severely deflated American prices and wages and employment. It seems to me clear that the way out of the depression is to combat and overcome the deflationary forces. Therefore, I regard the action now taken as being the best possible course under existing circumstances.[31]

Morgan's endorsement was echoed by other prominent bankers. General Charles G. Dawes, former head of the Reconstruction Finance Corporation, declared, "It is the only thing that could be done and, in my judgment, it will have a good effect upon commodity prices. It will assist generally in the necessary readjustment between commodity prices and debts." Melvin A. Traylor, president of the First National Bank of Chicago, added, "Personally, I have been of the opinion for some time that the only way to equalize our exchanges with foreign countries was to suspend gold shipments."[32] "Congratulations on gold embargo," he wrote to Roosevelt. "You now have the aces in your hand. Good luck."[33]

The reaction of the business community was far more mixed than the pronouncements of these prestigious bankers would suggest. While the *New York Times* reported that "Midwest agriculturalists, industrialists, financiers and merchandisers" were united in supporting what they divined as the beginning of controlled inflation, New York itself was anything but united.[34] "Up to a few months ago," the *Journal of Commerce* remarked, "Wall Street was unified on currency policy. Its program was a balanced budget, sound gold standard money and credit expansion, if at all, through Reserve Bank purchases of Government securities and through R.F.C. aid to banks." The consensus on these fundamentals of orthodox internationalism was now shattered by the uncertainty about whether Roosevelt's move meant that he was now definitely committed to inflation. While Wall Streeters conceded the necessity of some monetary expansion, they justified it in a number of significantly different ways. For some, easier credit and a cheaper dollar promised expanded business, both in foreign trade and domestically. Others feared that an artificially cheapened dollar, while undoubtedly favorable to the export trade in the short run, might lead to disastrous competition—a descending spiral of depreciating currencies—among nations loath to lose their markets. The more politically minded simply pointed out that a controlled policy of expansion was tactically expedient since it might defuse the momentum for uncontrolled inflation. But whatever rationalization was used, it was becoming increasingly evident that Roosevelt was shifting his position away from his initial conservatism in order to assume the leadership of the inflation forces since, as the *Journal of Commerce* correctly remarked, "the other alternative he faces may well be the creation of a majority 'inflation bloc' in both houses of Congress that could spell the definite end of his leadership."[35]

The inflationary wind from Congress was indeed blowing hard when it could bend not only the chief executive but such seasoned stalwarts of orthodox internationalism as J. P. Morgan et al. But whatever hope Roosevelt and his business allies might have entertained of containing the congressional inflationists (now joined in the omnibus Thomas Amendment) by any tactical maneuver short of accepting the substance of their demands soon proved illusory. And the first to abandon illusions, if he had ever harbored any, was President Roosevelt.

Roosevelt's capitulation to the inflationists came with dramatic suddenness. On the evening of April 19, meeting with his close advisers Woodin, Hull, Douglas, Moley, Warburg, Feis, Pittman, and Bullitt, he told them that he had accepted the Thomas Amendment. They were appalled, but the decision had been made. All that really remained for them to do was to work out the details of the compromise.[36] The Thomas Amendment was quickly revised by an unlikely team, including Senator Thomas, Secretary of the Treasury Woodin, Undersecretary of State Phillips, Raymond Moley, Budget Director Lewis Douglas, and Senators James F. Byrnes (D–S.C.) and Key Pittman (D–Nev.).[37] Within two days the job was done. Now the administration's farm bill, with the agreed-upon Thomas Amendment, was presented to Congress as an administration-sponsored measure.

The revised Thomas Amendment, composed of four sections, provided for credit expansion through the Federal Reserve System by the traditional device of open market operations. The Federal Reserve Board was specifically instructed to purchase up to $3 billion in government securities to effect this objective. If the board failed or was unwilling to execute this policy, the Treasury was authorized to issue $3 billion in unsecured greenbacks to pay for maturing government obligations. This was another way of doing the same thing—expanding credit—but using unconventional means. The third provision, the most controversial of all, authorized the president, if he so chose, to reduce the gold content of the dollar by up to 50 percent. The last section permitted foreign debtors the option of repaying the United States in silver, valued at 50 cents an ounce, up to a total of $100 million (later amended to $200 million).

The Thomas Amendment was introduced in the Senate by Elmer Thomas himself, playing the improbable role of spokesman for an administration measure. His initial strategy was "to ask that it 'lie on the table' subject to being called up later." His intention was to avoid delay by circumventing the regular procedure of referring the measure to committee for a hearing. This tactic required a unanimous consent agreement, and both Senator Fletcher, chairman of the slighted Banking and Currency Committee, and the Republican minority leader, Senator Charles McNary of Oregon, objected. "This amendment," McNary insisted, "involves matter probably more important than any referred to the Senate in the last decade. . . . Senators should have the right to give important thought to such a measure." [38]

Senator Thomas, in his remarks on the amendment, hardly endeared himself to the conservative opposition or, for that matter, to the Roosevelt administration. "If the amendment carries," he announced, "and the powers are exercised in a reasonable degree, it must transfer $200,000,000,000 in the hands of persons who now have it, who did not earn it, who do not deserve it, who must not retain it, back to the other side, the debtor class of the Republic." [39] Furthermore, Thomas was convinced that the amendment rendered the administration's proposed farm legislation obsolete and unnecessary. "This amendment," he specified, "will put wheat back to the dollar price. We won't have to operate the farm bill. We won't have to use the mortgage refinancing features. This reflation will bring higher prices than would the commodity relief provisions of the bill. The rise in prices will solve the farmers' mortgage problems." [40] With such an ally as this, what had Roosevelt to fear from the Republicans?

"President Roosevelt's program for inflation," Senator David Reed of Pennsylvania, the leader of the Republican opposition, stated, "reminds me of nothing so much as a child playing with dynamite." [41] Later, he added a sober afterthought: "Anything Mr. Hoover was known to favor could not pass Congress. Now the circumstances are exactly reversed. We would pass Mother Goose through the Congress if Mr. Roosevelt asked us to." [42] During the debate on the Thomas Amendment, Reed mused that the best way to stimulate business would be to have Congress adjourn immediately. "We passed our emergency banking bill," he remarked, "we passed the economy bill, and for the thirsty we passed the beer bill. Our program properly was finished then. We have kept on going, with all this currency tinkering, until we have scared the business people half to death." [43]

Republican leaders, who consulted with the astute and articulate Ogden Mills for advice on formulating their strategy, expressed their principled opposition to inflation in general and to the Thomas Amendment in particular in a formal statement issued by Senators Reed and Wolcott (Conn.), and Representatives Bertrand Snell (N.Y.), the minority leader, and Robert Luce (Mass.), the ranking member of the Committee on Banking and Currency. It was an eloquent restatement by unreconstructed adherents of orthodox internationalism in its pure form, and it provides a convenient summary of the similar reaction of those in the business community who rejected expediency and the tactic of compromising principles in the hope of taming the inflationists.

"The administration's inflation bill," they began, "violates the most elementary principles of sound monetary, credit and financial policies. It is better designed to defeat than to promote business recovery." And those who would bear the burden of loss, they insisted, were not the well-to-do, "who are in any event best able to take care of themselves," but the wage earners, the salaried workers, and those on fixed incomes. Then, in a direct rebuke to those conservatives who supported the measure as tactically necessary, they stated: "It may be urged that the President will not exercise the authority granted. Then why does he ask for it? And surely those who are powerful enough to force him to agree to this legislation will be strong enough to compel him to make it effective." They criticized in particular the gold provision, declaring it was clearly unconstitutional. "But aside from the constitutional feature," they remarked, "it is unthinkable that there should be vested in any individual the arbitrary power to alter at will the value of money which so directly and vitally affects all human relationships, obligations, activities, rights and property." Inflation, they warned, would destroy business confidence and stability, and they invoked the well-known specter of the German experience after World War I as an object lesson in the frightful consequences of an inflationary program. In place of Roosevelt's misguided, dangerous policy they proposed their own program, which consisted of "cheap long-term money" to "encourage the revival of heavy

49

industries and the purchase of capital goods."[44] Despite this moving testimony in defense of orthodoxy, the Congress was listening to other voices, voices demanding that something more be done than echoing past wisdom. In response, the Democratic leadership prepared a steamroller to flatten the opposition to their determined swing toward economic nationalism.

In the Senate, the Thomas Amendment was given the right of way by the defeat of the Frazier Amendment, 44 to 25. The administration secured the silverites by agreeing to include in the Thomas Amendment a provision authorizing the president, at his discretion, to remonetize silver at some fixed ratio to gold.[45] On April 28 the Senate adopted the Thomas Amendment by a vote of 64 to 21. The attempt to attach an amendment providing for the immediate payment of the veterans' bonus, a proposal Roosevelt strongly opposed, was defeated 60 to 28. The farm bill then passed, 60 to 20.

The House leaders eased the way by a special rule limiting debate to six hours and prohibiting amendments from the floor. The House then voted 307 to 86 to accept the Senate's version of the Thomas Amendment. After a brief struggle in conference, occasioned by the futile attempt of the Senate conferees to attach the cost-of-production plan as an amendment, the bill was adopted and signed by Roosevelt on May 12.

Thus the tripartite struggle over inflation among business, the Congress, and Roosevelt was resolved temporarily by the compromised provisions of the Thomas Amendment. But this compromise, more significant perhaps than most others, was merely one of the many that characterized the so-called honeymoon period of the First Hundred Days. It demonstrated vividly what some historians have called Roosevelt's political pragmatism as well as the pragmatic nature of the New Deal. Among the other measures which Roosevelt and the Congress struggled over during the special session were the immediate payment of the veterans' bonus, the Frazier Amendment, the resurrection of 16 to 1, the guaranteed cost of production, a nationwide mandated thirty-hour work week, and a huge public works program suggesting a "compensatory spending" impetus to the economy. We shall return to these issues and their political resolution later, but it should be emphasized here that they all won, lost, or were compromised within the operative reality that was Roosevelt's particular brand of political pragmatism.

FOUR

Relief as Recovery

RELIEF OF DIRE ECONOMIC DISTRESS during the Great Depression has been portrayed historically in a variety of deceptively straightforward ways. In part, this was the outcome of the sharp differentiation that was made of New Deal policies; they were designed for relief, recovery, or reform. The New Deal thus became a trinity of distinct programs which were rationally categorized by their differing functions and institutional constituencies. When one spoke of recovery or reform, therefore, the reference implied institutions and occupational groups, that is, banking and bankers or industry and businessmen. Relief, on the contrary, meant individuals. This conjured up to critics a mental image not of the aggregate known as the labor force, but of dejected unemployed men kept afloat by federal subsidies in the form of either direct money grants or make-work projects. Above all, relief was regarded by critics as charity or, more commonly and pejoratively, the dole. For conservative opponents of the New Deal, the dole was an unwanted import from England, symbolizing to them the road to individual degeneracy and national decay.[1]

If one were to accept this invidious definition of relief, then the proper focus of a discussion of New Deal relief policies would be obvious. It would involve principally the Federal Emergency Relief Administration (FERA), the short-lived Civil

Works Administration (CWA), and the more permanent Works Progress Administration (WPA), with a sidelong glance at such related programs as the Civilian Conservation Corps (CCC), the National Youth Administration (NYA), and perhaps some of the activities of the Farm Security Administration (FSA). The commanding figure in this relief bailiwick was the highly visible, energetic, and controversial social worker turned government administrator, Harry Hopkins. It was he who headed successively the FERA, the CWA, and the WPA, and in the process he became, along with Rexford Guy Tugwell, one of the major targets of the more vitriolic critics of the New Deal.[2]

The limitation of this conventional definition of relief and its attendant policies is that it hides more than it illuminates of the nature of the New Deal, particularly the scope and meaning of its recovery program. For the term "relief," conceived as state alms to the indigent unemployed, conceals the sweep of the government aid that was actually given to individuals, groups, and institutions alike. Semantics aside, the Roosevelt administration undertook an unprecedented and gigantic rescue effort which in its full course ended up by aiding Americans and institutions of all sorts and conditions. As Broadus Mitchell's perceptive analysis recognizes, Roosevelt attempted to "socialize" the losses of individuals as well as those of financial and business institutions, thereby taking a momentous step beyond Herbert Hoover.[3] The implication of Mitchell's insight was not only that federal aid to the unemployed was as socially necessary and justified as that given to bankers and businessmen; it suggested also that the recipients of federal relief included far more than the unemployed. In particular, it included the very class that was most vehement in its denunciation of the dole.

The more realistic perception of relief, consequently, is one that takes account of all the elements of the extremely broad undertaking by the Roosevelt administration to sustain the basic fabric of the nation's economic system. Alvin Hansen, the distinguished Harvard economist, termed this effort a vast "salvaging operation"; and its beneficiaries included banks, railroads, insurance companies, large and small businesses, mortgage and real estate firms, cities and states, homeowners, farmers, *and* the unemployed.[4] In effect, New Deal relief through its spending and lending policies spread far and wide, pervading all the interstices of American life.

Beyond its broad reach, New Deal relief was also more than relief as it has been usually defined. Relief was also recovery, or, more precisely, it was an essential precondition for a recovery program. The major objectives of New Deal relief, therefore, were to end the devastating and crippling process of deflation; to lighten the intolerable burden of accumulated debt, which was made doubly unmanageable by impaired income and a dollar which had significantly appreciated in value; and to preserve the network of institutions that were essential to a functioning free-enterprise economy. The main anticipated results of a successful relief program included the economic preservation of both debtors and creditors and the financial institutions which served them, the reestablishment of business confidence, the unimpaired functioning of the credit mechanism, the resumption of an expanded production, and the temporary alleviation of distress due to unemployment. In short, the relief operations were designed to preserve the essential institutions of the free-enterprise system as a necessary prerequisite to its return to full recovery performance. Relief was thus phase one of the New Deal recovery effort.

It is perhaps now evident that the majordomo of New Deal relief was not Harry Hopkins at all. Hopkins, in effect, ran a subsidiary enterprise specializing in only one aspect of relief—the unemployed. Instead, the commanding figure in the broadest range of relief activities was in fact the Texas banker Jesse Jones, head of the Reconstruction Finance Corporation (RFC), the first among relief agencies. A brief account of Jones's stewardship of his expanding empire, the RFC, provides perspective on the wide range of New Deal relief policies, the distribution of federal relief, and the intimate connection between relief and recovery, and helps us understand more concretely the essentially evolving, makeshift character of the New Deal and its recovery policies.

By the end of 1937 Congress had greatly enlarged the authority of the RFC by amending it some thirty times.[5] This was, in one respect, a remarkable personal tribute to its director, Jesse Jones, and an acknowledgment of the powerful connections he enjoyed on Capitol Hill. Beyond that, it was a clear measure of his influence among leaders of the business community.[6] The continual process of expansion that characterized the RFC during the Roosevelt years eventually made it the world's largest, most powerful bank.[7] As Roosevelt attempted to patch one point of weakness after another in the economic system, he repeatedly turned to Jones and the RFC. In Jones he found a man ever willing and fully able to take on new responsibilities. These accumulating functions were often discharged directly by the RFC itself, or they were spun off either to established agencies or to newly created bodies designed to accomplish a specific objective, such as the Commodity Credit Corporation.

Jones described the extensive scope of RFC activities and its methods of operation in a speech during the early days of the New Deal. "It is our expectation," he explained,

> that the home-loan banks will soon relieve us of loans to building and loan associations and that the new Farm Credit Administration will take care of loans to Federal land banks, joint stock land banks, livestock credit corporations, Federal intermediate credit banks, and regional agricultural corporations.
>
> That will leave the Reconstruction Finance Corporation with banks, trust companies, mortgage companies, insurance companies, railroads, self-liquidating loans, and loans for marketing and exporting farm products.[8]

In subsequent years, the RFC extended its relief functions even beyond this formidable beginning; but at the outset, its first priority was to rescue and to preserve the banks.

Roosevelt's dramatic closing and quick reopening of the nation's banks in March 1933 successfully reassured depositors and ended the immediate panic runs on the banks. This was essentially a psychological achievement which, if it were to be sustained, required more concrete, long-term assistance to the banks. Before recovery could begin, it was crucial to restore the soundness of a banking system battered by three years of economic depression. To carry out this preliminary task, and permit the banks to resume their vital lending function, Roosevelt turned to the RFC. "The government needs the willing and confident cooperation of its banks," Roosevelt informed Jones, "and is willing to go into partnership with them on a limited dividend basis, permitting the banks to end the partnership at will, but in the meantime making it easy for them to furnish the credit necessary for the recovery program."[9]

Jones spelled out the specifics of Roosevelt's proposed partnership to the bankers. Referring to the banks' large losses, which required bankers to reduce their surplus, reserve accounts, and capital stock, Jones explained in a national broadcast on August 1, 1933, that "the Government is now willing further to repair these losses and in effect to carry the slow assets by the purchase of preferred stock in sound banks on a very favorable basis, thus providing additional liquidity for new loans while at the same time building up the capital account."[10] The government, in short, was now going beyond its established practice of making loans to endangered banks to a new practice of investing money in them by buying capital stock. One controversial consequence of this innovation was that the government, through the RFC, became a stockholder in banks and thus part of bank ownership and management. In this capacity, the government actively participated in the bankers' central function of decision-making.[11] It was this aspect of the Roosevelt-bankers partnership—rather than the bankers' repeatedly stated lack of need for additional capital—that provoked so much opposition from the banks. To overcome this hostility, Jones undertook a long campaign of persuasion aimed at gaining banker cooperation. He finally succeeded in October 1933, some seven months after Congress had authorized the RFC to invest in the capital stock of commercial banks and trust companies, when the officers of a prestigious New York City bank, the Manufacturers Trust Company, agreed to accept the RFC's offer of a $25 million capital investment.[12]

This transaction opened the floodgates and was the beginning of a large-scale relief operation that ended only after touching thousands of banks; in the process it restored them to a condition of financial soundness. The potential significance of this program beyond relief per se was aptly stated by Jesse Jones. "The completion of bank reconstruction," he remarked in June 1934, "will mean more perhaps, in sustaining recovery, than any of the emergency measures. Without a sound banking system and a strong banking structure, we cannot sustain recovery."[13] "It is my firm conviction," he later added, "that without the RFC's repair work in banks through putting capital into them, our entire banking system would have failed."[14]

On November 6, 1934, Jones wrote to his friend and fellow Texan, Vice-President John Nance Garner, reporting with satisfaction on the RFC's bank work. "We have almost finished the preferred stock job and loans to closed banks, having used approximately a billion dollars for each purpose. Now if we can encourage the organization of trust companies that will come to the relief of the real estate situation on some sound basis, with the least possible assistance from the Government, another important step will have been taken toward ultimate recovery."[15] By October 1937 the RFC had aided 6,103 banks by its capital investment program, using slightly over one-half billion dollars each for national and state banks.[16] In a speech to the members of the American Bankers Association in 1938, Jones bluntly told them how badly they needed this assistance. "Much has been said," he remarked, "about banks taking RFC preferred stock capital that did not need it, and, since we are being frank today, I might tell you that of the 6,119 banks in which we put capital, as far as we in the RFC have been able to figure, less than 20 banks in the United States did not need the capital they took."[17]

In addition to the RFC's twin policy of providing relief to commercial banks by loans and by capital investment, it also added a third method of aid with the creation of the Federal Deposit Insurance Corporation. A primary purpose of the FDIC was to provide a supplementary stabilizing device for the banks, preventing the reoccurrence of bank runs by guaranteeing the deposits of some sixty million Americans. While limited initially to $2,500, the guarantee of deposits was progressively enlarged subsequently. Nonetheless, the FDIC, which went into effect on January 1, 1934, had had a highly uncertain legislative career. Both its enactment and later its successful implementation owed a great deal to Jesse Jones's persuasive endorsement, congressional clout, and administrative audacity.[18]

Bankers strenuously objected to the proposed guarantee of deposits, using a variety of arguments against it. They contended that the experiment had been tried in the past by several of the states and that it had always failed. They also argued that such a guarantee actually functioned to encourage faulty bank practices by shielding incompetent bankers from the consequences of their mistakes. Perhaps closest to the bone, however, was the bankers' objections to the method of financing the guarantee.[19] While it was commonly understood that the FDIC meant a government guarantee of deposits, the bankers knew better. The burden of providing the funds for sustaining the FDIC fell most heavily upon the banks themselves. In establishing the original capital stock of the FDIC, the federal government contributed $150 million, the Federal Reserve banks put in $140 million, and the insured banks another $150 million. But thereafter the insured banks were subject to additional assessments as they were needed, and the size of a bank's levy was determined by the bank's total deposits, so that the large banks paid more, the smaller banks less.[20] Thus the FDIC was, in an important sense, misnamed. The guarantee was backed up, in fact, by the private banks collectively and not by the federal government.

This new demand upon the banks' resources occurred precisely at a time when bankers were obsessed with the idea of maintaining an inordinately high degree of liquidity, a means of self-protection they saw as being undermined by the FDIC. They feared that the large banks would be called upon to provide the funds to sustain weak, small banks; if a debacle like March 1933 reoccurred, the demand for additional assessments might drain their resources and break them.[21]

In spite of the bankers' heated opposition, coupled strongly with President Roosevelt's initial disapproval of the deposit guarantee proposal, its proponents finally prevailed in Congress. Jesse Jones played an instrumental part in this outcome. An early advocate who had supported a previous attempt to enact the measure during the Hoover administration, Jones joined forces with the equally committed vice-president, John Garner. In collaboration with Senator Arthur H. Vandenberg (R–Mich.), who proposed the plan as an amendment to the Glass-Steagall Banking Bill, they maneuvered it through Congress. It was signed into law by Roosevelt on June 16, 1933.[22]

The enactment of the FDIC, however, turned out to be the easier part of a difficult undertaking. Jones estimated that when the nation's banks were reopened by Roosevelt after the bank holiday, perhaps as many as 5,000 out of the 12,817 national and state banks needed further relief to make them financially sound. With the approach of the deadline for implementing the FDIC, scheduled for January 1, 1934, some 2,000 of these banks remained in what Jones wryly called "the hospital group"; that is, they were still unsound. Since the secretary of the treasury, Henry Morgenthau, had to certify that all banks participating in the FDIC were sound, it appeared that an unenviable public disclosure was inescapable. Jones resolved this crisis by boldly proposing that if Morgenthau certified these banks as sound, he would make them all solvent within six months. By Jones's own account, however, solvency was not achieved by all banks doing business until fourteen months after they had been officially reopened by Roosevelt in March 1933.[23]

In the course of successfully rehabilitating the nation's private banking system, the RFC loaned $2 billion to the banks and invested another $1.35 billion in their capital stock. In all, Jones cited a figure of $4 billion in aid to financial institutions.[24] With the banking system stabilized, President Roosevelt and Jesse Jones expected the bankers to begin serving as active agents of the administration's recovery program. To remove any doubts on that score, the president and Jones repeatedly exhorted the bankers to do their duty.

"Loans can and will be made," the president insisted in his message to the American Bankers Association in September 1933. "I want you to know," he added, "that we rely on your organization for its co-operation in furthering the free flow of

59

credit so essential to business enterprise." "Only if this is done," he emphasized, "can employers do their full part in the great recovery program now under way."[25] A year later Roosevelt appeared in person to dramatize his appeal to the bankers to participate actively in the recovery program through a more liberalized loan policy. He also attempted to assure the bankers that the government's deep involvement in lending was temporary, and that it would withdraw from the field as soon as the banks resumed the functions that had been taken on by the federal agencies. "And when that time comes," he stated, "I shall be only too glad to curtail the activity of these public agencies in proportion to the taking up of slack by private owned agencies." "The time is ripe," he concluded, "for an alliance of all forces intent upon the business of recovery."[26]

Jesse Jones added his persuasive voice to that of the president's in trying to win the bankers' support for the recovery effort. It was a voice that mingled encouragement with warnings that if the banks failed to perform their lending function, the government inevitably would be drawn further into the business of banking. Such a development might well advance what bankers wanted to avoid, a planned economy. Reminding the bankers of their primary economic role, Jones declared:

> In the nature of our economic system, the banker is the leader in practically all phases of business for the reason that he holds the credit purse strings. The activity of business and industry depends in large degree upon the measure of actually available current credit.
>
> There is no ally that [President Roosevelt] needs quite so much to achieve and maintain recovery as the banker. In fact, as I see it, if the banker fails to grasp his opportunity and to meet his responsibility, there can be but one alternative—government lending.[27]

Despite this plain talk, the bankers' disinclination to lend persisted, and this was widely resented. "The common cry almost everywhere," Jones told them, "is that the banks are not lending. We get it on every side. Your representatives in Congress continually get it."[28] Why then did the bankers ignore all these admonitions and persist in their reluctance to lend?

In part the bankers' problem was that the depression trauma had rendered them fearful and timid. They also faced a very thin demand for loans by equally fearful businessmen. But Jones exposed a further difficulty, an occupational trait, when he remarked that "bankers take themselves very seriously. They try to make their job as hard as possible, while lending is really simple."[29] A more basic factor perhaps was that bankers were habitually wary of government, or, as Jones put it, "bankers seldom like the way government is run." They especially disliked the way the Roosevelt government was run, a judgment that hardened over time. "One characteristic of bankers," Jones observed, "is that probably 95% of them don't like the New Deal, and while they would not intentionally 'cut off their nose to spite their face' . . . they naturally pull back."[30] He might have added that bankers were remarkably impervious to advice on how to run their business. Government advice was undoubtedly associated in their minds with government planning, or at least with the suspicion that one led to the other. In any event, Jones lacked the time for speculation; too many other relief problems were queued before his door requiring action. Foremost among these, in Jones's opinion any way, was the prostrated real estate market.

"The two big problems still confronting the RFC," Jones declared in October 1934, "are some necessary assistance to railroads, and the reestablishment of a nation-wide market for sound real estate mortgages." Of the two, he added, "real estate mortgages constitute our really big problem."[31] It was important, among other things, as the largest form of indirect investment by the American people. More than $35 billion was invested in urban loans of all sorts, while the Home Owners' Loan Corporation had another $3 billion invested in home mortgages. Among the investors heavily committed in this field were commercial and mutual savings banks, trust companies, building and loan associations, life insurance companies, and other institutional and individual investors.[32] As a result of the depression, this sector of business enterprise had gone into "total eclipse," and it remained immovably fixed there. "Even after the banking structure had been made sound," Jones later wrote, "and agriculture was again moderately prospering, and most of the water had been wrung out of railroad finances, the real estate mortgage market remained immobile, congealed with fear."[33] Jones's objective was to unfreeze these loans by bringing new capital into the business. New investment, he explained to the members of the Real Estate Board of New York, would "bring measurable relief to property owners needing funds with which to meet maturing mortgages, and to lend to distressed mortgage certificate holders; also to make loans for new construction where the new construction is needed."

This task required persuasion and federal funds. Specifically, Jones offered bankers and businessmen the same type of funding the RFC had used to rescue the banks, capital investment, but on even more generous terms. The RFC was prepared to match $25 million of privately raised capital with $75 million of government funds to establish mortgage companies. This relief venture, begun in 1934, went badly. In December of that year Jones told the members of the Bond Club of New York City that "we at the RFC have been trying to interest bankers and businessmen . . . throughout the country in establishing or rebuilding mortgage institutions, and I am ashamed to admit the lack of interest and cooperation shown."[34]

The inability of private enterprise to rise to Jones's challenge confronted the Roosevelt administration with what was becoming a familiar problem. Should the government allow an important economic function that was a necessary part of the recovery process to go under by default, or should it step in where business feared to tread? In a sequence that was often repeated, the government chose to proceed with the task by facing it alone. In the spring of 1935 the Reconstruction Finance Corporation Mortgage Company was created, supplemented in 1938 by the RFC-owned-and-operated Federal National Mortgage Association.[35]

The Roosevelt administration faced an identical problem, but in a more significant way, with the nation's commercial banks and trust companies. It was anticipated that the completion of bank relief would restore the bankers' confidence and result in active lending to business and industry. What occurred, however, was a demonstration that between relief and recovery there existed an intractable human gap. Frightened bankers preferred to invest in the safe and highly liquid securities of the federal government rather than risk their funds in commercial loans. While this created an exceptionally strong market for the offerings of the Treasury Department, it was counterproductive, to say the least, to the recovery program. Once again, when persuasion failed the New Deal moved forward into the very center of business enterprise by making direct loans to business and industry.

On June 16, 1934, the Senate and the House approved the administration's bill to authorize federal loans to industry, and the president signed it on June 20. The act permitted both the RFC and the Federal Reserve Board to provide loans for working capital to small and medium-sized enterprises on a long-term five-year basis, later changed to ten years. Initially the RFC had $300 million for this purpose, and the Federal Reserve Board another $280 million. By June 1939 the board, which operated under more restrictive provisions than did the RFC, had loaned $179 million, compared with $434 million by the RFC. By the time the United States entered World War II, the RFC had made twelve thousand such loans, for a total of $848,400,000.[36]

The RFC thus became by increments a great engine of relief during the 1930s. Beyond the activities detailed here, it is only necessary to cite a few additional facts and statistics to complete the story of the RFC's remarkable achievement. During the depression, the RFC loaned over $1 billion to 89 railroad companies comprising two-thirds of the nation's total mileage; it made $90 million in loans to 133 insurance companies; and it loaned another billion and a half to farmers. It aided cities, cooperatives, and individuals further by creating new lending agencies, such as the Export and Import Banks, the Rural Electrification Administration, and the Disaster Loan Corporation. In all, during the years prior to World War II the RFC lent a total of $10.5 billion.[37]

"No one," Jones recalled about the beginning days of the RFC, "had the faintest idea as to the extent that it would be called upon to assist business and banking—banking in every line—and our activities have reached . . . every citizen of the United States."[38] This large claim was no exaggeration. RFC relief spread out like a rippling wave in a quiet pond. In saving the railroads from bankruptcy and receivership, for example, the RFC also saved those institutions, notably insurance companies, which held the $11 billion in railroad bonds outstanding. In addition it aided localities throughout the country whose income included railroad taxes. Through this interlocking process, RFC relief effectively sustained the nation's property owners and its owners of capital. The only ones excluded from these benefits were those who held no equity in anything, not even a job. These were the folks who were ministered to by Harry Hopkins. It is instructive to compare the government's investment in its unemployed workers with the help it gave its RFC recipients.

In Harry Hopkins America's army of unemployed workers found a tireless champion, an eloquent public advocate, and a skilled political infighter. At the depth of the depression, which coincided with Roosevelt's coming to power in March 1933, there were fifteen million unemployed men and women. To meet this emergency, Roosevelt established the first of his unemployment relief agencies, the Federal Emergency Relief Administration, and he brought Hopkins from New York to head it. The FERA was, in effect, a middleman in the relief business, funneling a half-billion dollars from the federal government to the states and cities. These in turn actually administered the distribution of the funds by direct relief; that is, they made cash grants to those on the relief rolls. The government was thus coming to the rescue of the public welfare agencies and the private charity organizations, which had previously borne the brunt of unemployment relief, by supplementing their depleted funds.[39]

The needs of the unemployed, however, were far greater than this first venture was capable of covering. Hopkins, who foresaw a desperate winter for the unemployed, persuaded Roosevelt to create another agency, the Civil Works Administration, to take over unemployment relief for the 1933–34 win-

ter season. Unlike the FERA, the CWA was a federally administered program, and it used work relief instead of direct money
handouts. Four million unemployed were provided work at
minimum wages by the CWA on a host of created jobs
throughout the nation. It is a measure of the novelty of federal
work relief for the unemployed and the intense criticism that it
generated within conservative circles that Roosevelt ended the
CWA in the spring of 1934.[40] The problem, however, remained acute and came home to roost the next year.

It was then that Hopkins won his case with Roosevelt for a
permanent work relief program. That victory was publicly certified when Congress passed the Emergency Relief Appropria-
tion Act of 1935, granting Roosevelt discretionary authority to
spend $5 billion for relief. The Works Progress Administration
actually received only $1.4 billion of this sum, since Roosevelt
siphoned off the remainder to numerous other government
agencies. Yet work relief now was launched as a permanent
venture, one that provided desperately needed help for three
and a half million blue-collar, white-collar, and professional
people.[41]

The WPA, which was one of the early casualties of World
War II, eventually spent $10 billion for relief.[42] In retrospect,
it was among the best-spent billions of Roosevelt's New Deal.
This was approximately identical with the sum lent by Jesse
Jones's RFC during the same period. It is long past time to
bury the invidious distinctions which conservative contemporaries so readily made between Hopkins's relief and the relief,
by whatever name, that was delivered by Jones. Both were
functionally imperative, not only for the survival of their beneficiaries but also for the success of Roosevelt's larger purpose,
national recovery, and beyond that, political stability.

New Deal relief was thus a complement to the more explicit
recovery policies that were enacted during the First Hundred
Days. The failure of the recovery measures, particularly the
Public Works Administration, the Agricultural Adjustment Administration, and the National Recovery Administration, to
achieve the quick recovery that had been anticipated put great
political pressure on President Roosevelt to adopt more drastic

measures. He was especially concerned with the demands of farm spokesmen and the danger of social disorder that was threatened by the militant farmers themselves. It was in large part the need to buy time for his recovery policies to attain acceptable economic returns for farmers that prompted Roosevelt to turn to a series of monetary maneuvers for quicker results. It is the political expression of these monetary policies which forms the subject of the following four chapters.

FIVE

Economic Nationalism

"THE COURSE OF THE FIRST WEEK," Roosevelt confided to Colonel Edward M. House regarding the beginnings of the New Deal, "was almost automatically laid out for me because of the banking emergency but in spare moments, with the help of Lewis Douglas, who, by the way, is in many ways the greatest 'find' of the administration, I got the Economy bill launched and have followed it up with simple messages on one topic at a time." He continued:

> While things look superficially rosy, I realize well that thus far we have actually given more of deflation than of inflation—the closed banks locked up four billions or more and the economy legislation will take nearly another billion out of Veterans' pay, departmental salaries, etc. It is simply inevitable that we must inflate and though my banker friends will be horrified, I still am seeking an inflation which will not wholly be based on additional government debt.[1]

On the following day, April 6, 1933, Roosevelt wrote in a similar vein to farm leader and impatient inflationist John Simpson, "Please let me assure you that I am just as anxious as you are to give the dollar less purchasing power and farm credit more purchasing power."[2]

Roosevelt's remarks reveal his acute sensitivity to what contemporaries called the price problem—the imperative need to raise the price level, particularly commodity prices—and his hesitation and uncertainty as to the most expedient method of attaining his purpose. There could be no doubt in Roosevelt's mind regarding where his director of the budget, Lewis Douglas, stood. Within the Roosevelt administration, Douglas was among the most steadfast of orthodox internationalists, a dogged advocate of a balanced budget and a committed exponent of the traditional gold standard. Nor could there be any question about Simpson's credentials as an inflationist leader. Roosevelt's dilemma can be stated in two ways. How was he to raise prices and still honor his campaign pledge to balance the budget? Or, how was he to balance the budget and still meet his commitment to the farm leaders to raise agricultural prices? More simply, his dilemma was which way to go and whom to please: Douglas and the internationalists, or Simpson and the economic nationalists?

Characteristically, Roosevelt hoped to satisfy both groups and to achieve general economic recovery by devising a program which somehow blended inflation and a balanced budget. This explains the popularity of the euphemism "controlled inflation" within administration circles and, perhaps, Roosevelt's ready acceptance of the distinction made between the normal budget and the emergency budget. More important, this ambiguity accounts in large part for the initial confusion and outright contradictions of much of the early New Deal. Although Roosevelt did not explicitly acknowledge the contradictions between these two disparate approaches to recovery, or the fundamental differences that separated economic internationalists and nationalists, he was forced eventually to choose between them in the course of administering policy.

Roosevelt's first use of his presidential powers to influence Congress conformed closely to the maxims of orthodox internationalism. Congress responded to his bidding by enacting the Emergency Banking, Economy, and Beer acts. Conservatives, incredulous at this unexpected stroke of good fortune, were as delighted as doting grandparents with the first steps of the New Deal. The editor of *The Commercial & Financial Chronicle,* the purest among orthodox internationalists, was as unstinting in praising Roosevelt as he was soon to be in criticizing him:

> Few months in our country's history have been as epoch-making as March 1933, and probably never since our transition from an agricultural to an industrial state has such a gamut been run from paralyzing fear to renewed hope and encouragement. . . . The most impressive fact is the change in business psychology apparent today compared to that prevailing during the chaotic period of a month ago. Trade is still far from normal . . . but impressive steps forward have been made and it is once more possible to plan intelligently, to attempt to forecast future developments in industry with some degree of confidence and to renew belief in the institutions which have been our safeguard in past years.[3]

The Guaranty Trust Company of New York, commenting on the surge in business confidence in its March report, observed that "a large share of the credit for this truly notable record must go to the Federal Administration, which met the emergency with a calmness and vigor that inspired the people with the confidence essential to the success of its program." Businessmen, surprised and pleased, now spoke of recovery "with a new feeling of confidence in the essential soundness of the nation's financial structure."[4] The National City Bank of New York, in its monthly report for April, remarked with satisfaction that "it is demonstrated that sound measures, however drastic, will win the co-operation of the people."[5]

By late April this lavish acclaim was subsiding perceptibly, dampened by the uncertainty awakened by Roosevelt's compromise with the inflationists over the Thomas amendment. The gyration in business expectations induced by the headlong movement of Roosevelt's New Deal toward inflation was well expressed by the editor of the *Journal of Commerce*. "When Roosevelt promised in his inaugural address," he wrote, "to give the country a currency 'adequate but sound' it was taken for granted that he meant to maintain the gold standard and to pursue fiscal policies that would put an end to deficit financeering." As Roosevelt moved "to complete the deflationary cycle by the scaling down of fixed charges," businessmen were reassured. "It looked," he remarked wistfully, "as if the die had been cast in favor of policies essential to maintenance of a sound currency and a sound fiscal policy."[6] But where was Roosevelt now heading? In what direction would he set his administrative course?

On this score, businessmen should have been heartened—at least in the beginning. For Roosevelt, in addition to legislative conservatism, also followed a conservative approach in his initial administration of policy. This is particularly evident in the uses that Roosevelt made of monetary policy as his first method of raising commodity prices. And here, perhaps, a clarification should be made regarding the political alignments on the price problem. Business analysts, bankers, and businessmen were not opposed to the *objective* of raising the price level. In fact, they stressed the necessity of an upward adjustment of prices, citing approvingly Great Britain's commitment to this same objective. The political dispute arose over the proper *method* of arriving at a mutually sought-after goal. It was over the choice of methods that a deep political cleavage developed between orthodox internationalists and economic nationalists.

For conservatives the permissible monetary method for raising prices was to follow the traditional procedures of the past under the auspices of the Federal Reserve System.[7] These devices included lowering the discount rate at which the member banks borrowed from the Reserve banks, and the more potent procedure of undertaking large-scale open market operations. By buying government securities, the Federal Reserve System increased the reserves of the member banks, thus providing them with a base of excess reserves upon which to expand credit—the assumption was that the member banks would respond to excess reserves by expanding their loans to business. Theoretically, at least, if the Federal Reserve System, through its Open Market Committee, carried out a $3 billion open market purchase of government securities (as, for example, the Thomas Amendment stipulated), thereby increasing bank reserves by the same amount, actual credit might expand as much as tenfold, to $30 billion. No one, of course, expected that what was theoretically possible would actually happen in this precise ratio; but, depending upon the extent of one's fervor and conviction, more or less credit expansion was expected. The enthusiasts expected more, the more historically minded expected less.

The recent historical record itself was not at all encouraging. In summarizing the past failure of open market operations, Colonel Ayres stated:

> In 1930, the bonds held by the Reserve banks increased by 43%, but contrary to theory the loans of the member banks shrank by 7%. The results in 1931 were even worse, for the increase in the bonds was 12% and the shrinkage in the bank loans was 20%. In 1932 the Reserve System made a determined and systematic attempt to stimulate credit for the member banks, but again without success. The bond holdings were lifted 127%, but the bank loans decreased 21%.[8]

This disturbing discrepancy between optimistic theory and intractable performance was one of the realities of the Great Depression. Frightened bankers, worried about protecting their banks' liquidity, were simply not going to loan large sums to businessmen, who in turn saw little prospect of making a decent return on any investment. But since few, then or now, pay much heed to the past, theory and not history guided men's actions. Roosevelt was no exception. In his search for an effective and quick means to raise agricultural prices, he tested out once again the traditional monetary devices, without, however, closing the door conclusively on his future consideration of the more radical alternatives available to him in the Thomas Amendment should conventional methods fail.

Roosevelt's acceptance of the Thomas Amendment had been an obvious political compromise. As such, it did not signify that he agreed with the specifics of the inflationists' recovery program; much less did it guarantee that he would implement their proposals in policy. Like most political compromises, this one helped Roosevelt to avoid an impasse, or even an outright defeat, but it did not make him an instant convert to one set of policies. Nor did it mark a decisive turn in his course or that of the New Deal. It simply won him time, a political pause, during which he might puzzle out whose advice best fit his own political instincts, perceptions, and needs. For the advice that he was getting within his administration from his official advisers, as well as that offered by the ever-present entourage of unofficial ones, reflected in microcosm the struggle in the country at large between those imbued with either the international or the nationalistic persuasion.

In administration circles, the principal advocates of policies that conformed to orthodox international thinking were Will Woodin; Lewis Douglas; Dean Acheson, the assistant secretary of the treasury; Professor Oliver M. W. Sprague of Harvard, former adviser to the Bank of England and currently adviser to the Treasury; and James P. Warburg, a New York financier attached to the State Department as economic adviser. Their adversaries included Henry M. Morgenthau, Jr., a close friend of the president's and head of the Farm Credit Administration; George F. Warren and Frank Pearson from Cornell University; and James Harvey Rogers, professor of economics at Yale. These two groups of advisers, representing conflicting viewpoints and contrasting policies, particularly in regard to monetary matters, were engaged in a protracted struggle to win over the president to their respective recovery policies. The first public glimpse of this internal dispute occurred during the World Economic Conference which met in London during June and July 1933.

Here the internationalists clearly had the initial advantage. The mere fact that the conference met at all demonstrated that Roosevelt had not abandoned interest in the possibilities offered by an international approach to world recovery, that he had not, as yet, accepted in toto the nationalists' contention that the only place to start the recovery process was at home, and that an international meeting was merely another exercise in futility. In addition, the long interval of waiting for the conference to commence—from when it was first arranged by Hoover to the time it finally met under Roosevelt—permitted expectations to rise to an extravagant degree.

This waiting period was well used by internationalist-minded business institutions such as the International Chamber of Commerce and the Bank for International Settlements to publicize the importance of the meeting, to promote their own preferred agenda of issues, and to stress how crucially necessary it was for the assembled nations to arrive at an agreement on fundamental matters which would serve as the impetus to world recovery. Roosevelt himself did much to foster these high expectations by his invitation to selected heads of state to visit him in Washington for preliminary discussions. The ensuing procession of foreign leaders to the White House, in April 1933, generated additional drama and fanfare. It also gave a powerful boost to the hopes of American internationalists that Roosevelt was determined to resist the heavy political pressure put upon him by the economic nationalists.

In early April the Chamber of Commerce of the United States made it clear to the Roosevelt administration that it shared the assumptions and objectives of the internationally oriented business organizations. Henry I. Harriman, president of the Chamber, wrote a well-publicized letter to Secretary of State Cordell Hull, who was to head the American delegation to London, setting forth his organization's position on the priority items that required international agreement and cooperative implementation. These included the familiar roster of war debts, monetary instability, unbalanced budgets, governmental extravagance, and protective nationalistic obstacles to world trade. A new element in the Chamber's recommendations for removing these barriers to world recovery, however, was the stress it laid upon adopting a hard bargaining attitude toward foreign nations. That is, while the Chamber urged the government to make concessions, it demanded that the American negotiators extract a quid pro quo in return.[9]

The main American bargaining lever centered on the emotion-charged issue of the unresolved wartime debts owed to the United States. Here the Chamber suggested a horse trade. The United States was to agree to a modification of the terms of repayment, meanwhile continuing to acquiesce in the postponement of actual payments due from those nations which had already defaulted or were soon likely to default. In return, the debtor nations were to negotiate trade agreements with the United States and remove exchange controls, thereby permitting American producers a wider access to foreign markets "on a fair competitive basis." This preoccupation with opening up foreign markets was also the predominant factor in the Chamber's suggested use of the other bargaining levers which it saw available to the American negotiators: the continuation of American capital investments in foreign countries and the return of the United States to the gold standard. American agreement on these issues was to be contingent upon a willingness by European governments to remove exchange restrictions and other devices hampering foreign trade.

The American government was also exhorted to adopt a variety of policies all intended to provide assistance to the nation's businessmen in expanding their trade opportunities. These included the demands that American exporters be permitted to function outside the restrictions of the antitrust laws, and that the state cease its competition with private business enterprise—while at the same time the Chamber insisted that the government continue its subsidizing of the American merchant marine. The Chamber also requested that steps be taken to assist in stabilizing the price of silver, a suggestion addressed to all and sundry but most likely included for domestic political consumption.[10]

Not all internationalists were as uniform in their advice as these business organizations, or as consistently hostile to all ideas associated with the enemy camp of economic nationalists. Professor Jacob Viner, a University of Chicago economist who was soon to serve as an influential adviser to the Treasury under Morgenthau, tried to combine ideas associated with both groups. In specifying the minimum which needed to be accomplished if the London Conference was to succeed, Viner attempted the difficult feat of blending traditional objectives with what he termed "regulated inflation." There were four essential subjects to which the London conferees needed to address themselves closely, according to Viner. The first was to lighten "the weight on debtors and on the international monetary mechanism of the burden of international debts, private as well as public." This could be done, singly or in combination, by writing the debts down, by freeing world trade, or through an international agreement to raise prices. The second goal was a "substantial" lowering of trade barriers, while the third was another international agreement to halt "the process of deflation." Here Viner suggested that consideration be given to "proposals for a world-wide regulated inflation until a world price-level has been established at some specified level above the present one, and then for a general restoration of the gold standard, managed on an internationally co-operative basis." This last proposal actually extended to the entire world the nationalists' domestic price objective, without, however, specifying their preferred standard—the reestablishment of the 1926 price level. Finally, Viner called for "the restoration of international capital movements," purged of their recent abuses and regulated to avoid an excessive reliance on unstable, short-term loans.[11]

Viner, in his analysis and recommendations, took issue with the most conservative internationalists, the bitter-end deflationists, who argued that the deflationary spiral of the preceding three years should be permitted, even encouraged, to proceed on its downward course until it reached rock bottom. Presumably at that point the economy, completely purged of its weak and inefficient business-financial units, could go no other way but upwards. Instead, Viner favored a middle way—the alternative method of controlled inflation. But Viner was highly critical of Roosevelt's inconclusive posture regarding deflation versus inflation. "If," he insisted, "recovery is to be sought through price inflation, the Administration should say so, should reveal which of the many possible procedures it intends to adopt, and should indicate just how far it plans to go in this direction." It was precisely this kind of specificity which Roosevelt, committed as he was to administrative flexibility, was invariably at great pains to avoid.

The American delegation to London consisted of Secretary of State Cordell Hull, a lifelong apostle of lower tariffs as the cure to all the world's important economic ills; Senator Key Pittman, chairman of the Foreign Relations Committee and as single-minded as Hull in his own pursuit of a cure, domestic or foreign, for the problems that sorely beset the American producers of silver; Senator James Couzens (R–Mich.), the millionaire expartner of Henry Ford who, like Roosevelt, had the price problem on his mind; Samuel D. McReynolds (D–Tenn.), chairman of the House Foreign Affairs Committee; James C. Cox, the Democratic presidential nominee and Roosevelt's running mate in the 1920 election; and Ralph W. Morrison, a wealthy Texan.[12] Warburg went along as financial adviser to the delegation.

Roosevelt also sent to London two financial specialists to confer with foreign treasury officials and representatives of central banks on monetary matters. Professor Sprague and George L. Harrison, the governor of the Federal Reserve Bank of New York, were both high priests in the service of orthodox internationalism. While Roosevelt intended that in some way the discussions of the official delegates and that of the special mission of financial experts would be kept separate, he was no more successful in this than he was in his attempt to prevent all mention of the war debts within the conference itself. In fact, as it turned out, the tentative agreement on monetary stabilization, worked out by the central bank and treasury representatives, became the tail that wagged the dog, propelling the conference to an abrupt end.

Warburg, who assisted Sprague and Harrison in devising the stabilization formula, described the outcome of this conference as a "fiasco," while Raymond Moley, the head of the Brain Trust and Roosevelt's all-purpose adviser, in subsequent years argued the damning thesis, now widely accepted, that Roosevelt simply did not understand what was actually happening in London. According to Moley, Roosevelt piled misunderstanding upon mistake upon error, both before and during the conference, until the meeting was submerged by political ineptitude, intellectual confusion, and gross diplomatic bungling.[13] It should be recalled, however, that when Moley personally intervened in this affair by his dramatic trip to London, to be heralded in the European press as the "savior" of the conference, he came at the peak of his reputation as Roosevelt's most influential adviser. By the time he left London, after what Moley called Roosevelt's "bombshell message," which abruptly rejected the monetary agreement Moley had helped fashion, Moley had been personally repudiated and publicly humiliated. His self-esteem was shattered beyond public repair. Consequently, Moley's account of Roosevelt's naiveté and ignorance in this episode should be treated with the skepticism that is appropriately accorded any man who has been used as a sacrificial lamb.

It is undeniable, however, that the American delegates were a badly mismatched team, both personally and programmatically. Hull, an inflexible internationalist, was already dispirited by the time he arrived in London. He had expected to hold a strong hand in the bargaining for tariff reductions, in the form of legislative authority to negotiate reciprocal trade agreements. Instead Roosevelt informed him in midpassage that he had decided that the closing days of the special session were not an opportune time to push for new tariff legislation, which he feared would be divisive.[14] The issue of lowering tariffs or continuing the policy of domestic protection was another major dispute in the as yet unresolved struggle between internationalists and nationalists within the Roosevelt administration. Nor did Hull get clear and consistent guidelines from Roosevelt detailing the specific objectives of his mission. From first to last Roosevelt was oscillating between opposed policies, attempting to juggle them together into some form of synthetic harmony instead of making a decisive choice. Consequently, internationalists at London and elsewhere might well be pardoned their presumption in assuming that Roosevelt intended the conference to be a major factor in his recovery plans, that his explicit words of international cooperation could indeed be taken at face value as his settled purpose.

In retrospect, at least, Roosevelt's confusing, groping course during this time toward a resolution of the choice between internationalism and nationalism can be reconstructed. In April, Roosevelt took the country off the gold standard while Ramsay MacDonald was on the high seas to visit him for preliminary discussions. The unhappy Britons were faced with a fait accompli. Roosevelt's decision, prompted primarily by domestic political considerations, provided him incidentally with a new and strong bargaining chip in dealing with the British and the

French. Later in the same month, Roosevelt's acceptance of the Thomas Amendment equipped him with a whole new armory of monetary weapons.

On May 7, in his second fireside chat, Roosevelt made it unmistakably clear that he was determined to raise American price levels. "The Administration," he stated,

> has the definite objective of raising commodity prices to such an extent that those who have borrowed money will, on the average, be able to repay that money in the same kind of dollar which they borrowed. We do not seek to let them get such a cheap dollar that they will be able to pay back a great deal less than they borrowed. In other words, we seek to correct a wrong and not to create another wrong in the opposite direction. That is why powers are being give to the Administration [in the Thomas Amendment] to provide, if necessary, for an enlargement of credit, in order to correct the existing wrong. These powers will be used when, as, and if it may be necessary to accomplish this purpose.[15]

Roosevelt's commitment here was unequivocal. The "when, as, and if," however, indicated that he was still poised in uncertainty regarding the method he would use to achieve his goal.

But again, internationalists listening to Roosevelt's speech can be excused for thinking they understood Roosevelt's mind and assuming that he intended to achieve his price objective by international means. "I want to emphasize to you," the president stated in this regard, "that the domestic situation is inevitably and deeply tied in with the conditions in all the other nations of the world. . . . We can get, in all probability, some measure of prosperity return in the United States, but it will not be permanent unless we get a return to prosperity all over the world." The means to achieve world prosperity were then particularized, in international terms, as intimately tied to the realization of four complementary objectives of American foreign economic policy:

> First, a general reduction of armaments and through this the removal of the fear of invasion and of armed attack, and, at the same time, a reduction in armament costs, in order to help in the balancing of Government budgets and in the reduction of taxation.

Secondly, a cutting down of the trade barriers, in order to restart the flow of exchange of crops and of goods between nations.

Third, the setting up of a stabilization of currencies, in order that trade and commerce can make contracts ahead.

And, fourth, the re-establishment of friendly relations and greater confidence between all nations.[16]

But beneath the surface of Roosevelt's articulated internationalism, all was in flux. The push and pull on Roosevelt by his close and divided advisers, for example, was nicely summarized in two memoranda submitted to him for defining the objectives of the American delegation to London. Professor Rogers urged the cause of the economic nationalists, while James P. Warburg pushed the agenda of the internationalists and the State Department. These two memos reflect more accurately the president's unsettled state of mind than do his more coherent public pronouncements.

Rogers's memo of April 23 went to Roosevelt through Moley, and it proposed three major points for the American agenda:

1. That something be done immediately to get adequate purchasing power into the hands of ready spenders. Unless this is done very promptly, the dollar will recover to approximately par, the temporary impetus from the gold embargo will disappear, and a second banking crisis will become imminent.

2. That even inflationary measures (other than independent devaluation of the dollar, which is apt to start competitive devaluations in other parts of the world), to be effective, must provide for getting new funds to ready spenders.

3. That should drastic inflationary measures be utilized, their control should be carefully provided in advance.

Rogers conceived of these as a suitable vehicle to arrive at a number of definite objectives that would serve the American interest. Here he suggested specifically that "through some stimulus to business, raise world prices by an agreed upon percentage *and by no more.*" He also wanted the delegation to "secure international cooperation in major money and central bank policies," by which he meant an agreement for "international devaluation" of currencies with built-in controls for subsequent "credit expansion and contraction." His third objective was to start on "a long-run policy of gradual downward revisions of tariffs and of all other trade barriers." Most economic nationalists would strongly demur on this last policy objective even though it was couched in terms of the long run. As for that political and economic albatross the war debts, Rogers counseled "liberal concessions" in return for the cooperation of the debtor nations in his program.[17]

Warburg's lengthy memo was presented to Roosevelt as the "second draft of American policy on monetary and economic topics to be discussed in bilateral conversations and eventually at the Economic Conference."[18] A straightforward, uncompromising exposition of the major goals sought by orthodox internationalists, it included a pointed warning against any resort to economic nationalism. Warburg discussed six objectives, five of which involved monetary issues requiring international agreement and coordinated implementation by central bank and treasury officials. Warburg's monetary recommendations were a logical, integrated package deriving their substance and spirit from the status quo ante, the halcyon days before World War I. He called for promoting world monetary stability by establishing "a uniform legal gold reserve ratio for all the major countries." Warburg suggested a 30 percent ratio as the central bank bullion reserve. This was deliberately set below the existing average of national reserves in order to encourage a worldwide expansion of credit. "The United States Government believes," he stated, "that one of the most important things to be accomplished is to prevent a rushing about in the world of a large quantity of homeless money." To achieve stability, Warburg proposed establishing uniform buying and selling points for gold with a 5 percent spread, to replace the existing system of relying on the physical transport of gold in response to import and export points.

Silver, which was currently selling at the basement price of 27 cents an ounce, was to be assisted in a small, guarded way. The overall policy statement itself was hostile to the larger ambitions of the silverites: "The United States Government is opposed to any form of fixed-ratio bimetallism and is further opposed to any proposal for artificial raising of the price of silver, just as it is opposed to any valorization scheme in any commodity." But according to Warburg the government was not averse to suggesting means that might bring the price of silver more in line with the general commodity price level, something in the vicinity of 50 cents an ounce. This might be done by encouraging a limited monetary use of silver in subsidiary coinage, and by recommending its use as an optional, additional reserve of 5 to 7 percent above the 30 percent gold reserve. In effect, Warburg was proposing the creation of a modest market for silver. This was to be supplemented by an agreement among the major silver-producing nations to limit their output and by persuading the Indian government to refrain from dumping large amounts of silver on the market.

The three remaining monetary objectives, involving exchange restrictions, central bank money policy, and the gold standard, were presented by Warburg's memo somewhat in the form of axiomatic principles. "It is the view of the United States Government that it is in the interests of all concerned to remove all artificial exchange restrictions as soon as possible." This would require, as a necessary preliminary step, the reconstruction of the debt structure by scaling down national debts. The American government tendered its good offices in assisting the debt-burdened nations in their negotiations with both government and private creditors. The second proposition declared that "the United States Government is in favor of close cooperation between the various central banks in their money policy." Specifically, Warburg urged that all nations cooperate in coordinated central bank open market operations. The last proposition read: "The United States Government believes that the maintenance of an international gold standard in some form is an essential to world recovery."

Beyond these strictly monetary matters, Warburg proposed something akin to a worldwide compensatory spending program, or what he termed a "synchronized expenditure program":

The United States Government believes that the general price level cannot be raised except by means and measures which will ultimately restore the willingness of individuals to engage in the normal risks of trade and that this willingness alone can keep the industrial machinery operating at a point where the natural sources of employment provide employment for all requiring work. The United States Government believes that a continued process of paying people to do nothing without a program for the rehabilitation of industry and commerce must lead to progressively greater unemployment; and if carried to its ultimate extreme, must lead to strangulation of industry by inordinate taxation, the strangulation of imports to protect threatened budgets, the ultimate unbalancing of budgets, with the final result of uncontrolled inflation and complete chaos.

The sound means of raising prices, according to Warburg, included clearing "the channels of international trade," and a two- to four-year coordinated plan of simultaneous national expenditures to stimulate reemployment. This could be done "either by direct Government expenditure or in the form of subsidies to private interests."[19]

Most of what Warburg recommended to the president had been said before, and it would be repeated endlessly by publicists, economic analysts, academic economists, bankers, industrialists, corporate leaders, and conservative politicians, but seldom was it stated with such clarity. The notable exception to the pervading international and orthodox tenor of Warburg's advice was his endorsement of the Keynesian emphasis on public spending to compensate for the insufficient level of private expenditure, a notion which orthodox internationalists would soon combat with the same tenacity they showed in their long fight against inflationist proposals.

In mid-May Roosevelt cabled a message to the European governments on disarmament, including, incidentally, his thoughts on his monetary plans for the London Conference. "The Conference," the president recommended emphatically, "must establish order in place of the present chaos by a stabilization of currencies, by freeing the flow of world trade, and by international action to raise price levels."[20] It was such internationalist statements as these which led Neville Chamberlain, the British chancellor of the exchequer, to remark later in a speech to the House of Commons that Roosevelt had had a major change of mind during the course of the conference itself. "There came a time in the United States," Chamberlain astutely observed, "when public sentiment closely connected the depreciation of the dollar with the rise of commodity prices. It was then impossible for the President to agree even to temporary stabilization without running the risk of checking the policy to which he had set his hand." [21] When Roosevelt at long last found that he could not ride two horses to his goal, he was forced to surrender one. That he chose the domestic means of control over commodity prices as surer and quicker than the more elusive international approach demonstrated that immediate national self-interest exerted a strong pull on Roosevelt. He was hardly unique in this respect, since the conference itself, rhetorically dedicated to international cooperation for the realization of orthodox ends, was in actuality an arena of competing national economic aspirations.

Internationalism was eloquently introduced in the opening speech of the conference by the British prime minister, Ramsay MacDonald. "The economic life of the world," he declared, "has for years been suffering from a decline which has closed factories, limited employment, reduced standards of living, brought some States to the verge of bankruptcy and inflicted upon others recurring budgets that cannot be balanced. The machinery of international commerce, upon which the vigor of the human life of the world and the prosperity of the nations depend, has been steadily slowed up." A principal factor in the spread of world depression was the tempting but delusive recourse to economic nationalism. MacDonald vividly portrayed the mutually destructive consequences of this exclusionist ideology:

> One cause of the later phases of the deterioration is the fact that the nations, left to pursue a policy of national protection, have been driven to resort to measures which, while offering some temporary relief from the pressure which threatens them, add to the general stagnation of world trade and so intensify the influences which increase our trouble.
>
> No one . . . can doubt for a moment that the experiences of the last few years have proved that a purely national eco-

> nomic policy in the modern world is one which, by impover-
> ishing other nations, impoverishes those who pursue it. No na-
> tion can permanently enrich itself at the expense of others.
> Mutual enrichment is a condition of individual enrichment.
>
> Nationalism in the sphere of politics may be essential to
> human freedom. Self-sufficient nationalism in economics is the
> death knell of advancing prosperity.[22]

MacDonald's measured attack on what Alvin Hansen has called
"the beggar-thy-neighbor" policy of economic nationalism out-
matched in eloquence Roosevelt's best efforts, but the two heads
of state were equals in their pursuit of the economic self-interest
of their respective nations.[23] Nor were the uses of economic
nationalism entirely unknown to them.

At the outset of the conference Roosevelt spoke the language of internationalism; by its close he was acting the part of
an economic nationalist. This shift can be briefly chronicled.
The immediate precipitating factor which forced Roosevelt to
choose between opposed methods of raising prices was the ex-
peditious manner in which Harrison and Sprague concluded
what they conceived to be their mission. On June 10 the American, British, and French central bank and treasury representatives held their first meeting. By the 16th the bank officials
had worked out a technical procedure to limit exchange fluctuations between the dollar, pound, and franc, reporting their
agreement to the treasury representatives. Governor Harrison,
with Roosevelt's approval, then arranged to sail for New York
on the 18th.[24] But Roosevelt did not approve his handiwork.
Woodin, assisted by Moley, issued a press release on the 16th
denying that any stabilization agreement had been reached.
"Any proposal concerning stabilization," they announced,
"would have to be submitted to the President and to the Treasury. . . . The discussions in London in regard to this subject
must be exploratory only and any agreement on this subject
will be reached in Washington, not elsewhere."[25] This rejection
of the first stabilization agreement was explained by Roosevelt
the following day in a cable to Hull.

Roosevelt objected to the declaration that "the governments
and banks of issue of United Kingdom and United States have

stated that stabilization of their currencies on gold basis under proper conditions forms the ultimate objective of their policy." He pointed out that he wanted "worldwide" accord on stabilization—that is, agreement by the sixty-six participating nations and not merely by a few. He was also worried that the British and French, unlike himself, would not construe the agreement merely as "general and permissive," and that this misunderstanding might lead to charges of "bad faith" when the Americans failed to accept the Europeans' interpretation. Roosevelt's policy, in short, was to preserve his flexibility, and he made this abundantly clear:

> As a general principle, I am at present opposed to any agreements aimed at close stabilization of pound and dollar with small leeway either way, especially at present approximate levels.
>
> It is my thought that at this time we should avoid even a tentative commitment in regard to any definite program by this government to control fluctuations in the dollar.

The limit Roosevelt was willing to go on stabilization was merely an informal statement to the British that should the pound "rise to an excessive point" the American government would take some unilateral corrective action. But should the dollar appreciate instead, causing a drop in commodity prices, Roosevelt was emphatic: "We must retain full freedom of action under Thomas amendment in order to hold up price level at home."[26]

Sprague, Warburg, and Cox replied to Roosevelt, assuring him that the ultimate objective of the stabilization plan was to include all nations. They denied the likelihood of being charged with bad faith, and they maintained that the proposed dollar-sterling rate range was not too narrow. This was preliminary to their main argument: an agreement was essential if violent fluctuations were to be prevented. "If we refuse to cooperate in reducing fluctuation immediately," they concluded,

> it will be interpreted here as meaning first that having sent special representatives to discuss temporary stabilization we have now changed our mind or, second that the American representatives have exceeded their authority to present [the] whole program.[27]

Despite these protestations Roosevelt remained unmoved, and on the 22nd publicly explained the American position in a message released by the American delegates:

> The American Government at Washington finds that measures for temporary stabilization now would be untimely.
>
> The reason . . . is because the American Government feels that its efforts to raise prices are the most important contribution it can make and that anything that would interfere with those efforts and possibly cause a violent price recession would harm the conference more than the lack of an immediate agreement for temporary stabilization.[28]

On the 28th Roosevelt was warned in a cable from Acheson that his attitude on stabilization might force the gold countries—Switzerland, Holland, and Belgium, led by France—off gold if monetary fluctuations were not controlled. He replied complacently, "I do not greatly fear bad setback to our domestic price level restoration even if all these nations go off gold."[29]

In spite of Roosevelt's explicit public messages and his private instructions and warnings, on the 30th Moley telegrammed another proposed stabilization agreement, one that he and Sprague had worked out and that Moley now endorsed and recommended to the president for approval. The crux of this second proposal was contained in the first of its four provisions:

(1) The undersigned governments agree
   (a) That it is in the interest of all concerned that stability in the international monetary field be attained as quickly as practicable.
   (b) That gold should be reestablished as the international measure of exchange value it being recognized that the parity and time at which each of the countries off gold could undertake to stabilize must be decided by the respective governments concerned.[30]

A thoroughly exasperated Roosevelt, whose own emissaries had now joined the clamoring foreign crowd insisting that he agree to a temporary stabilization agreement, answered in language that everyone understood. "In regard to suggested joint declaration," he cabled Hull on July 1,

I must tell you frankly that I believe the greater part of it relates primarily to functions of private banks and not functions of governments. Other parts of declaration relating to broad governmental policies go so far as to erect probable barriers against our own economic fiscal developments. As to paragraph 1(a) . . . this language assumes that immediate stabilization in international monetary fields will create permanent stability. This I gravely doubt because it would still allow a country to continue unblanaced budgets and other financial operations tending to eventually unsound currencies. For example France.

As to paragraph 1(b) we must be free if gold or gold and silver are re-established as international measures of exchange to adopt our own method of stabilizing our own domestic price level in terms of the dollar regardless of foreign exchange rates.[31]

Roosevelt was opposed to any formula for temporary stabilization because it would interfere with his primary purpose of lifting the domestic price level, a purpose that was favorably served by continuing the existing doubt regarding the future value of the dollar. "It would be particularly unwise," he explained, "from political and psychological standpoint to permit limitation of our action to be imposed by any other nation than our own. A sufficient interval should be allowed the United States to permit in addition to the play of economic forces a demonstration of the value of price lifting effort which we have well in hand." Then, giving full vent to his resentment of foreign nations who had long been playing the nationalistic game, he added:

It would be well to reiterate the fact that England left the gold standard nearly two years ago and only now is seeking stabilization. Also that France did not stabilize for three years or more. If France seeks to break up conference just because we decline to accept her dictum we should take the sound position that economic conference was initiated and called to discuss and agree on permanent solution of world economics and not to discuss domestic economic policy of one nation out of the 66 present. When conference was called its necessity was obvious although problem of stabilization of American dollar was not even in existence.[32]

This blunt message was hardly unclear in its meaning; nor was Roosevelt's economic reasoning confused—its import could be readily understood by internationalists and economic nationalists alike. Roosevelt followed up his cable with a public message on July 3, the so-called bombshell.[33] Roosevelt here spoke as an undisguised nationalist, and he gave in addition the first public indication that he was seriously considering the nationalists' objective of permanently stabilizing the value of the dollar through the device of the "compensated" or "commodity" dollar:

> The sound internal economic system of a nation is a greater factor in its well being than the price of its currency in changing terms of the currencies of other nations. . . .
> So, too, old fetishes of so-called international bankers are being replaced by efforts to plan national currencies with the objective of giving to those currencies a continuing purchasing power which does not greatly vary in terms of the commodities and need of modern civilization.
> Let me be frank in saying that the United States seeks the kind of dollar which a generation hence will have the same purchasing power and debt-paying power as the dollar we hope to attain in the near future. That objective means more to the good of other nations than a fixed ratio for a month or two in terms of the pound or franc.[34]

Roosevelt well understood the old adage: when on the defensive, take the offense.

The conference itself, upon which these efforts and expectations had centered, was inconclusive on all the major issues it considered: gold, monetary stabilization, tariff revision, production control of staple commodities, and the price-debt problem. Only on the minor issue of silver did the assembled nations reach an accord. This failure was not due to any message, however rude, that President Roosevelt addressed to the gathering. The conference failed because the national self-interests of France, Great Britain, and the United States were basically at variance with each other. France, determined to remain on the gold standard, insisted upon a stabilization agreement based on the gold standard as a necessary precondition for her agreement on other economic issues. The British were uninterested in monetary stabilization at this time since the depreciated value of sterling was paying off handsomely in increased exports, particularly in the Far Eastern markets. They were even less interested in a downward revision of tariffs, because this would have put them in direct conflict with the imperial preference system adopted within the British Empire the year before at Ottawa. This was economic nationalism on a grand scale, and it was a policy strongly supported by the staple-producing Dominions seeking relief from competing agricultural exports, particularly those of the United States. The United States itself, or, more precisely, Roosevelt, having been given nothing, returned it in kind. Roosevelt would not jeopardize the downward movement of the dollar on the foreign exchanges and the attendant upward movement in American prices by agreeing to any stabilization proposal, no matter how innocuously expressed. Until a larger interest or a greater threat arose to overshadow these conflicting national aspirations, it was unrealistic to expect anything but failure from such international conferences.

The significance of the London Conference, however, is neither its failure nor the well-publicized peccadilloes and undiplomatic behavior of the American delegates. It is historically important as a bench mark in the evolution of the early New Deal. Roosevelt's backing and filling was a sign that he went into the conference still undecided in his own mind whether to follow the advice of the internationalists or the nationalists. In London, the committed internationalists, especially Sprague, Harrison, and Warburg, attempted to force Roosevelt's hand. They were assisted, ironically, by the nationalistic Moley, who blundered into an unfamiliar arena to help work out what he regarded as an innocuous compromise on monetary stabilization to keep the conference alive. Roosevelt, unwilling to have the decision made for him, rejected the compromise. This effectively ended the conference, but not Roosevelt's time of hesitation. His main concern was clearly with the domestic movement of American prices, and if the London episode clarified

anything at all, it was that Roosevelt would not tolerate anything that might interrupt the upward movement of prices and
the downward valuation of the dollar—at least, for the time
being.

SIX

The Battle of the Monetarists

WITHIN THE ROOSEVELT ADMINISTRATION, the struggle among
the monetary advisers did not cease with the end of the World
Economic Conference at London. While the president had made
it clear that he would not be deterred from pursuing his goal
of raising domestic commodity prices, he had not as yet officially decided whose side he was on. But Roosevelt's decisive
rejection of the temporary stabilization agreement was more
than a straw in the wind indicating the direction in which he
was moving. It was a serious setback to the influence and prestige of a powerful set of advisers who, officially at least, had
jurisdictional claim over monetary policy. Institutionally, this
group represented the Departments of the Treasury and State,
the Federal Reserve Board, the Federal Reserve Bank of New
York, and the Bureau of the Budget. Ideologically, they were
spokesmen for what Warburg called the "stability-confidence
school of thought"; that is, they were basically orthodox in their
economic reasoning and internationally oriented programmatically. Politically, these advisers, who became known as "the
monetary group" within the administration, took their stand
against economic nationalism and its advocates (whom Warburg labeled the "inflation school of thought") in a short but
decisive battle to win over Roosevelt to their monetary program. The struggle itself, which spilled over from the London

Conference, reached its peak of intensity during August–September 1933.[1] Roosevelt resolved it on October 21, ending his long hesitation.

The president's official advisers reacted to London by concluding, among other things, that Roosevelt was getting monetary advice from far too many quarters. Warburg in particular assumed the lead in attempting to reestablish the administrative departments and agencies' sole responsibility for advising the president on monetary policy. He undertook, as well, the task of lecturing Roosevelt on the economic orthodoxies of monetary theory as well as the dangers of heretical doctrine. This immediately involved him in an ideological duel with Professors Warren and Rogers, who were also busily lecturing Roosevelt, with the aid of statistical tables, on the economic advantages of a purported quick remedy for the domestic price problem. Warburg confronted his adversaries on July 28; then, on August 8, the three debated their viewpoints at a lunch with Roosevelt at Hyde Park. In the meanwhile, on August 2, Warburg had sent to Roosevelt the first of a number of memoranda staking out the administrative claim of the Treasury and State Departments and asserting the economic legitimacy of orthodox monetary policy.[2]

Warburg's memo, titled "Domestic Currency Problem," was a lucid exposition of the viewpoint advocated by the monetary traditionalists, accurately reflecting their dismay over the fallout from London and their sense of urgency in attempting to dissuade Roosevelt from adopting the "academic" and "untried" theories of their opponents.[3] "The Administration has never faced a more serious situation than it does today," Warburg declared gravely. "The entire recovery program, which is the heart of its policy, is jeopardized by uncertainty and doubt in the monetary field." Specifically, Warburg warned that lack of confidence in the future of the dollar was undercutting the administration's current efforts to stimulate general industrial recovery. The National Recovery Administration—the central vehicle for recovery—simply could not succeed "if there is fear of currency depreciation of an unknown amount and fear as to monetary experimentation." He also cited the "tremendous flight of capital" from the country induced by the prevailing anxiety. The fear of inflation, he continued, was no longer acting as a stimulus to buying, production, or trade—the scare tactic of what others called "psychological inflation" had already boosted prices and production well beyond realistic levels.

To this catalogue of domestic "menaces" Warburg added another from the international field. In a direct allusion to the unfortunate consequences of London, he remarked that internationally "the feeling that we were embarked on a well-ordered program is rapidly shifting into a feeling that we are fumbling about in the dark, and the result of our present undefined monetary policy will inevitably be further monetary chaos in other countries." His particular concern was that the administration's unpredictable monetary behavior might force the gold countries off the gold standard, plunging all countries into a "vicious circle of progressive devaluation" that would go well beyond safe limits.

Warburg's immediate purpose in drawing this dark picture was to persuade Roosevelt to follow the advice of the members of his official family. He recommended specifically:

> That all monetary ideas, projects and studies be concentrated in one place, and it would seem logical that this place should be the Treasury Department in consultation with the Federal Reserve Board.
>
> That it be decided now what authorities are to be consulted in preparing a definite monetary program; that these authorities be instructed to collaborate immediately; and that this group, the existence of which should preferably not be known, be given not over a month to prepare a definite recommendation to the Treasury.

Warburg then briefly outlined the monetary program that should be followed by Roosevelt. The setback suffered by the internationalists at London was now to be redeemed by a similar program which included the new factor of a definite devaluation of the dollar. "The United States Government desires not later than October 1st," Warburg stated in anticipation, "to fix the amount of devaluation which is desired in order to bring about the necessary adjustment to the price level, allowing for a subsequent variation of not over 10%." This could best be done by international agreement with Great Britain—the rest of the countries would then easily "fall in line." Warburg left to the proposed monetary group the determination of the exact amount of American devaluation, and the precise definition of the new, improved gold standard to which the United States would return.[4]

In mid-August Roosevelt responded by authorizing the creation of a monetary group consisting of Woodin; Acheson; Douglas; Sprague; Harrison; Eugene Black, governor of the Federal Reserve Board; George Peek, head of the Agricultural Adjustment Administration; Walter Stewart, economist and former adviser to the Bank of England; Herbert Feis, economic adviser at the State Department; and Warburg. The monetary group, which met in New York on August 17 and 28, engaged in a collaborative effort. Warburg, in a "suggested agenda," took the position that monetary uncertainties were seriously hindering business recovery; they could be removed by firmly deciding what type of dollar was intended for the future, and also by establishing "how big a dollar." Later he supplemented these proposals by another memo highly critical of the NRA, an operation, he stated, "so uncertain that it makes it almost impossible to formulate a monetary policy at the present time."

The Federal Reserve Bank of New York, in its staff analyses and reports to Governor Harrison, also formulated a strategy for recovery, and was even more critical than Warburg of New Deal recovery policies. It agreed with Warburg's basic contention that the NRA was in serious trouble and that a main consideration of the monetary group would be to devise ways to remove monetary uncertainty, at least, from the thorny path of the recovery program. But in the judgment of J. H. Williams, staff economist, Warburg's proposed stabilization plan was "premature":

> The public has apparently learned that discussion of the currency means "devaluation" which means "inflation," and it therefore proceeds (a) to put down the dollar and (b) to put up prices of stocks and commodities. As Mr. Warburg says,

this movement has gone too fast and too far, and I feel that it is time to unteach the public that there is a close connection between the dollar and prices and production; the connection is, in fact, not very close except as the public is instructed that it is and acts on the instruction.[5]

Consequently, Williams suggested that an effort be made to divert public attention from monetary policy to the domestic recovery program of the NRA:

I think that if Washington would cease giving out intimations about "devaluation," "inflation," or "reflation," but address itself singly to the N.R.A. activities, the dollar would gradually rise because of its inherent strength combined with seasonal weakness of sterling, and this gradual strengthening of the dollar would be found consistent with improving business conditions and firm or gradually rising prices based upon the turn in the business cycle which, it is now clear, occurred in the world at large last summer.[6]

On August 29 the secretary of the treasury sent Roosevelt a fourteen-page document, "The Interim Report on Monetary Policy," the end product of the monetary group's deliberations, unanimously agreed to by all its members.[7] "Monetary action alone," the experts began deprecatingly, "cannot bring about national recovery." This assertion that monetary means were only complementary to a number of other economic devices for regulation of the economy was consistently argued by orthodox internationalists within and without the government throughout the years of the Great Depression. It also differentiated them sharply from the economic nationalists and the inflationists who were convinced that the key to recovery was to be found in a bold exercise of unconventional monetary methods. The traditionalists not only denied the primacy of monetary policy for inducing recovery, they also minimized its impact upon price behavior itself. They pointed out, for example, that the depreciation of the dollar since March 1933 had not affected all prices, not even all agricultural prices. While staple commodities, which figured prominently in the export market, responded to the downward movement of the dollar in the foreign exchanges, other agricultural products, such as livestock, butter, eggs, and milk, were unaffected. The crux of the problem, according to the monetary group, was that if prices were to be raised further and then held there, this would require "a general broadening of industrial activity, with its attendant lessening of unemployment." This development was the responsibility of the National Recovery Administration. The NRA's main objective was to increase mass purchasing power by raising industrial wages and by expanding public works expenditures. The proper role of monetary policy was merely supplementary to the NRA: that is, the policy of the Federal Reserve was to create a favorable environment for the success of the administration's other economic recovery policies. Monetary policy, in short, was only a handmaiden in the service of more potent economic instrumentalities.

The members of the monetary group, in thus assuming such a modest role for monetary policy, were attempting to make an important political point. They were telling Roosevelt that their rivals were misguided men, promising the unattainable and in fact endangering the prospects for a sound recovery by frightening businessmen and destroying confidence. Their own prescription, which avoided these pitfalls, was a three-stage procedure: the "immediate," the "transition," and the "ultimate" programs of monetary policy.

The immediate program was designed to achieve two objectives: to prevent any strengthening of the dollar, and to cause an expansion of credit, timed to synchronize with the "purchasing campaign" of the NRA. This was to be done by "a fairly vigorous program of open market purchases by the Federal Reserve Banks," with an additional increase scheduled to coincide with the opening of the NRA program. These moves would create a favorable monetary "environment" for the direct recovery policies.

The group also took the precaution of rejecting explicitly a number of alternative monetary devices for the immediate future, including devaluation of the dollar, the creation of an equalization fund, the free import and export of gold, and the issuance of Thomas Amendment notes. Devaluation was premature because "the trend and velocity of price movement and purchasing power are not yet clearly enough established to permit finality in devaluation." They also wanted first to explore the possibility of cooperation with Great Britain before undertaking what they intended to be the first and final devaluation. Their criticism of the technique of manipulating the dollar through an equalization fund, modeled on that used by the British, was based partly on the constitutional ground that it required congressional action to protect the Federal Reserve System against loss, and partly on their anticipation that this tactic would provoke retaliation. They objected to regulating the dollar through the free import and export of gold because it would drain gold from abroad and provoke protective measures such as gold embargoes. The resort to issuing greenbacks, they stated, "would be harmful to the whole recovery program" because it would frighten businessmen; it would be difficult to control politically, running the "grave danger of uncontrolled inflation"; and it was likely to result in a depreciation race.

The transition program was to be marked by "the initiation of conversations with the British . . . designed to secure, if possible, the adoption of a common policy with regard to a trade recovery, prices, and currency revaluation." Specifically, they recommended that agreements be worked out with the British on the following issues: a clear understanding on the necessity of raising prices further; a clarifying statement to the British that the American recovery program consisted of three components—the NRA, public works, and a coordinated open market policy—and an effort to persuade the British to adopt a similar program; negotiation of trade agreements and, if possible, a revision of the Ottawa Agreements; a settlement of the British debt owed to the United States; and a mutual understanding "as to the eventual monetary standard to be adopted," that is, the gold bullion standard. The consequences of failing to reach a general accord with the British, they predicted, would be "drastic inflation here, further chaos abroad, default of debts, increased restrictions on trade, and very likely competitive devaluation with social and political upheaval."

The ultimate program was indefinitely scheduled; implementation was to take place only after the achievement of domestic trade recovery, that is, after the NRA realized its recovery goals. Then the improved gold standard would be established. This, in the judgment of the group, was the "best means of approximating a money unit of 'constant purchasing and debt-paying power'"—quoting here Roosevelt's announced aims for the future dollar. The critical word here is "approximating," since the members of the group, with the possible exception of Rogers, did not believe that the dollar, compensated or not, could be stabilized once and forever. "The group does not believe," as they put it, "that under this or any other monetary standard price and business stability can be attained in the absence of far-reaching reform in the conduct of banking and investment business."[8]

Roosevelt's own thinking about the price problem and the place of monetary measures in the general scheme of the recovery program can be glimpsed in two letters he wrote during August. To Nicholas Murray Butler, president of Columbia University, he revealed his irritation with New York bankers and orthodox international advice:

> There exists, of course, a group—most of them your friends and mine—who would like to see a categorical statement as to the exact level, to the last cent, of the proposed purchasing power of the dollar, together with a definite prognostication with dates and figures as to the ultimate relative value of the dollar, pound and franc. The difficulty, of course, is that in a program such as this we must feel our way towards the general objective. Conditions are changing and will change from month to month in such a way as to require new methods or modifications of existing methods. The main fact for the pessimists and cynics is that we are actually getting somewhere and that we propose to keep that ball rolling.[9]

To David Stern, editor of the *Philadelphia Record,* he confided, "Confidentially, I don't think you need worry about our going back to the gold standard for a long, long time! Like you, I feel that much can be done by going after the bank credit problem."[10] Neither of these comments, of which the monetary group knew nothing, was propitious to the group's purpose of persuading Roosevelt to adopt a safe international program.

Warburg, the moving spirit of the monetary group, was the most active in attempting to keep pressure on the president for a favorable decision on the group's program. On September 20 he wrote to Roosevelt, announcing dramatically, "I believe that this is probably the last moment at which drastic inflation can be forestalled." He pointed out that since the interim report, the dollar had dropped further, to something less than 65 cents in gold, that "pressure for drastic inflation is increasing continuously and it begins to look as if Congress would take the bit in its teeth in January provided nothing is done before." He continued to insist that there could be no further benefit from allowing the dollar to descend in value; it could only cause great harm to the common people.[11]

Warburg suggested that a national campaign be launched to mobilize the "latent" but "dormant" majority opposed to inflation. "The five or six largest insurance companies," he pointed out, "could alone reach between fifty and seventy-five million policy-holders." He also urged Roosevelt to devalue the dollar immediately at the existing rate, using the authority granted him by the Thomas Amendment. Roosevelt "could, in so doing, pass back to Congress the permissive power contained in the Thomas Amendment and relieve himself of the pressure under which he now finds himself." Later, when he came to write his autobiography, Warburg recalled his meeting with the president the next day. After repeating his plea against inflation, Warburg was stopped by Roosevelt's reply: "If we don't keep the price of wheat and cotton moving up, I shall have marching farmers."[12] It was not the first or the last time that Roosevelt would rest his case on that particular assertion.

A week later the secretary of the treasury sent the president the final report of the monetary group, a one-page document with three recommendations.[13] The Treasury Department was to prepare immediately for discussions with Great Britain to stabilize the dollar in terms of sterling; the Federal Reserve Bank of New York was to be authorized "to prevent the dollar from depreciating below the 4.86 sterling rate and the present gold rate"; and open market operations to prevent the strengthening of the dollar were now deemed "unnecessary."

Within two days, a thoroughly aroused Roosevelt replied to Woodin in an unusually blunt memo:

> I do not like or approve the report of the special monetary group.
>
> 1. They have failed to take into consideration the United States, and look at things, I fear, from the point of view of New York and banking. The first recommendation for discussions with Great Britain is premature; Great Britain is not ready to enter into this discussion.
>
> 2. The effort to prevent the dollar from depreciating below 4.86 is unsound from the American point of view unless the pound weakens with the dollar in its relationship to gold. If the pound and gold remain at substantially the present price I should hope to see the dollar go to $5.00 or more in relation to the pound.
>
> 3. Open market operations should most certainly continue, both from the point of view of the exchange situation and the banking and credit position.
>
> Tell the committee that commodity prices must go up, especially agricultural prices.
>
> I suggest that the committee let you and me have the recommendation of how to obtain that objective and that objective only.
>
> You and I understand this National situation and I wish our banking and economist friends would realize the seriousness of the situation from the point of view of the debtor classes—i.e., 80 per cent of the human beings in this country—and think less from the point of view of the 10 per cent who constitute the creditor classes.[14]

The members of the monetary group, so sternly admonished to turn their attention to the politically charged issue of raising prices—and to that alone—complied with the president's command, but only after Warburg had prodded them into action. Warburg, who had been ill, missed the group's meeting after the rejection of their program. On October 12 he wrote Acheson, expressing dismay that nothing had been done to answer Roosevelt's question: how to raise prices?[15] "I feel very strongly," he stated, "that the group should answer the question as best it can and not let the matter go by default even though the answer which I think has to be given will in all probability be rejected by the President." Warburg's fighting spirit was up, and he felt that the time had arrived to match Roosevelt's blunt language and, perhaps, jolt him off his course toward economic nationalism. Warburg urged that Roosevelt be told the unvarnished truth: that the entire recovery program was not working and could not work unless it was reoriented on the sound but admittedly slow recovery principles of orthodox internationalism.

The report to the president, he insisted, should come down hard on six basic propositions, presented without further equivocation with political factors. They should go on record as being opposed to any further depreciation of the dollar. The current 35 percent depreciation had already reached the point "of diminishing return," and it was breaching Roosevelt's public assurance that "we seek to correct a wrong and not to create another wrong in the opposite direction." The middle class was now on the brink of being wronged. The uncertainty regarding the dollar should be ended decisively by an international accord on a "modernized gold standard." The two essentials for a permanent price rise, a sound banking system and a smoothly functioning capital market, required strengthening the capital position of the banks and "immediate action to revise and liberalize the securities bill so as to make it possible for conscientious bankers to underwrite and sell sound securities to the investing public." The group should insist "that price-fixing and wage-fixing are inimical to an economic system built upon the principle of profit." These should be purged from the NRA. If these recommendations were followed, and "if a clear position is taken not to pursue further the course towards State Capitalism on which we are now embarked . . . then a rise of the price level is inevitable and will take place in an orderly manner, provided nature is allowed to take its course without constant application of palliatives." The final point, Warburg stated, was "that complete recovery can only take place on the basis of world recovery, and that world recovery in turn depends upon the free flow of goods and services between nations."[16]

Warburg, in insisting that this viewpoint with its attendant recovery program be put unequivocally on record, had no illusions about its reception by Roosevelt. "I realize," he admitted, "that such a report will not find favor with the President because in its very essence it envisages a long and necessarily slow process of recovery, whereas what he wants from the group is a recommendation which will produce immediate tangible results." But what the president wanted, in Warburg's judgment, was economically impossible—and he should be so told.

On October 21 Dean Acheson, the undersecretary of the treasury, delivered to Roosevelt the final memorandum of the monetary group, titled "How to Raise Prices."[17] This document, an exemplary analysis of the factors affecting not only the price problem but the larger issue of economic recovery, represented the conventional wisdom at its best. No effort was made to evade the issues by invoking natural law as a sanction for doing nothing. Nor, on the other hand, did the group curry favor by promising more than they believed could be achieved. Their recommendations, which went far beyond the confines of monetary policy into the broader area of general economic recovery policy, were perhaps as far as a group of committed orthodox internationalists could in good conscience go.

"A sustained and well-balanced rise in the general level of prices," the experts began, "can be accomplished without great delay." But the realization of this objective went beyond the reach of monetary measures. An increased price level, they cautioned, "will come only with expanding business and increased employment. In the final analysis, prices do not rise except in response to purchases. Hence purchasing power in the hands of spenders is of fundamental importance. In its absence, even inflationary devices cannot bring a lasting rise."

Historically, they declared, *"effective* inflation" has been of only two types, induced either by unbalanced national budgets or by a public works program financed by a credit expansion. In effect, the two were really one. "In the final analysis, they consist in the turning over of new funds to spenders *without concurrently recovering equal sums from other spenders."* The huge military expenditures of World War I, for example, functioned as a gigantic public works undertaking. It was financed by the

Treasury borrowing from the people, who borrowed from the commercial banks, who in turn borrowed from the Federal Reserve Banks. The key to the effectiveness of this procedure, in peacetime as well as wartime, was that it operated to put new funds into the hands of ready spenders.

In addition, there were other types of inflation, the principal ones being exchange depreciation, devaluation, the fixing of the price of gold, and the issuing of greenbacks. The common element in all of these was that they were relatively untested empirically, and consequently their effectiveness was "problematical and indeterminate." However, their results could be theoretically evaluated by reference to the crucial criterion of whether or not they would deliver new funds to ready spenders.

All of these alternatives were rejected on various grounds for the United States. The effectiveness of exchange depreciation, for example, had already reached its limit; and devaluation, its logical terminal point, was politically dangerous since forcing the remaining European nations off gold "might greatly increase political chaos with far-reaching results which cannot be foreseen." The technique of fixing the price of gold—the alternative, they knew well, that Roosevelt was seriously considering—was carefully assessed:

> At no great expense to the government, currently produced domestic gold—just as any other local product—might be purchased, if legal authority exists, at any price considered wise. If the price were placed high, it would no doubt be interpreted as an indication that devaluation to at least a corresponding degree would later ensue. Because of resulting exports of capital and short-sales of American exchange abroad, therefore, the dollar would very likely depreciate by a like amount in the foreign exchange markets of the world. How long such a result, mainly psychological, would last it is of course impossible to forecast—but probably not more than a very few weeks. Like a first issue of greenbacks, it is largely a "scare" device and would later have to be extended into far-reaching and perhaps premature commitments. Once the American public should realize that early devaluation was not contemplated, the dollar, in the absence of effective income

expansion, would doubtless again recover. Only an extension, at great government expense, of our gold-purchasing operations to other parts of the world, or definite devaluation, with all the commitments involved, would then continue the desired low rate of the dollar.

The resort to the printing presses by issuing greenbacks, a program associated with Congress, which was then not in session and therefore not an immediately pressing factor to be considered, was more abruptly dismissed. "Because of the great confusion in the minds of the public regarding monetary phenomena," the group conceded, "the issue of greenbacks has much psychological importance." Greenbacks were popularly associated with currency inflation rather than credit inflation. The short-term speculative results might therefore be considerable, but, they added, "the long-run economic effect on prices would again depend on the extent to which new incomes were put into the hands of ready spenders."

With the alternatives disposed of and, as the group added, "with a full appreciation of the extreme emergency, political as well as economic, with which the country is faced," they advised a program of "indispensable" measures to attain four ends: "reducing the exchange value of the dollar; removing existing obstacles to business and credit operations; stimulating directly business and credit operations; and disposing constructively of existing surpluses of commodities."

The rationale offered in support of this program was, taking the measures in order, that first the dollar should be manipulated to weaken it, as a "temporary expedient" to aid farmers during crop marketing time. The operation itself was to be carried out by the Federal Reserve Board following the techniques successfully used by Great Britain; that is, the board would be authorized "to import gold, to deal in foreign exchange and in American government securities held abroad, or to use other devices at their command." This should be done in the open and in consultation with the British and the French. The suggested limit to American depreciation was not to exceed $4.86 in terms of sterling.

The group was profoundly pessimistic regarding the current availability of both short- and long-term credit through the banking system and the securities market:

> Our commercial banks, many insolvent, many others in wretched financial condition, and all faced with impending rigid examinations, are not lending, and apparently will not lend, to struggling American industry. At the same time, our capital markets are virtually stagnant and long-term credits in many cases are unobtainable. The major sources, therefore, of purchasing power, which in periods of economic health is turned over currently to American business, have almost completely dried up.

In addition to offering these veiled criticisms of New Deal banking reforms, they also severely criticized NRA policies, in particular the widespread practice of increasing business costs *before* an expanded market for new production was available. This cart-before-the-horse procedure, they pointed out, "is not only adding greatly to business uncertainty and retarding future commitments, but at the same time, because of the resulting premature rises in the selling prices of certain industrial products, is fast shutting off the demand for them by large sections of the buying public."

The remedy suggested involved rehabilitation of the banking system by reversing the policy of the Reconstruction Finance Corporation, which was further strengthening the strong banks instead of concentrating on the weaker ones that needed to bolster their capital position by selling preferred stock to the RFC. This would "avoid another banking crisis at the end of the year." They also wanted the immediate release of the billion dollars in depositor holdings tied up in closed banks, adding to the sum of badly needed new purchasing power. They urged that the liability features of the Securities Act be amended so as to restart "the flow of long-term capital to industry." The NRA should abandon economically restrictive policies; in particular they suggested that "the unsuccessful price and wage-fixing elements could be allowed gradually to fade out of public prominence and be discarded." The alternative policy of extending these price and production controls to cover all of

American industry was emphatically rejected, since this was judged "most unfortunate and inconsistent with an economy based on private profit." Finally, they supported a vigorous attempt to negotiate reciprocal trade agreements in exchange for generous concessions on the war debts.

The group recommended for achieving its third objective that the public works program be expedited; that the government lend at 2 percent to the railroads for financing improvements, and to home builders (up to 85 percent of the value of new houses); and that it institute a system of bonuses to heavy industry as a direct stimulus. The surplus commodity problem could be dealt with by government purchase of agricultural surpluses for disposal as direct relief to the unemployed, and by "the sale of such products to Russia and China" on the best terms that could be gotten.

Monetary policy, in this scheme for economic recovery, was to play a minor part, modeled after the example of Great Britain. "The policies . . . recommended can be pursued satisfactorily if, and only if, public confidence in the money unit is sufficient to make possible private as well as Government credit on a large scale and at reasonable rates of interest."[18]

The monetary group thus not only advanced its own recovery program but also provided a devastating critique of the recovery program of the New Deal. Roosevelt gave his answer the very same evening of the day he received the report. In a public broadcast, he announced his decision to try out the gold experiment, publicly rejecting the program of the orthodox internationalists and accepting instead the advice of the economic nationalists. "In the end," Warburg reminisced, "it was not conviction that the Warren theory was right so much as the fact that Warren offered a program of action—a program more suited to the immediate political necessities—that carried the day."[19] The monetary group held the stronger ground in economic theory; politically, for the moment, they were irrelevant.

During this first year in office, Roosevelt was subject to converging political pressures. These stemmed in part from the partisans of opposed approaches to recovery among his official advisers, while another, greater source was a similar cleavage that characterized the many public advocates who energetically argued and lobbied in support of stability, business confidence, and internationalism or, conversely, for governmental initiatives, inflation, and nationalism. This intense discharge of political energy played upon Roosevelt with full force. The Congress, which itself received a full measure of pressure from constituents and organized groups, leaned heavily in turn on the president, giving additional urgency to presidential decision-making. One needs to add to these direct pressures the strong influence of indirect pressure which the national economy—or, more precisely, the direction of movement of economic indicators—exerted alike upon partisans, Congressmen, and ultimately, Roosevelt. Here there was an inverse correlation between the direction of the indicators and the intensity of public response: upward motion soothed, while downward movement brought agitated objection. Roosevelt, the political magnet for all these pressures, remained serene but politically sensitive, especially as he looked over one shoulder to check if the farmers were indeed falling into marching ranks while over the other he kept a weather eye on the Congress. And all together, they watched the economic indicators.

Among the indicators most closely followed by economic commentators in their analysis of the economy and the administration's recovery policies were those dealing with industrial production, employment, purchasing power and consumption, prices, and the cost of living. Initially, the overall behavior of the economy was highly favorable to Roosevelt's program. That is, until July 1933, when the rapid progress of recovery suddenly reversed itself and many of the advances slipped away.

From March until July, industrial production (January 1931 = 100) rose from its lowest point of 69 to 96. As Colonel Ayres pointed out, industrial production had "recovered in three months the losses of 30 months."[20] Wage increases for continuously employed industrial workers just matched the 8.8 percent increase in the cost of living for the year. For the Roosevelt administration *the* political barometer was the performance of the agricultural sector, where prices paid the farmer rose nearly 60 percent from February to July, while the prices of goods the farmer bought increased only 7 percent. The farmers' gross income for the year, including the government subsidies provided by the AAA, increased about 24 percent.[21]

In July this upward movement broke sharply and the decline continued to November. The break in production and prices wiped out two-thirds of the increase in industrial production; in agriculture wheat was below 70 cents a bushel and cotton below 9 cents a pound by October. Secretary of Agriculture Wallace predicted that at these prices farmers were "likely to get impatient, and demand a strong dose of inflation."[22] Indeed, that is exactly what farmers, their representatives and spokesmen were demanding, and they directed their protests to the White House. Roosevelt's mail provides a vivid profile of the inflationist reflex response of the nation's farmers to declining prices, as well as delineating the economic and political context in which Roosevelt weighed the competing advice of his advisers.

As prices fell, the volume and the intensity of letters to the White House rose. Individuals speaking for themselves or reporting to the president their personal observations on conditions among farmer folk; representatives and senators, back home among their constituents, mirroring the distress of farmers and their belief that only inflation would save them; inflationary leaders in the Congress urging their colleagues to write to Roosevelt *immediately;* and the organized group pressures of farm organization spokesmen joined by dissident businessmen and industrialists, associated primarily with the Committee for the Nation: all these pleaded, urged, recommended, or demanded that Roosevelt use the inflationary powers that he already possessed, or some others—anything and everything that might conceivably restore the upward movement of commodity prices.

"Permit me to suggest," Senator John H. Bankhead (D–Ala.) wrote on July 20, "that you give notice of an intention to revalue the dollar. If agricultural and other prices receive further shocks we may lose all our gains. Don't let them whip us."[23] In late August, as the price drop persisted, he became more alarmed:

We are greatly distressed at the price and prospective price of cotton. Increased acreage, increased fertilizer and ideal weather have ruined us. Last year thirteen million bales were produced. It is my judgment, after the best investigation I can make, including a motor trip through Alabama, Georgia, South Carolina and part of North Carolina, and notwithstanding the first government estimate of twelve million three hundred thousand bales, that we will produce more cotton this year than we did last year. The price now is under nine cents. When hedging comes on the market in full swing, I fear the price of cotton will go substantially below eight cents a pound. With the higher prices under the Industrial Recovery program, eight cents cotton means doom to the South and destruction of purchasing power by thirty million people whose purchasing power is necessary to the success of your recovery program. It looks dark to us.

Bankhead saw only two ways to save the South: "inflation, or the definite indication of it in such way as to bring about increased prices in anticipation," or his own plan to license all ginners and restrict the amount of cotton ginned to 50 or 60 percent of the 1931 crop, which had amounted to seventeen million bales. This might give the farmer "the pre-war exchange price of twelve and a half cents"—enough to get by. "I know your reluctance to [use] any form of compulsory action," he added, "but we have passed that stage in the Industrial Recovery program. If industrial employees are to be benefitted by quasi compulsory action, and where necessary by compulsory action, I sincerely hope you can see your way clear to extend the same doctrine to the protection of the cotton producers."[24] In October, the day before Roosevelt's public announcement of the gold experiment, Bankhead offered some further advice on tactics:

Anticipation of higher prices through currency expansion is much more appealing to the speculative element (whose buying puts prices up) than expansion of credit. One is quick; the other long, drawn out in its effects.

The recent general understanding that there will be no inflation of prices through currency expansion is retiring from trade many of those who recently anticipated such action. It will deter others from buying *now*.

My suggestion:

Regardless of what action you may finally take, dangle before the public in some appropriate way a suggestion that currency expansion or a devaluation of the gold dollar may take place at any time. Such action, if made strong enough, will help tide over until your other measures for increasing prices have time to become effective.[25]

Senator Hugo L. Black (D–Ala.), while denying that he was joining "in the widespread request for an immediate inflationary program," nonetheless emphasized the need of doing something to raise agricultural prices. "I have never subscribed to the theory that inflation of the currency would cure all of our ills," he wrote, "nor do I subscribe to such a theory now. I am of the opinion, however, that it is vital to your program, and vital to millions of farmers, to do everything possible to bring about an increased farm price *while the farmers hold the crops*. I am alarmed at the inexcusable increase in the price of necessary commodities of a manufactured nature, without a corresponding increase in the farm prices."[26]

Senator Elmer Thomas, the tireless prophet of inflationary recovery, responded to the drop in prices with his typical energy. On August 12 he wired the President, pointing out the statistics on declining credit and circulating money, the increased value of the dollar—all corroborating his long-held conviction that the proper objective was a higher price level and the means to that objective was cheaper, more plentiful money. "Should you agree with my analysis," he remarked, "then I respectfully suggest that the present policy of the Federal Reserve be halted and the reverse policy inaugurated."[27] On August 24 Thomas made his point more explicit by publicly releasing a letter to Eugene R. Black, governor of the Federal Reserve Board.[28] This was a blistering attack on Federal Reserve policies past and present. "The Federal Reserve system was established," he informed its head, "to prevent financial crisis. Its obligation is to take decisive action, particularly when a crisis can be foreseen. Nevertheless the Federal Reserve has been inactive during the worst monetary crisis in our history." Specifically, he blamed the system for the banking crisis of 1932–33, for the continued tie-up of $7.5 billion in deposits in closed banks, and for its persistent opposition to going off the gold standard, despite the example of Great Britain. Closer to home, Thomas attacked the Federal Reserve for thwarting his own recovery strategy:

> Primarily for the purpose of forcing us off the gold basis and preventing the disasters which have ensued because we remained anchored to gold, I have sponsored since 1931 bills for issuance of Treasury notes to bring the urgently needed relief to our people. However, I was defeated in these efforts by the Federal Reserve, which were [sic] directed by large Wall Street deflationists.

Then, turning to the present price crisis, he offered some advice to the governor and, incidentally, a barb for the president:

> The gold embargo has accomplished something toward restoring our national solvency, but further steps are absolutely necessary if solvency is to be attained. The dollar must be still further reduced from its gold parity in order to raise prices and create confidence by restoring normal values to commodities, securities, farms, homes and real estate. Europe has had to go through this same process. We cannot escape it, notwithstanding all the other palliative measures we have taken.[29]

By September, Thomas had broadened his personal crusade by launching a mass congressional telegram campaign, designed to shower Roosevelt with the inflationary message. To all members of Congress, Thomas telegrammed the following appeal:

> Senators Harrison Chairman Finance Fletcher Chairman Banking and Currency Smith Chairman Agriculture are urging President Roosevelt to use rational inflation immediately as means of increasing commodities prices and to assist farmers producers weak and closed banks and NRA program if you concur in such recommendation please wire me here so that your message may be presented to chief executive.[30]

In the House, John E. Rankin (D–Miss.) led a similar campaign, urging representatives and senators to wire Roosevelt in support of an "immediate expansion of the currency in order to raise farm prices." The stress on immediate action was to ensure that the increase in price occurred while the farmers still had possession of their crops. "If farmers are forced to sell their cotton and other farm products at the present low price levels," Rankin concluded, "it will bring disaster not only to the South but to the entire country." "Be sure, he added, "to wire at once."[31]

Roosevelt, in response to the deluge of telegrams and letters, soon developed a stock answer:

> I have been glad to have your telegram, but I do not think that you are drawing a wholly accurate picture of the present situation, especially in view of the fact that price levels have increased and are continuing to increase and that re-employment of the unemployed continues.
>
> That does not mean that agricultural price levels are high enough or that re-employment can stop. I hope that if you are in Washington this autumn you will come to see me and let me give you some rather interesting figures covering not only your State but the country as a whole.[32]

To those he was more intimate with, Roosevelt was more blunt. To the majority leader of the House, Joseph W. Byrns, he wrote:

> Please don't encourage conversation and complaints in your section or in any other section which are not based upon a complete knowledge of the facts. I would like to see fifteen cent cotton just as much as you would, but it is not bad to have raised cotton from four and a half to nine and a half cents in this short period. It is not bad to have added three hundred and fifty million dollars to what the cotton farmer got for his crop over what he got last year.
>
> I know you will forgive me if I write you very frankly, as I have, but I know you will agree with me that it is time for team work.[33]

Politically, neither of these replies was a sufficient answer to those, like Representative John J. McSwain (D–S.C.), who were not part of the form letter campaign but wrote Roosevelt thoughtful letters on their observations of conditions back home:

I have been watching the development of the Recovery program with great care. I have visited retail stores, talked with the poor people on the streets, conversed with bankers and manufacturers, read every line printed in newspapers or magazines on the situation, and believe that I am justified in expressing to you the opinion that now is the time to use the power of actual reflation in order to stimulate buying, encourage manufacturing, and thus bridge over the set-backs, confusion and dislocations incident to the work of N.R.A. and of A.A.A.

Now, just as we are entering the autumn, is a critical time with these two new great agencies for recovery. The people have great hope and confidence, but are beginning to insist upon visible and tangible evidence of actual economic recovery in terms of dollars and cents, in terms of decreasing unemployment, in terms of purchasing power, in terms of increased prices for basic farm commodities, such as cotton, cotton seed, tobacco, wheat, oats, corn, hog meat, cattle meat, and dairy products.[34]

While Roosevelt listened to this disturbing news from congressmen and senators back home, the message was reinforced by the leaders of organized farm and inflation groups. If nothing else, Roosevelt must have been overwhelmed by a sinking sense of redundancy.

The leaders of the nation's major farm organizations reacted to the price crisis by calling a conference which met in Chicago on September 18–19. Represented were the American Farm Bureau Federation, the National Grange, the National Committee of Farm Organizations, the Farmers' National Grain Corporation, the American Cotton Cooperative Association, the National Livestock Marketing Association, the National Cooperative Milk Producers Federation, and the editors of *The Farmer* and the *Prairie Farmer*. On the 25th they sent Roosevelt a memorandum detailing their deliberations. They emphasized three demands: the harmonizing of the operation of the NRA with that of the AAA; the speeding up and liberalizing of Farm Credit Administration procedures for servicing the farm mortgage debt; and the granting to farm organizations and cooperative associations of an official recognition comparable to that granted organized labor by the NRA.[35]

The critical issue of farm prices, dealt with in the first resolution, was presented in a statement which combined an expression of the agrarian bias, with its supposition that general recovery would develop out of the prior recovery of agriculture; a criticism of the NRA on the familiar ground that it was raising the cost of living faster than the farmers' income; and a statement of faith in inflation as the sure remedy to the price and recovery problems. "It is the conviction of farm people," the resolution read,

> that the first step in any program of national recovery is to restore farm purchasing power. This opinion is also shared by many leaders of industry. While entirely sympathetic to the objectives of the NRA Act, farm people are convinced that its operations today have worked to the disadvantage of Agriculture, in that the disparity which has for years existed between the exchange value of farm commodities and the goods and services that farmers must buy has actually been increased.
>
> [We] . . . feel justified in calling upon the President . . . to use the great power vested in him and at once restore the price level of all farm commodities. . . . If this restoration of price parity or proper exchange value of farm products is not accomplished at an early date . . . the entire recovery program is in grave danger.
>
> . . . the quickest and easiest way to bring this about is to immediately launch a program of inflation along the lines that have been repeatedly suggested by the Farm organizations of the United States. Further delay threatens the success of the recovery program and destroys the hope which has been the sustaining force of agriculture during the past three years.[36]

John Simpson, president of the Farmers' Educational and Co-Operative Union, was absent from and unrepresented at this gathering. The position of his organization, which was by far the most critical of New Deal recovery policies of all the major farm groups, was delivered directly to Roosevelt in two angry letters. C. N. Rogers of Iowa, a member of the executive committee of the Farmers' Union, expressed a growing disillusionment with New Deal agricultural policies:

> I believe that up until recently the majority of the farmers, regardless of what organization they belonged to, had confi-

dence in the New Administration, that the economic condition would be corrected. . . . The sentiment I find amongst the thousands of farmers I come in contact with is that they have never believed that Mr. Wallace's program would succeed in reestablishing farm prices based on an average cost of production. The sentiment which seems to prevail amongst the rank and file of farmers is that there must be a fixing of prices for that portion of the farm commodities that is consumed in the United States. . . .

There is a growing sentiment all over the United States against destruction of food commodities as well as cotton when there are so many of our own people who are sadly in need of clothing and food, and it is my opinion that unless there is something done immediately to restore the buying power of the American farmer that the NRA movement is doomed to failure and I am afraid if the NRA movement fails, that it will be almost impossible to prevent a revolution that will be hard, if not impossible to stop.[37]

John Simpson caustically added his own bitter judgment:

Your "Brain Trust" goes from one folly to another. They evidently do not speak the farmers' language neither do they understand it. The farmers ask for cost of production; and your "Brain Trust" . . . indicate they are going to lend them more money. . . .

The best your "Brain Trust" could produce as a remedy to restore prosperity is summed up in three words: drink, borrow, and destroy. There is not a ten year old farm boy . . . so ignorant as to believe anyone can drink himself into prosperity, borrow himself into prosperity, or become prosperous destroying property. . . .

Mr. President, the crooks who were running this government in 1920, and who have apparently not moved out of the basement in Washington, destroyed prosperity in less than ninety days. They destroyed prosperity by withdrawing credits and deflating the currency.

You can restore prosperity by undoing what they did in 1920, and you can do it in twenty-four hours. The minute you remonetize silver by proclamation, the minute you cut the gold dollar in two by proclamation, the minute you announce all public debts coming due will be paid with full legal tender non-interest-bearing currency—the next morning after you make these three proclamations, the prices of farm products will go back to what they were in May, 1920.[38]

The most prominent bridge between Roosevelt and the inflationists was the Commitee for the Nation. The leaders of the major farm organizations were among its members and supporters, it also had influential links with Congress and, by way of Professor Warren, a direct line to Morgenthau, the White House, and Roosevelt. The committee, organized early in 1933, had from the time it issued its first report in March consistently urged the whole array of inflationary policies, including the abandonment of the gold standard and devaluation of the dollar, as the essential means of raising the price level and recovering the nation's foreign trade.[39] One measure of the committee's influence was that it quickly established itself as the wellspring of ideas for all inflationists. It deluged Congress and the White House with letters, telegrams, and reports studded with arguments and data which were, in turn, freely quoted by farm leaders, members of Congress, and President Roosevelt himself.

In the monetary field, the committee's basic position was that the dollar was seriously overvalued in terms of both gold and foreign exchange. A strong currency resulted in low prices for domestically produced goods, the repayment of debts in highly valued dollars, and prohibitively priced American exports. This meant that the dollar return to the producer of goods was low and, consequently, that the value of a debt in goods was high. This relationship has been more graphically explained by the familiar argument that farmers, for example, contracted their debts for the equivalent value of 100 bushels of wheat, corn, or whatever, and now had to repay those debts with 200 or more bushels of the same product. In foreign trade, a strong dollar meant that it took more pounds, francs, yen, etc., to purchase dollars in foreign exchanges, thereby making American goods noncompetitive. The solution to these problems, according to the committee, was simple: devalue the dollar and thereby raise the price level. In April the Committee urged that gold be revalued from the long established price of $20.67 an ounce to $36.17 (a 75 percent increase), which they thought would then raise the commodity price level to that prevailing in 1926. In October the committee upped this first to $40.00 an ounce, and then to $41.34.[40]

The committee's analysis and its advice to Roosevlt are nicely summarized in two of its letters to the president. On May 17, when the committee was worried that Roosevelt might follow what it termed the "deflationists'" program at London, it reminded him that while "the world determines the value of gold . . . each country can and should fix for itself . . . the number of grains of gold in its monetary unit required to give it the domestic price level suited to its needs."[41] In this regard, two "fundamental essentials" had to be kept firmly in mind:

> 1. That we revalue the dollar to a point that will take care of American interests between Americans in America—that is, give us our 1926 price level.
> 2. That provision be made for changing the price of gold in the future so as to maintain a dollar of stable purchasing power that will protect us from future disruption of our price level.

The similarity between these two principles and Roosevelt's "bombshell" message is obvious. Nothing less was at stake, according to the committee, than the survival of capitalism:

> The capitalism of Western civilization with its institutions of freedom is built upon the principle of the freeest and widest possible exchange of goods and services upon the basis of prices. Each individual is free to produce what he can or sell his services and to enter short and long-term contracts upon the basis of a monetary unit which serves as a medium of exchange. The value, or purchasing power, of this unit expresses itself in all prices, the average of which, weighed as to importance of each commodity, is the price-level.
>
> Modern civilization is so complicated that a change in the commodity price level has far reaching results beyond the power of the human imagination to foresee. Individuals and economic groups within a nation are thrown into disequilibrium. Trade between nations becomes increasingly difficult. The world wide drop in price level that has taken place during the past four years has weakened the structure of capitalism itself. . . .

Compared with a stable price level—domestic and international—all else is of secondary importance. Only upon the basis of a stable price level can the exchange of goods and services, within nations and between nations, take place at the highest possible intensity—which is the essence of prosperity.[42]

On October 21, the day of the monetary group's final report and Roosevelt's announcement of the gold experiment, the committee urged its case again, clothing its arguments in potent traditional symbols: the agrarian myth, the national self-interest, and a surefire program of recovery through monetary manipulation:

Farm strikes are merely symptoms of a general condition both critical and dangerous to our institutions. Ever since the founding of our republic, prosperous, land-owning farmers have been the real backlog of our national stability. . . .

Never in history has the economic position of the farmer been so deeply undermined. Never have so many farmers lost their homes. . . .

Our farmers' distress is due to the fact that we, instead of beginning to follow England's example two years ago, still persist in following Montague Norman's advice to the Federal Reserve and the U.S. Treasury to keep the dollar high. . . .

Our Committee again urges you to use before it is too late the power conferred on you by Congress to raise adequately the price of gold and the price level. Our Committee's ten months of exhaustive research show that either a steady increase in the price of gold or immediate revaluation to $41.34 (50 percent cut in gold content) is the only measure by which we can deal successfully with the problems of farm relief, reemployment and national solvency.[43]

Undoubtedly, this is but a pale reconstruction of the converging inflationary pressures brought to bear upon the president. But once again, Roosevelt carefully avoided a showdown; instead he chose to match formidable political pressure with adroit political maneuver. Gold and silver provided the next arenas in the ongoing battle for and against inflation, confronting Roosevelt with dangerous political mine fields which somehow had to be traversed.

SEVEN

The Politicization of Gold

ROOSEVELT ANNOUNCED HIS DECISION to experiment with gold in a nationwide radio broadcast on a Sunday evening, October 21, 1933. "Our dollar," he explained, "is now altogether too greatly influenced by the accidents of international trade, by the internal policies of other nations, and by political disturbances in other continents. Therefore, the United States must take firmly in its own hands the control of the gold value of our dollar. This is necessary in order to prevent dollar disturbances from swinging us away from our ultimate goal, namely, the continued recovery of our commodity prices." This was nothing less than an acceptance of the go-it-alone philosophy and its preoccupation with national self-sufficiency. Roosevelt had adopted the role of economic nationalist in earnest. "This is a policy," he asserted disarmingly, "and not an expedient. It is not to be used merely to offset a temporary fall in prices. We are thus continuing to move toward a managed currency."[1] Seemingly, this "policy" was designed to achieve express economic objectives by the application of a planned economic program. But scratch the surface of an economic discourse by Roosevelt and underneath can be found the political factors and motivation which were the decisive considerations.

The underlying economic theory and rationale for Roosevelt's new venture in the use of monetary policy as the means of lifting the domestic price level were provided by two members of the Cornell University branch of the Brain Trust. George F. Warren, professor of agricultural economics and farm management, and Frank A. Pearson, professor of prices and statistics, were long-time collaborators in the analysis of prices. As chance would have it, they succeeded in arresting Roosevelt's attention and fixing it for a brief space on their theory of the relation of gold to prices. Roosevelt's decision to try out their ideas catapulted the obscure professors to national prominence and subjected them, Roosevelt, and the gold experiment to the withering criticism of outraged economists and dumbfounded monetary experts. One can only admire Roosevelt's audacity in blithely bypassing traditional expertise; President Hoover's rejection of the advice of one thousand economists by signing the Hawley-Smoot Tariff seems timid by comparison.

"One of the chief criticisms of this work," Warren and Pearson complained in defense of their price analysis and explanation of the cause and cure of the Great Depression in *Prices* (1933), "is that it is so simple that it cannot be true. Truth is always simple. Ignorance is mystical."[2] The charge of grossly oversimplifying complex economic phenomena, and of then using this to justify an equally simplistic and erroneous recovery program, was soon to become the major motif in the public debate which raged over the gold experiment. Unlike most economists, who were at pains to emphasize the complicated interplay of multiple variables—economic and psychological—in price movements, Warren was preoccupied with identifying and isolating the one causative factor. The conviction that there was a single cause was central not only for understanding and controlling prices, he believed, but also for demystifying the origin of the depression. And this cause, once known, suggested the cure.

"The economic catastrophe in which we find ourselves," Warren stated in defining the critical issue, "is due to a fall in commodity prices." The major problem to be resolved, therefore, was: "What made prices fall?" Warren impatiently brushed aside professional economic obscurantism by denying that prices had collapsed because of any of the "115 assumed causes."

Among the principal factors thus summarily dismissed from consideration he included overproduction, technological efficiency, the business cycle, high tariffs, lack of business confidence, and international economic complications.[3]

Warren insisted that contrary to common supposition, there were four factors in the determination of prices. "The price of wheat," he explained, "is the ratio of the supply of wheat and demand for it to the supply of gold and the demand for it." This major proposition of the Warren theory applied equally to all commodities. The essential relationship involved both commodities and gold; but gold, which was both a commodity and a monetary measure, was the decisive consideration.[4]

Warren eliminated three of the four factors in price as causative elements by subtracting those which showed no significant statistical change over time. He denied, for example, that there was an over-production of commodities. "There is a great difference," he explained, "between over-production and under-consumption due to unemployment. If the trouble is over-production, it can easily be cured by cutting production. If it is under-consumption, we must find a way to put the unemployed to work so that they can consume, rather than attempt to cut production to what an unemployed man can buy."[5] According to Warren, the statistics on production for the seventy-five years prior to World War I showed a "stable increase" of "the world physical volume of production of all basic commodities" of about 3.15 percent per year. "Since 1915," he added, "the rate has been distinctly less." The difficulty, in short, did not rest with an oversupply of commodities—a conclusion that might have given pause to those associated with Roosevelt who were committed to the economics of scarcity and its administrative expressions in the AAA and the NRA, where the emphasis was distinctly on cutting back excess production.[6]

Nor, for that matter, could the real trouble be ascribed to the second factor—the demand for commodities. Obviously, the effective demand for all goods was abnormally low in the midst of the depression, but the confusion here was between cause and effect. "The fall in demand for commodities and the consequent low prices," Warren asserted, "are a result, not a cause of depression."[7] With the supply and demand for commodities thus eliminated, the only portion of the equation that remained was gold.

Warren maintained that the existing supply of gold was "sufficient to support prices at about the pre-war level with all the world back on a gold basis, and gold used with pre-war efficiency." However, this condition solved neither the price problem nor the depression, since the prewar price level was approximately 50 percent below what Warren judged was necessary to permit debtors to repay the $203 billion in accumulated private and public indebtedness. "The price level must be raised to the debt level," Warren insisted, "or the debt level must be lowered to the price level. This is a matter of grim reality that cannot be cured by psychology, confidence, or government lending."[8] Further deflation was clearly out of the question, and to attempt to bring about recovery by increasing the supply of gold was dismissed on the ground that this would require a 50 percent advance in the normal gold supply—a manifest impossibility.[9] Since the supply side of gold offered no ready solution, that left only the question of the demand for gold, its consequences, and its resolution.

Warren's treatment of this critical factor was presented historically rather than by his customary statistical approach. During World War I, the nations of the world went off the gold standard, the demand for gold as a consequence fell, and prices rose. This condition persisted into the postwar years, during which debts were contracted at the higher price level. "Beginning in 1925," Warren continued, "gradual efforts were made to return all nations to a gold basis. Americans took a leading part in urging and financing this return, not realizing that the return of demand for gold would raise its value and cause a price collapse. France returned to the gold basis in the spring of 1928, and the gold panic was on."[10] These events and decisions made clear not only the reason for the price collapse but *the* cause of the depression itself and its unresolved persistence. As Warren put it, "The depression was caused by the fourth factor in price—demand for gold. This was so low as to allow prices on a gold basis to double. This was followed by a demand so high as to cause the present depression."[11]

What, then, was to be done?

Warren's proposed remedy was as forthright and· uncomplicated as his explanation of the cause of the depression itself. If simplicity and truth were indeed synonymous, here was a marvelous demonstration of simple truth. "The dollar," Warren declared in a celebrated utterance, "has to be rubber either as to weight or value. It cannot have a fixed weight and also a fixed value." Warren proposed to manage the dollar in such a fashion as to "give it a fixed value and a rubber weight."[12] "Rubber dollar" quickly became a derisive epithet among critics of the commodity dollar. Derived from Professor Fisher's earlier compensated-dollar proposal, the commodity dollar was strongly pushed by Warren and given Roosevelt's public blessing. The new dollar, by whatever name (compensated, commodity, rubber, or, as Al Smith sarcastically dubbed it, "baloney"), was to be a thoroughly managed one. By varying its gold content in accord with the movement of the wholesale price index, the managers aimed to secure a dollar "with a purchasing power as nearly constant as possible."[13] The value of the dollar, in short, would be stabilized in terms of the quantity of goods it could purchase over a period of time. Technically, in the proposed detailed management of the dollar,

> if prices rose 0.1 per cent in a week, the weight of gold purchasable by a dollar would be increased 0.1 per cent until any rise was corrected. If prices fell 0.1 per cent, the weight of the gold purchasable by a dollar would be decreased 0.1 per cent. There would be a small difference between the buying and selling price of gold. This is an all-commodity dollar rather than a one-commodity [i.e., gold] dollar. It would be independent of business cycles.[14]

But before the dollar could be stabilized in this manner, it had first of all to be depreciated further, presumably to that value which would restore the 1926 price level or, more probably, to whatever point was satisfactory to President Roosevelt.

In mid-October Warren warned Roosevelt of the dangerous consequences likely to come from the recent strengthening of the dollar. "When such violent recovery in the dollar occurs," he pointed out, "violent crashes in prices of commodities are

inevitable."[15] Warren also sent Roosevelt a "suggested procedure" for increasing the price of gold. The central recommendation here was contained in his second point:

> Purchase newly-mined gold at prices that are gradually ad-
> vanced until the desired price level is reached.
>
> If necessary to control the dollar, purchase limited amounts
> of foreign gold or sell limited amounts of gold to foreign
> countries.
>
> As a start, it might be well to reduce the dollar by stopping
> control over the flight of capital, giving out rumors of infla-
> tion, and other means to get as near $35.00 as possible very
> quickly. Then set an initial buying price at about $35.25 and
> gradually raise this price.
>
> An increase in prices to the legal limit of $41.34 will prob-
> ably be sufficient if adopted soon. If not, a higher price is not
> improbable.

The gold experiment began on October 25, after having
been delayed several months while Roosevelt impatiently awaited
legal clarification of his authority to purchase newly mined domestic gold at varying prices. At the time the legal price of gold
was $20.67 an ounce, its current market price was $29.06, and
the initial pegged price was $31.36. Roosevelt, who directed the
operation, was assisted at a daily morning gathering by Morgenthau, Jones, and Warren. As Arthur M. Schlesinger, Jr., de-
scribes it, "While Roosevelt ate his eggs and drank his coffee,
the group discussed what the day's price was to be."[16] Thereafter the price was raised each day by differing amounts, a tactic adopted to confuse speculators in gold and foreign exchange. The RFC, acting as Roosevelt's agent, bought the gold
by selling its own debentures; but after a four-day trial, it was
obvious that the gold purchase scheme, confined to domestically mined gold, was not working as planned. As the editor of
The Commercial & Financial Chronicle remarked, "The foreign
markets failed to follow the American price, and, indeed, moved
lower, with the result of establishing two prices, the American
price and the foreign price, and with the difference between
the two constantly widening."[17] This result impelled Roosevelt
to broaden the purchase program from the domestic to the international gold market.

On October 29 Roosevelt summoned to the White House an imposing group of monetary specialists, including Governor Harrison, J. E. Crane, and Fred I. Kent from the New York Federal Reserve Bank, Jones, Morgenthau, Acheson, Black, Henry Bruere (a New York banker, friend, and financial adviser), and Professors Warren and Rogers. Roosevelt's purpose was neither to consult nor debate the issue with the assembled talent; it was to demand their support of the gold experiment in its new, expanded international phase. Crane, who wrote a report of this gathering for the files of the New York Federal Reserve, captured the tense drama of the confrontation, which stripped away the economic layers camouflaging the underlying political realities:

> The President said that the meeting had been called to consider the machinery by which the R.F.C. could buy gold in foreign markets. . . . He referred to the course of deflation and described briefly the situation of the country as he found it last March. At that time . . . he was convinced that we could deflate no further without the danger of an uprising, that it was imperative to get prices up and have some inflation. He was convinced that this program required prompt action, that the country would not wait for results over a period of years, that even now it was absolutely necessary to put up agricultural prices within the next few months . . . in order to avoid a march of the farmers on Washington. He said that he did not know anything about economics but felt he knew something about politics and from that standpoint prompt action was required. . . . He had decided last Sunday to use a new method in trying to raise commodity prices. . . . There were doubtless many opinions on the efficacy of that method . . . and it was evident that there was much complaint and objection. He said he did not like to hear so much complaining . . . that all those associated with the Administration were in one boat in the matter of getting recovery and that if any one was not willing to pull a willing oar he ought to get out of the boat at once.
>
> The present expedient . . . of raising the price of gold in order to depreciate the dollar further and put up basic commodity prices, had not worked in the past few days. . . . He had decided . . . to take the next step which was to buy gold in foreign markets. . . . He indicated clearly that he was not

seeking opinions on the policy but merely asking about the mechanical steps which should be taken. . . .

The President said that he thought it imperative to get agricultural prices up before Congress meets and that if we did not he was fearful of what Senator Thomas and the other inflationists might do. . . .

The President said that he thought we might get by in this country without an uprising or serious social disorders in the west if prices of wheat, cotton, etc., could be put up moderately and held between now and April.[18]

At the close of this meeting, it was publicly announced that the administration would extend its gold purchase program to foreign markets—which meant, in effect, the London gold market. The Federal Reserve Bank of New York served as the buying agent for this phase of the experiment, which began on November 1. Unlike the domestic-mined gold purchases, the foreign gold ones were made at the existing world market price. Two weeks later, on November 12, Roosevelt met with the same group to assess the economic and political effects of the expanded gold experiment.

Roosevelt professed to be satisfied with the results of the program. But it was clear from the president's discourse that the economic and political effects were inextricably intertwined in his thinking. He cited the current dollar price of gold, wheat, corn, cotton, and common stocks with satisfaction, but he quickly added that while the danger of militant farmers in revolt descending upon Washington was less acute now, the "fundamental difficulty persists." That meant that commodity prices, while somewhat improved, were still not high enough to break the potentiality of the "marching" fever. Specifically, his immediate goal was $1 wheat and 10 cent cotton. Revolt apparently was measurable and hinged on fractions. The gold experiment, in short, was to be pushed further.[19]

The bankers present understood Roosevelt perfectly, and they objected promptly and forcefully. "Governor Harrison, Mr. Bruere, Secretary Woodin and Governor Black all pointed out to the President the real danger that further depreciation of the dollar would demoralize the government bond market and result in a breakdown of the government's credit." Harrison in particular urged Roosevelt to stop the program or, at the very least, slow it down. He doubted that further forced depreciation of the dollar would have much effect on prices—certainly not enough to compensate for the undoubted harm to the government's credit "and to general business recovery because of fear and uncertainty about the dollar." The bankers were attempting once again to recall the president to the traditional confines of orthodox internationalism, with its familiar emphasis on currency stabilization.

In reply, Roosevelt showed that he too understood the bankers perfectly, and that while he also thoroughly understood their economics, they needed some schooling in the political consequences of their economic advice. As J. E. Crane of the New York Federal Reserve recorded it,

> The President said that he thought the immediate effect of currency stabilization would be higher government bond prices and lower prices for wheat and cotton, that he did not think the country would stand for lower wheat and cotton prices now, and that if he undertook to stabilize the dollar wheat would drop five cents the first day. . . . He did not think he could give any assurances about keeping the dollar stable or consider *de facto* stabilization of the currency until wheat was at one dollar, cotton ten and a half cents and corn fifty-five cents.

Instead of unilateral stabilization, Roosevelt proposed that the nation's big bankers bankroll the government's commodity lifting program:

> The President stated that a few hundred millions of dollars would be all that would be needed to maintain the prices of these commodities at the levels suggested and that if the banks of the country would agree to stabilize these prices at such levels for the next few months he would be willing to halt further depreciation of the dollar and to stabilize around present levels.

Roosevelt added that he hoped this idea would be given "serious consideration." Whether he took his suggested trade-off seriously himself, or whether he was merely making a blunt political point, the idea itself was stillborn. After this diverting interlude, Roosevelt turned from the farm problem per se to the even bigger problem of farmers *and* Congress in alliance:

> The President indicated clearly that he anticipates trouble with Congress when it convenes in January and that Congress will probably make a drive for $1.25 wheat and fifteen cent cotton. He feels that if he has tied his hands by legal devaluation of the dollar he will be in a hole with Congress and unable to handle them, but that if he can keep wheat and cotton and corn for the next few months at $1, 10½ cents and 55 cents respectively and has not used the powers given him under the Thomas Amendment, he will be able to deal with Congress effectively because he thinks his veto power would be sufficient under those circumstances to prevent Congress kicking over the traces.[20]

Roosevelt thus administered a double dose of fear and anxiety to his monetary experts: the provocative image of marching farmers united with a runaway inflationist Congress. He also demonstrated once again that in an economic argument he could hold his own with the best of them. And when he inevitably shifted the discourse to economic means for the realization of political ends, he left them all far behind—if not exactly open-mouthed in admiration, certainly breathless. It was evident, in any case, that the monetary experts would have to endure the gold experiment some while longer.

While Roosevelt's orthodox advisers vainly attempted to stop the president's headlong plunge toward the political manipulation of the dollar, like-minded men outside the government bestirred themselves to arouse public opinion in support of the opposition. Walter Lippmann, an ever-sensitive barometer to incipient movements, early on raised a "Danger Signal" concerning the political implications of the president's political use of monetary policy.[21] The time had come, he forecast, for the American people to examine critically Roosevelt's "political regime," which he defined as "the concentration of authority in the hands of the Executive and the moratorium on organized criticism of and opposition to the exercise of that authority." Lippmann's own allegiance was to this protest-to-be, and he suggested one main line of attack on Roosevelt by the opposition movement which he was attempting to call forth. "When Congress passed the Thomas amendment," he recalled,

> it vested in the President what is virtually the whole power of the Government under the Constitution to regulate the value of money. Inasmuch as alterations in the value of money are alterations in the distribution of wealth, affecting the economic status of every one and the economic relationship of each man with all other men, the regulation of money is one of the greatest of all the powers of a sovereign state. The exercise of this power involves the deepest questions of social justice.

Lippmann doubted that Roosevelt had "social justice" in the forefront of his mind as he juggled with the dollar price of gold in the early morning hours; and he was disturbed by the "coincidence" of the gold experiment occurring "at a time of acute farmer protest." "The raising of the price of half a dozen commodities by manipulating the National dollar," he stated, "would be an unwarranted use of the power over money." Since this was, in fact, Roosevelt's acknowledged objective, Lippmann's purpose was to warn the President of the political consequences:

> Once let the conviction crystallize in men's minds that the powers concentrated in the President are not being used in a widely National spirit, the political truce will collapse. Men will say that if these powers are allowed to respond to the agitation of one group of producers, then every one else must organize and agitate to defend or promote his own interest.

Lippmann found this development a "deplorable prospect." The assumption here was that Roosevelt was subverting an existing classless management of money by disinterested private bankers for a new and dangerous type of management by public officials for the economic advantage of particular classes—in this case, farmers and debtors.[22] This contention, a favorite argument of orthodox internationalists, was one of the more durable conceits of their public rhetoric. Yet however, well worn by usage, this charge of politicizing monetary policy was repeatedly thrown like a political tomato in Roosevelt's face.

Edwin W. Kemmerer, research professor of international

finance at Princeton, was perhaps the most prestigious and persistent public critic of the administration's monetary policies. A familiar figure at congressional hearings, he was active on the podium and in the press in opposition to the least hint of unorthodoxy. As an experienced adviser to foreign nations on reorganizing their monetary systems, Kemmerer had for years been an active participant in the management of money. "All currencies in recent years," he remarked, "have been more or less managed, even the gold standard currencies themselves, over which a moderate amount of management is commonly effected through open-market operations, variations in the discount rates of central banks and other central bank devices." But while central bank management was permissible, political management was different in degree and kind. "The great danger," he cautioned,

> is that a highly managed currency will flounder on the rocks of politics. Prices, wages and debts are "affected" with such tremendous class interests that when once a currency has broken away from its customary metallic basis the danger is that its control will cease to be rational or scientific, despite the good intentions of the administrative authorities, and will become a football of politics.

The public management of money and public confidence in the dollar were mutually exclusive; the former inevitably destroyed trust in the latter—they interacted only to promote uncontrolled inflation. "If the public once loses confidence in its money," he added, "controlling inflation is like controlling a hurricane." [23]

These criticisms were expanded upon by other influential business spokesmen and economic analysts, such as Colonel Ayres, Benjamin Anderson, Moody's Investors Service, the National City Bank of New York, and aroused professors at Yale, Swarthmore, and elsewhere. [24] While the gold experiment was the immediate cause of this discontent, it also provided a convenient vent for the pent-up grievances which had been accumulating about the New Deal. Beyond the conventional objections—such as the traditionalists' distrust of any political tampering with the currency, the disbelief in the commodity dollar, and the disturbance caused to business confidence and long-term investment—more basic suspicions about Roosevelt and the New Deal now emerged. Moody's, for example, reported that private capital was deeply discouraged, but this was only partially due to "the utter lack of knowledge as to what the future value of our monetary unit may be. . . ." It suspected that the profit motive and the capitalistic system itself were being attacked and undermined by such New Deal policies as "price-fixing and production-control schemes, direct Government competition with utility companies, criticisms of high profits in certain industries, attempts to reduce salaries in others, dictation of corporation policies toward union labor."[25]

The gold experiment, whose effects spilled over from the domestic to the international arena, also provoked storm signals from abroad. The earlier repeated warnings of Roosevelt's monetary group that tampering with gold would lead to competitive devaluations and economic warfare now seemed on the verge of realization. When Governor Harrison first informed Montague Norman, head of the Bank of England, that the gold purchase program was to be expanded to foreign markets, Norman "hit the ceiling." He feared that the American policy would "bring about complete currency and exchange chaos in Europe." "London and the Continent," he told Harrison, "were thoroughly frightened."[26] The *London Economist* responded more specifically by bluntly stating:

> There is a point beyond which we cannot remain indifferent to an artificial cheapening of the dollar. . . .
>
> If we consent to this artificial stimulus, American exports might make serious inroads upon the precariously improved condition of our export trade. Still less can we afford to have sterling driven up by an influx of capital fleeing from the United States.
>
> Hitherto, the exchange equalization account has not attempted to manipulate the exchange value of sterling except by neutralizing temporary disturbances. But that policy, formulated without regard to the possibility of currency warfare, might be made an instrument of national policy, and in the

changed circumstances the British Government might reluctantly be forced to adopt a more aggressive policy.[27]

Sir Robert Horne, former chancellor of the exchequer, repeated the message to the members of the New York Bond Club: Great Britain would protect its foreign trade from the incursions of an artifically cheapened dollar.[28]

The burden of attack upon the gold experiment was quickly taken up by business groups who broadened the criticism from individual protest into an organized national movement. Among the more influential organizations which were instrumental in mobilizing this opposition were the Chamber of Commerce of New York State; the Committee on Monetary Policy, based in Chicago; the Economists' National Committee on Monetary Policy, organized on November 17 in New York City and composed of one hundred monetary economists; the Federal Advisory Council of the Federal Reserve Board; the Chamber of Commerce of the United States; and the National Association of Manufacturers.

Two days after Roosevelt began foreign gold purchases, the New York State Chamber launched its drive to arouse national public opinion against monetary experiments. In a special meeting which reached out far beyond its own membership to enlist commercial, civic, trade, and professional groups in its cause, the Chamber adopted resolutions that directly contravened administration policy. "The Chamber believes it is of the greatest importance to business recovery that the Administration clearly and unequivocally announce that it will not adopt an automatic commodity dollar or similar currency experiments, but will adopt a policy directed towards the return to a gold standard." Only stable money would restore business confidence, expand "the volume of business done at a reasonable reward," reopen the flow of investment, and increase the national income. Recovery and the restoration of a gold standard were one and indivisible.[29]

Later in the month, the Federal Advisory Council lent its influence to the protest movement by publicly issuing a set of resolutions highly critical of the administration. In impeccable orthodox style, it declared that a higher price level was a result, not a cause, of an increase in national income and the volume of business and employment, and that monetary uncertainty would neither correct "existing discrepancies in the price level" nor bring about a sound, lasting recovery. The council charged "that this uncertainty tends and has tended to depress the market price of government securities and corporate and municipal bonds, which in turn has affected and will continue to affect adversely the entire economic structure and thus stand in the way of recovery." Furthermore, this would make it difficult for the government to finance its large and increasing expenditures and debt. Under these conditions, long-term investment would be further discouraged to the direct detriment of the durable goods industries—a sector with a large and difficult unemployment problem. Stable money, it insisted, required international cooperation—an improbable prospect except if negotiated on the basis of gold. "History shows," it concluded, "that the further currency inflation goes, the more difficult it becomes to control and that it invariably results in untold losses to great masses of the people and the ruin of national credit."[30]

The Chamber of Commerce of the United States, representing 1,600 business organizations with an estimated membership of 900,000 businessmen, was the largest, most influential spokesman of the business community. It now departed from its position of supporting the president by joining forces with the opposition. Its resolution, issued on the same day as the Federal Advisory Council's, urged Roosevelt "that there be an immediate announcement of intention of an early return to a gold basis, with complete avoidance of monetary experimentation, currency manipulation, greenbackism and fiat money and with complete recession from theoretical or arbitrary ideas of 'price-index' fixation of the value of gold." The Chamber must have found the taste of opposition pleasant, since it also used the occasion to criticize government competition with business, particularly in the housing and public utility fields, and it made some passing swipes at the NRA for not giving business and the trade associations what it regarded as their due influence, especially on the issue of the code authorities' jurisdiction over labor disputes.[31]

By December the business bandwagon was virtually complete when the National Association of Manufacturers, at its annual convention, recommended that the president assure the nation of his intention to return to a modified gold standard as soon as he could manage it "without jeopardy to the people of the United States."[32] The NAM's unusually gentle language was only slightly exceeded by F. M. Law, president of the American Bankers Association, who identified Roosevelt with those like himself who advocated sound money. "I firmly believe," he stated, "that Mr. Roosevelt, with his conservative background and record, and with his knowledge of history and economics, would have the same abhorrence and fear with regard to the issue of fiat money that the most ardent member of the sound money group would have." "Thus far," he added, "the President has employed the mildest and safest of the types of inflationary powers granted him by Congress."[33] If the choice narrowed between the president and Congress on the money question, Roosevelt still remained the clear preference.

Within the administration itself, several prominent advisers who had been closely involved with monetary policy from the start indicated unmistakably that they were indeed reluctant oarsmen on Roosevelt's nationalistic boat. Acheson, Warburg, and Sprague departed suddenly from the government. Acheson, who was close to Lewis Douglas, left in silence after virtually being pushed out by Roosevelt, but Warburg and Sprague immediately joined the opposition as leaders of the rapidly accelerating criticism of Roosevelt's nationalistic policies. Warburg soon became the darling of the conservatives as he went about energetically challenging Roosevelt's recovery policies, first in speeches and articles, then in two denunciatory books published in 1934, *The Money Muddle* and *It's Up to Us.*[34]

Sprague, in a public letter of resignation, complained that he had been shut out of the decision-making process, and that he had been unable even to talk with Roosevelt since returning from the London Conference. His "fundamental disagreement" with the gold policy was based on his conviction that it would not work in achieving higher prices, but that it would succeed in destroying the government's credit. "I believe," he informed Roosevelt, that you are faced with the alternative either of giving up the present policy or of the meeting of Government expenditures with additional paper money. You will then no doubt secure a rise in prices, for you will be faced with the distrust of the currency, already manifest in a growing flight from the dollar, but extending into a frantic desire to hold anything other than currency or securities yielding a fixed interest return.

"I have now reached the conclusion," he announced, "that there is no defense from a drift into unrestrained inflation other than an aroused and organized public opinion."[35] Sprague's immediate contribution to organizing the opposition was his book *Recovery and Common Sense* (1934). In it he publicly joined the list of monetary experts who denied that there was a purely monetary remedy for the depression. Roosevelt, in his preoccupation with a monetary-induced recovery, had stumbled into the wrong boat.

The president remained publicly unperturbed by the gold tempest, but privately his resentment toward his departed advisers and his vocal business critics seeped out. "All goes well here," he wrote to Robert Bingham, his ambassador to London, "though some of the inevitable sniping has commenced, led by what you and I would refer to as the Mellon-Mills influence in banking and certain controlling industries."[36] "I am glad," he remarked to the inflationist leader James H. Rand, Jr., "that you are at work on national broadcasts to counteract the somewhat unpatriotic propaganda we are facing," while to Senator Pittman he confided that "it is a good thing that our friends the enemy are firing off all their ammunition first."[37] Reporting to Secretary Woodin, who was gravely ill and bedridden, on the success of the civil works program in creating employment for four million workers, he added, "General sentiment is so much better that the affairs of the Spragues and Al Smiths of the East are being laughed at more and more."[38] The one public hint of the president's private feelings occurred in his Savannah speech, where he poked fun at "certain modern Tories" who opposed experimentation and the "doubting Thomases" who feared change.[39] Senator James F. Byrnes of South Carolina, who had heard rumors that the president was considering a public reply to his critics, counseled a benign silence, on the principle that "it is a pretty good rule not to do what your enemies want you to do." "I sincerely hope," he told Louie Howe,

> that he does not place himself on the defensive and engage in a debate with Messrs. Sprague, Smith, Baruch and Warburg.
>
> As a matter of fact, these critics have done us no harm. They have helped us by silencing the extreme inflationists of the Senate, who will give us more trouble in the next session than the few who hold and will express the views of Smith and Baruch.[40]

Nonetheless, Roosevelt did have his public defenders against the critical barrage of the monetary traditionalists. The defense, as motley a group as ever assembled in a common cause, included Professors Warren, Rogers, and Fisher, Senator William E. Borah, Father Charles E. Coughlin, William Randolph Hearst, financiers and industrialists associated with the Committee for the Nation, and the Monetary Reform League. The main argument of the defense was, in effect, that the gold program was working, and that more of the same would work even better.

In the midst of all this passionate furor, Governor Harrison warned Roosevelt of the imminent expected fall of the French government and its forced abandonment of the gold standard. To minimize the likelihood that the American gold program would be blamed as the cause, he urged Morgenthau and Roosevelt to cease raising the price of gold for a week. Harrison insisted "that there was nothing magic in the figure of $34.00 an ounce, and that they might just as well stop here rather than unnecessarily precipitate further difficulties here and abroad." It was an opportune time, he argued, to explore the possibility of a short-term stabilization of the dollar and the pound with the British. Roosevelt was unsympathetic to the French situation, remarking that it was their own fault because they had not balanced their budget in the last three years—an ungenerous criticism, considering Roosevelt's fiscal performance. Nor was the president much concerned about Harrison's pessimistic assessment of the government's credit, replying "that the government had lots of funds with which they could support the government bond market and he was not worried about that." Nonetheless, Harrison carried his point; Roosevelt agreed not to alter the gold price for a week, and then to "take stock" of the policy.[41]

On December 2 Harrison met with Morgenthau, who was just back from conferring with Roosevelt at Warm Springs, Georgia, together with Bailie and Oliphant of the Treasury, Warren, Rogers, and Crane. Morgenthau reported that Roosevelt was now "willing to discuss *de jure* stabilization with Great Britain." He added "that the President felt there was much to be said in favor of his fixing a new gold content for the dollar as he was authorized to do under the Thomas Amendment before Congress adjourned, and that if he exercised that power he felt he might be able to deal with Congress." Roosevelt thus effortlessly reversed his tactics and timetable on the stabilization of the dollar. Initially, he had planned to hold off stabilization until June 1934—that is, after Congress adjourned. Now he took the position that he could better control Congress by stabilizing *before* the session adjourned. In fact, he wanted "to do something" (i.e., to fix the gold value of the dollar) before January 1.[42] Harrison, who must have been as startled as he was delighted, moved quickly to sound out the British on the new policy. The British, however, proved intractable. Harrison told Roosevelt that while they would consider a temporary, short-term stabilization, they were opposed at this time to de jure devaluation and stabilization.[43] Roosevelt, who had hoped for simultaneous action with the British, was disappointed. It was the London Conference reenacted in private, but with a curious reversal of roles. Roosevelt would have to proceed on his own toward devaluation and stabilization of the dollar.

On January 15, 1934, the president sent to Congress a message calling for the devaluation of the dollar, and its stabilization at its new value on a modified gold bullion standard. The gold experiment was over. What had been won and lost?

Both Roosevelt and Warren claimed success for the gold experiment. Warren, predictably, justified the program statistically. "When February 1933 is 100," he wrote in *Gold and Prices*

(1935), "the price of gold for the six months after the price of gold was fixed was 169 and the *Journal of Commerce* index of 30 basic commodities averaged 167." According to Warren,

> Most of the advance in the price of gold occurred previous to the date on which control began to be exercised. The average price of gold for 30 business days preceding October 22, 1933, was $30.98. The advance to $35 which took place from October to the following February was only 14 per cent. For the month of January 1934, the average price was $34.27. The advance in February over January was 2 per cent. As would be expected, most of the advance in commodity prices occurred when the price of gold was advanced, because informal action was as effective as formal action.[44]

Warren listed the prices of farm products from February 1933 to March 1934, and he concluded that 110 advanced more than 69 points, while only 11 increased less than the increased price of gold.

Warren's claim for the economic vindication of his theory of the relation of gold and prices was hotly disputed by a near-unanimous consensus of professional economists. The most devastating criticism of the theory itself, its statistical and historical rationale, and the results of its practical application by the Roosevelt administration was that of Walter E. Spahr, professor of economics at New York University, in *The Monetary Theories of Warren and Pearson* (1934), and Charles O. Hardy, economist at the Brookings Institution, in *The Warren-Pearson Price Theory* (1935). The Warren theory emerged from these critiques figuratively torn limb from limb, drawn and quartered.

Roosevelt, who remained unscathed by the hubbub, claimed success on other than economic grounds. As usual, politics was at the front on his mind. And on this score he could not be confuted by economic experts. Economic science, or pseudo-science for that matter, was merely one means to a larger end. Roosevelt's forte and interest was in the management of men, and if he turned for a brief season to the management of gold and money, it was merely one of his many diversionary tactics in the manipulation and control of political realities. In this case, the political realities which he dealt with were an amalgam of highly volatile political pressures emanating from two fiercely competing camps; inflationists and sound-money men.

Roosevelt thus closed the gold circle: from an initial position of orthodox internationalism, which he carried into the London Conference, to a long excursion into economic nationalism thereafter, until he returned safe and sound to the gold standard and international cooperation and accord. In the process he made some limited economic gains, or at least avoided the catastrophic consequences so freely predicted, confounding nearly everyone mainly because everyone else was transfixed by the economic appearance of the gold experiment rather than its political outcome.

And Roosevelt, who proved his ability to play political chess so adroitly with gold, now turned his attention to the returning Congress. He would now test his genius for maneuver and control on the as yet unsubdued silver forces.

EIGHT

Roosevelt Parlays the Silverites

THE IMPACT OF SILVER on the politics of recovery during the New Deal was, if anything, greater than that of gold. Unlike the defenders of the gold standard, who had tradition and established usage on their side, the silverites were the innovators in monetary policy, the latter-day revivalists of a tradition that had lost out with William Jennings Bryan and the bitter presidential campaign of 1896. During the 1932 campaign Roosevelt's opponents attempted to discredit him and the proposed New Deal by linking him with the Bryan cause and legacy. Roosevelt, these critics warned, would out-Bryan Bryan.[1] Roosevelt was far too astute to be caught on that particular bramble, but he laid the charge to political rest during the campaign only to confront it anew, from the opposite side, during his presidency. That political problem, which he now faced, involved him in protracted maneuvering with the resurrected proponents of silver's cause who clamored insistently for him to, as the saying went, "do something for silver." Roosevelt, in effect, moved away from one side of a hot fire only to sit more uncomfortably at another. That ambiguous "something" demanded by the silverites plunged him into the complexities of a political issue which exerted a strong pull among his supporters, and its political resolution was anything but obvious or simple.

Silver, like gold, was both a commodity and a monetary

measure—or, at least, it was a monetary measure in some countries still, notably China, and it had once been in many others, including the United States. By the twentieth century silver had lost out to gold as the preferred, dominant base for national currencies, and in the next three decades it lost further. Its value as a commodity followed its downward course as legal money. In 1920 silver was priced at 133.9 cents an ounce; by 1929 it had plunged to 53.34 cents, and in December 1932 it reached its lowest point in history, 24.6 cents. If the depression was an added disaster for silver as a commodity, it also provided the occasion, or opportunity, for a new crusade for silver's monetary use. To the dedicated silverites, gold was the class money of Wall Street and privilege, while silver was ideologically the people's money. And they made large claims indeed for silver as a recovery panacea from the Great Depression.

The political objective of the silverites was, ideally, to remonetize silver in accord with the old war cry, unlimited coinage at 16 to 1. That is, the United States was to adopt a bimetallic standard consisting of gold and silver as the metallic backing for its currency, with silver valued at a ratio of sixteen ounces of silver to one of gold. The benefits claimed as a result of remonetization were, again ideally, both domestic and international in their effects. Besides raising the world price of silver by increasing demand for it, remonetization would expand the amount of money in circulation; it would achieve the elusive goal of lifting commodity prices, with all its beneficial side effects on debtors and producers of basic commodities; and it would revive world trade. Silver, in short, was the real golden key to recovery.

It was this monetary and ideological aspect of silver which provided it with political potency, and an appeal transcending the obvious self-interest of the silver producers. The enthusiasm for silver centered geographically in the South and West, including the seven Rocky Mountain mining states, but it was hardly confined to them. Among its supporters were agriculturalists and farm organizations, notably the Farmers' Educational and Co-Operative Union; exponents of inflation who were not particular as to the means to a fervently desired end; and monetary reformers such as those associated with the Committee for the Nation. Without its ideological ramifications as a recovery-reform measure, silver would have been of no interest to spokesmen for the veterans, the farmers, and the debtors. These constituted the potential components of a successful political movement if anyone with sufficient political wit could unify them behind a specific legislative program which effectively combined their diverse objectives into a rationalized whole. Actually, there was no lack of aspirants for this role, but the qualifications ran exceedingly high: success depended in the last resort on outmaneuvering President Roosevelt.

Roosevelt had a number of possible strategies to choose from as the means of neutralizing the political appeal of silver, or of controlling the content and scope of silver legislation if the issue came to that pass. He might, for example, feign a genuine interest in the recovery potentialities of a restored bimetallic standard as a more immediately effective version of controlled inflation. Or, at the other extreme, he could conceivably make an open alliance with the sound money forces in the business community and resolutely face down any silver tampering with gold. However, if he chose to deal with silver in the forum of public opinion, he might well try the strategy of attempting to alienate and divide the silver inflationists from the exponents of other forms of inflation, thereby isolating the silverites and rendering them impotent. Or, if Congress were regarded as the more favorable ground for contest, he might play off the Senate against the House, or vice versa—to prevent any silver legislation from issuing at all, to work out an acceptable compromise, or to hold enough votes to sustain his veto of any unacceptable legislation. One final possibility to consider: Roosevelt might concentrate on maneuvers to split the silver bloc itself by separating the uncompromising ideologues of remonetization from others of a more practical bent who would sacrifice theory for assurance that the price of the commodity silver would be enhanced, thereby improving the cash return of their constituents, the silver producers.

Another politician might have chosen *one* of these strategies, but we are dealing here with Franklin D. Roosevelt, and it was not his style to cast away plausible options carelessly. Nor did he lack the talent to carry off a performance that easily could have wrecked a lesser politician. Roosevelt, in effect, made gestures in all directions; figuratively, he danced lightly about all possibilities, to the utter bafflement of friend and foe alike. In the course of this complex ritual he effectively masked his roundabout methods of asserting political control not only of the silverites, but of that larger body of which they were a part— the inflationists.

By the 1930s the production, refinement, and ownership of silver were an American-dominated enterprise. Silver was primarily a by-product of copper, lead, and zinc mining—in the United States 80 percent of the silver produced was a by-product, while in world production this was the case for about 40 percent. Since 1920 Mexico, the United States, Canada, and Peru had accounted for 80 percent of all silver mined. Mexico's output was the largest, at 40 percent (1925–29), while the United States produced 24 percent; however, by 1929, through foreign capital investment, "American interests controlled 66 percent of the mine production of the world." In addition, refinery production was largely an American monopoly (77.8 percent), with the British a poor second (11.4 percent). Yet while Americans were by far the largest influence in silver, silver itself as a commodity was insignificant in the American economy. "The importance of silver to the United States," Y. S. Leong calculated, "may be gauged by its relative position among the 550 commodities sold at wholesale. Of the aggregate value in exchange derived from these commodities, silver contributes only one-tenth of one percent."[2] Silver's value, as Joseph Reeve sacrilegiously put it, was less than that of peanuts in the American economy. But despite its economic insignificance, silver was a power on the political scene long before peanuts.[3]

Silver's power derived, in the first instance, from the fact that although it was produced in a limited region (Utah, Idaho, Montana, Arizona, Nevada, Colorado, and New Mexico), these seven states had fourteen United States senators speaking and working on silver's behalf. In a Congress mesmerized by inflationary visions of quick recovery, the silver bloc was potentially the difference between yea and nay on important legislative matters, particularly those of an inflationist nature. Beyond this, silver commanded an imposing array of political talent and parliamentary experience. Among its most conspicuous leaders were Democratic Senators Thomas (Okla.), Wheeler, and Pittman and, on the Republican side, the formidable Borah.[4] In their relationship to Roosevelt, Thomas and Wheeler were outsiders, while Pittman, the epitome of the practical politician, was the insider—willing and eager to do some business with Roosevelt.

From the outset of the New Deal, Roosevelt worked closely with and through Pittman on all matters that touched upon silver. It was Pittman whom Roosevelt chose to send to the London Conference to negotiate an agreement that aimed to increase the price of silver. The ensuing agreement, which Pittman carefully defined as *not* a treaty (to avoid the bother of ratification by the Senate), provided for raising the price of silver by limiting the supply to the market of both newly mined and existing silver stocks. Pittman, who went to London accompanied by a Senate resolution (sponsored by Wheeler) urging the American delegation to promote bimetallism internationally, dealt with the ideological aspect of silver by ignoring it. It would not be the first or the last time that the Nevada senator sacrificed the monetary claims of silver for the sake of practical advantage to silver the commodity.

By December 1933 Pittman was becoming increasingly anxious at the president's delay in accepting the London silver agreement. Pittman reminded Henry Morgenthau that American acceptance only required a presidential proclamation; it was unnecessary to refer the matter back to Congress, since Roosevelt already had been granted full power to act. Furthermore, it would be exceedingly unwise to provide Congress with another opportunity to debate the money issue. "The excitement in the country relative to the remonetization of silver," the senator suggestively noted, "is growing rapidly, and this excitement would be greatly allayed, and many advocates of the remonetization of silver satisfied, if the President should take the action suggested."[5]

Roosevelt, for his part, hardly needed to be reminded that remonetization was much on the public and the congressional mind. On December 21 he issued a proclamation designed to "allay" the inflationary "excitement," and thereby officially adopted Pittman's advice and handiwork. This provided for removing from the market annually for four years twenty-four million ounces of newly mined American silver by government purchase. The government was to pay the legal price of $1.29 an ounce, retaining 50 percent of this as a seigniorage fee. The American producer, in short, would now receive one-half the legal price, or 64.5 cents an ounce. Since the prevailing market price was 43 cents, and the total domestic output for 1932 had been, curiously, twenty-four million ounces, the American producer was being given a guaranteed higher price for his entire product.[6] While Roosevelt, in a press conference, stressed that he was merely carrying out the plan agreed upon at London, the *New York Times* perceived another intent. "Capitol Hill," it reported, "reflected at least the partial success of another purpose, considered perfectly obvious here, the quieting of inflation demands by the silver bloc."[7] And in truth it was a beginning that other commodity producers might envy. But as the silver ideologues quickly pointed out, it was not remonetization. With gold currently at $34.06, bimetallism at 16 to 1 would have put silver at $2.13 an ounce. In any event, Roosevelt's first bid failed to allay the excitement, and this became evident when the Seventy-third Congress returned to Washington for its regular session in January.

Pittman, in a private forecast to Roosevelt on the probable political alignment in Congress, had predicted that the members would divide into three groups: Tories, radicals, and liberals.[8] As for the Tories, he expected that they

> will probably demand the immediate return to the gold standard; the repeal of the Act declaring contracts payable in gold contrary to public policy, and that such contracts may be settled in any legal tender money; that only gold, gold coin and notes secured by legal reserve of gold shall be legal tender; that the so-called Thomas Amendment be repealed; that the special budget for special emergency expenditures under Public Works Act and under similar Acts be repealed.

145

The radicals, he judged, would demand a 50 percent devaluation of the gold dollar; "that the soldiers' bonus certificates be cashed, and that their pensions and compensations be restored; that the wages of Government employees be increased proportionate to the increase in wages of non-Government employees; and our Government take the initiative in restoring bimetallism throughout the world." The Tories would be the smallest faction, the radicals the largest, and the liberals the crucial swing group. "The liberal group," he suggested, "will be in a position to perform the greatest service to the country if it is unified and well organized behind a constructive program that meets with your approval."[9] It was a perceptive analysis, and implicit in it was the assumption of combining conservative opposition to change with liberal moderation to undercut the radicals' drive for an outright inflationary program.

Congress, as Pittman predicted, quickly demonstrated that it was in an uncontrollable ferment, with its members determined to force Roosevelt's hand toward the use of more forceful inflationary measures. The House was the first to break loose from administration control, aided and abetted by that old silverite, Speaker of the House Rainey (D–Ill.). Representatives of the wheat belt organized themselves by state delegations to cooperate with the Western silverites. Representative Martin (D–Colo.), chairman of the Rocky Mountain group, was instrumental in the organizing drive; he planned to expand on this initial success by next organizing successively the representatives of the Southwest and the Pacific Coast, then moving eastward to create an effective national silver bloc.[10] In a related move, the governors of the silver-producing states created a silver committee and sent its chairman, George W. Malone, to establish quarters in Washington to lobby for remonetization. "The silver advocates feel," the *New York Times* reported, "that they have but one thing to do to force some action on the metal, and that is to agree upon a single plan."[11]

Nonetheless, interest in the House initially centered on two plans—the Dies and the Fiesinger bills. The Dies Bill provided for subsidizing the export of agricultural products by permitting foreign nations to pay for them with silver valued at a premium of 25 percent above its world price. The Fiesinger Bill authorized the purchase of silver to be used as a reserve against a silver currency issue—the purchases to continue (up to 1.5 billion ounces) until prices reached the 1926 level. The Speaker allowed the silverites a giant step forward by deciding to call up the Dies Bill under a special rule requiring a two-thirds majority to pass. Rainey thus effectively eliminated the competition of the Fiesinger Bill, achieving the long-sought unity around one plan. Martin Dies explained part of the success of his winning combination when he remarked:

> It is undisputed that many of the silver-using countries as well as all others need our surplus agricultural products. They cannot purchase our products with gold because they have no gold, they cannot exchange our products for their products on account of tariff barriers, and they cannot purchase our products with their silver money because, through the process of exchange of their money for gold they are compelled to pay too much for our products.[12]

Senator Thomas of Oklahoma exposed another aspect of the House uprising when he observed that "the House is expressing itself in favor of currency expansion. It doesn't care whether it comes through the bonus or through silver."[13] On March 19 the Dies bill passed the House by better than the two-thirds vote required, 257 to 112.[14]

In the Senate events followed a different course toward the same destination. The first major move here was an attempt to capitalize on the steadily mounting support for Wheeler's remonetization plan. The Montanan proposed this plan again as an amendment to the administration's Gold Revaluation Bill; the amendment's defeat by a mere two votes convinced the silverites that if they combined silver with a measure that had the support of the agricultural interests, a majority was assured.[15] And they quickly divined that the vehicle to realize this purpose was already at hand in the Dies Bill. At a meeting of twenty-three inflation-minded senators, a strategy was devised to broaden the Dies Bill from a primarily agricultural relief measure into a relief-recovery proposal by amending it to provide for the compulsory government purchase of 750 million ounces of silver, against which silver certificates would then be issued. This would permit farmers to dispose of their surplus staple crops on the world market while the silverites at long last would achieve remonetization on a grand scale.

The achievement of unity by silver, inflationist, and agricultural spokesmen around a specific bill came in spite of a series of blocking maneuvers by Roosevelt and Morgenthau. The president had attempted to avoid the coalescence of the inflationary factions by such diversionary tactics as the gold experiment, the acceptance of the London silver agreement, the Gold Revaluation Act, and a number of other minor concessions and implausible alternatives. Early on in the regular session, he flatly informed Congress that he neither wanted nor would he accept any silver legislation for the time being.[16] Morgenthau added his bit by telling the members of the House Banking and Currency Committee, who were holding hearings on another version of the Goldsborough Bill for monetary reform, that the administration's monetary program was an experiment, that the Treasury was operating consequently on a "day-to-day basis," and that Congress should refrain from interfering for at least a year—providing sufficient time to assess the results of the experiment.[17] Morgenthau also attempted to lull the silverites by announcing that he was sending Professor Rogers to the Far East to investigate the international and trade aspects of the silver question. Roosevelt, when he returned from his vacation in late April, met with the congressional leaders to reiterate his opposition to any monetary or inflationary legislation, including specifically the Dies Bill.[18] However, when all these tactics failed to check the gathering momentum of the silverites, the president abandoned opposition for the more flexible mode of political compromise.

In a series of bargaining conferences during April and May, Roosevelt and the Senate silver leaders gradually worked out a compromise silver measure. Roosevelt at first proposed that the Dies Bill be broadened "to include the promotion of industrial as well as farm products."[19] This suggestion was then elaborated into an even more grandiose scheme. Roosevelt's new idea

was to link "a domestic silver program with moves . . . for reciprocal tariffs and an international monetary conference."
Specifically, Roosevelt was offering a package which included
the eventual nationalization of silver at a price not exceeding
50 cents an ounce (that is, of existing stocks, exclusive of newly
mined domestic silver, which would remain at the current price
of 64.5 cents); a bimetallic currency reserve at the ratio of 75
percent gold to 25 percent silver; and additional executive authority to negotiate silver agreements for increasing the world
price of silver and improving the competitive position of American exports in world markets. In return for these concessions,
Roosevelt insisted that the execution of these provisions, both
as to methods and timing, must remain flexible.[20] This was
merely another way of telling the Congress that he would accept silver legislation only if it were cast in permissive and not
mandatory terms.

The committed silver ideologues immediately balked at
leaving the implementation of the compromised program to the
discretion of the president. They had already learned a great
deal about the practical ramifications of that strategy from Roosevelt's handling of the permissive inflationary provisions of the
Thomas Amendment. Wheeler publicly denied that the president had given any specific commitment on remonetization, and
Borah walked out in protest from a conference with Morgenthau over the issue of discretionary authority.[21] It was at this
unresolved juncture that Senator Pittman's persuasive talents
and his penchant for bargaining and compromise came into
full play.

Pittman, as a longtime student of silver, had his own preferred solutions for restoring the monetary and market value
of a metal which figured so prominently in his home state of
Nevada. During the course of his advocacy of silver, he had
visited China in 1925 and again in 1931.[22] In the early stages
of the silverites' renewed pressure on Roosevelt, he urged his
own matured scheme upon Morgenthau and the president. His
plan, in brief, was to open the fabled potential market of China
to American exports by increasing the exchange value of
Chinese money—silver. This could be accomplished by the

American government undertaking a worldwide unlimited coinage of silver. "We propose," Pittman argued, "to coin silver from anywhere, and to place the coined silver, or the bullion that we would have coined, in our treasury, and issue silver certificates in payment for it." Pittman estimated that speculators held between 400 and 500 million ounces of silver, and he conceded that most of this might end up in the United States. However, this prospect did not alarm him or detract from the usefulness of his plan. "In what way," he asked,

> would that disturb our economic system? Only 12 per cent of our circulating currency is silver. Based on the increased value of gold, it is only 8 per cent. In 1900 30 per cent of our total currency issued was silver. We could issue $1,800,000,000 of dollars in silver certificates and place them in circulation, and even then the proportion of our silver currency to our other currency would not exceed that of 1900.
>
> Why not try this plan? It is within the power of the President at any time, by proclamation, to terminate it. That is the reason why this plan has an advantage over any congressional legislation. An Act of Congress is inflexible, and sometimes is hard to repeal in the face of a filibuster. A Presidential proclamation can be annulled at any time. Why argue upon the theory as to what may happen with regard to our currency or our exports or our imports when the matter can be determined by actual experience without any danger whatsoever?[23]

While Pittman spoke in the clear tones of political pragmatism in support of his preferred program, he also readily assumed the familiar role of mediator between the silver bloc and the Roosevelt administration during the series of conferences which led to the Silver Purchase Act of 1934. Pittman informed the president that the inflationists were already dissatisfied with the recently enacted Gold Revaluation Act. They were convinced that it was being administered by the Treasury in a fashion calculated to minimize its inflationary impact. Silver legislation thus offered them yet another opportunity to make good on their long-held and consistently thwarted determination to devise an effective inflationary recovery program. It was Pittman's function to discern the consensus among the Senate's silverites and strike a bargain with Roosevelt that would avoid a futile, destructive political fight while at the same time advancing silver's cause another important step foward.

On April 22 Roosevelt met in "informal conference" with the silver senators; on the following day the silverites gathered together with the members of the Senate Committee on Agriculture, who were discussing the Dies Bill, to mull over the president's statements on silver. According to Pittman's report to the president, Senator Thomas summarized his understanding of the president's position by stating that while Roosevelt was "in sympathy with the desires and intentions of those who were supporting the Dies bill," he was not in favor of the Dies Bill itself. Thomas's impression was that Roosevelt preferred first "to work out something internationally" before proceeding with any silver legislation; "that you felt that mandatory legislation might tie your hands and it might be in the interest of the government to act immediately and in a more flexible manner." Thomas then launched into a familiar refrain by bluntly criticizing the administration's gold policy; the senators present agreed with his conclusion "that the devaluation of the gold dollar was futile unless the additional base was utilized for the purpose of supplying additional currency." However, at this gathering it was Senator Henrik Shipstead who spoke to the more immediate concern of the silverites, and he expressed "the concurrency of opinion" of the group. With his report Pittman enclosed a copy of Shipstead's remarks for the president's contemplation.[24]

Shipstead disposed of Roosevelt's maneuvers to forestall national silver legislation in favor of internatonal negotiatons by remarking, "I do not believe you can get an international agreement on silver." The Europeans just were not interested. Nor was the Minnesota Farmer-Laborite optimistic about the administration's recovery program or its future prospects. "I do not have much hope of recovery," he stated simply. In his mind, there were only three options for inducing recovery, and these were "controlled inflation," cutting the interest rates on debts in half, and "wholesale bankruptcy."

> I have favored the use of government credit to give us a
> breathing spell during which we could inaugurate policies for
> the liquidation of this indebtedness whose fixed charges are
> choking industry and agriculture. It has been said that the ex-
> penditure of Government funds would "prime the pump" of
> banking and private credit. Did you ever try to "prime the
> pump" that is cracked?

Nor was he impressed with the economic performance of the
Agricultural Adjustment Administration. In 1933, he pointed
out, "the farmers' income was six billion dollars." This year the
AAA's benefit payments would raise this to approximately $7
billion. "That is six billion dollars less than the income of agriculture in 1926, with their fixed charges as high or higher than
they were at that time." The main beneficiaries of AAA were
the cotton and tobacco farmers, but, he added, "they make up
a comparatively small part of our agricultural populaton." Besides the continued low prices for eggs, pork, butter, oats, and
wheat, farmers faced new burdens imposed by the NRA in the
form of higher prices for the things they bought. "Under the
price raising program the farmer will be gouged for more than
any benefit he will receive out of the agricultural program."
The farmers, he predicted, would be worse off at the end of
this year than last.

The solution to these conditions, he insisted, was not to be
found in federal relief. The crux of the matter was the unresolved issue of money and credit:

> Our credit system must be made to function. We tried to make
> it function for four years by blowing Federal credit into it but
> it is like pumping air into a tire that has blown out. . . . The
> way to pay debts is to give the debtor a dollar of the same
> purchasing power as the dollar he borrowed. The paralysis of
> our credit system must be attacked and in my opinion the most
> orderly way to attack it is by a domestic cheapening of the
> dollar at once to raise the price level of raw materials and
> through the proper control of the NRA keep the prices of
> finished products down until some purchasing power can be
> allowed to flow into the pockets of the great mass of the peo-
> ple.

> No one wants uncontrolled inflation. The remonetization
> of silver will give us a controlled inflation. I do not know
> whether it will give us sufficient inflation but I think it ought
> to be tried and at once.

Pittman's own conclusions regarding this meeting and the
consensus he perceived in it are highly reflective of his mediator role. He informed Roosevelt that he had "no doubt the Dies
bill will pass the Senate either with the present silver amendments or with some others." Pittman regarded this as an "im-
perfect act," and he added that it was loaded with great political danger for the president. "If you vetoed the act, and it could
not be carried over your veto in the Senate, it would undoubtedly embarrass members of the House and the Senate in their
support of your program in the coming campaign." Since Pittman saw pitfalls as well in Roosevelt's signing the existing bill,
he suggested his own strategy for resolving the dilemma:

> I have been giving considerable thought to the matter. I be-
> lieve that we can work out amendments to the silver provisions
> of the Dies bill, which, while in expression mandatory, will, in
> fact, be so flexible and so limited as to avoid entirely the dan-
> gers of mandatory legislation which you fear.[25]

Later, in May, after Roosevelt had decided to make the new
silver legislation an administration matter, Pittman offered some
additional parliamentary advice. "The situation," he wrote to
Morgenthau,

> is this: There is now pending on the calendar the House bill
> known as the Dies Bill. The proper parliamentary procedure,
> in my opinion, would be to have Senator Robinson, as Majority
> Leader, move at the proper time for the consideration of such
> bill. Then permit me to offer the Administration measure in
> the nature of a substitute for the Dies Bill. To accomplish this
> I would move to strike out all after the enacting clause, and
> substitute the Administration measure.

Pittman, who claimed credit for drafting the bill's provisions
for a 25 percent silver reserve and its requirement that silver
be paid for with silver certificates, as well as the stipulation that
these be put into actual circulation, was very anxious to sponsor

153

the bill. "I have a great ambition," he confided to Morgenthau, "as a closing act in the work that I have been doing with regard to Silver during the past 5 years, to offer this amendment [i.e., bill]." Pittman was concerned here with mending his political fences. The honor of sponsorship would refute a number of "false reports" which were politically damaging to him. "It was generally reported by my opponents in the State of Nevada, and throughout the West," he complained, "that the action taken by me at the London Conference has blocked the passage of the Wheeler Free Coinage Act, and was so intended; that I was in opposition to the aspirations of the Silver Bloc." The new silver legislation, which he helped so materially to design, ought by political right to bear his public imprint.[26]

On May 31 the adminisration bill passed the House without any material changes, 263 to 77.[27] In the Senate, the committed inflationists attempted on June 11 to broaden and strengthen the measure with major inflationary amendments. Thomas of Oklahoma proposed to increase the amount of silver which could be bought under the program by requiring that the silver purchased for reserve should be calculated at its market and not its monetary value. This first test of strength was defeated 65 to 17. Senator Long next offered the free coinage amendment, modified by the proviso that the president might set any ratio between silver and gold within the range of 16 to 1 to 70 to 1. This was rejected by 59 to 18. Shipstead's amendment, which would have added the Patman Veterans' Bonus Payment Bill to the measure, was then defeated 51 to 31. The bill then passed as Pittman had introduced it, 54 to 25—six Democrats joining sixteen Republicans in opposition.[28]

Roosevelt and Pittman could well afford to be pleased with their bargain. China, one of the chief purported beneficiaries of this act, did not see the outcome in the same light. Li Ming, chairman of the Bank of China, ironically thanked Congress for its friendship and concern for the welfare of China in a "thanks but no thanks" speech at the Bankers Club in New York City. Discussing the economic aspects of the measure, he predicted that it would cause great harm to China. "China," he explained in impeccable orthodox language, "does not suffer

from low value of silver. Her purchasing power is not measured by the value of silver she possesses, the same as America's
purchasing power is not measured by the value of gold you
possess." Purchasing power, he reminded the Americans dryly,
was directly related to productivity:

> China, like every other country, pays for her imports chiefly
> by her exports. The silver in her possession, no matter how
> big that amount may be, does not help much in her purchases
> abroad. The theory that by raising the price of silver China
> would be able to buy more in America or America would be
> able to sell more in China is not economically sound. The ef-
> fect, if any, would be very short lived as China could not long
> afford to pay for American imports of commodities with ex-
> ports of silver because she needs all the silver she has for her
> medium of exchange.[29]

The agitation for silver inflation did not suddenly cease with
the passage of the compromise act. Senator Thomas, together
with other committed ideologues, continued to propagandize
the money issue, monetary reformers gathered in conference,
and congressmen and senators pressed the administration for
larger purchases of silver at higher prices.[30] What did change
was the political context in which all this occurred. Silver was
now administratively contained. The determination of the volume of silver purchases as well as the support price of silver
domestically and internationally had been brought safely within
the confines of the Department of the Treasury. There the value
of silver could be measured by political scales, and its monetary
impact neutralized by the simple expedient of withdrawing from
circulation Federal Reserve notes sufficient to counteract the
new issues of silver certificates.

On August 9, 1934, President Roosevelt invoked the Silver
Purchase Act to nationalize silver, calling into the Treasury the
silver on the commercial markets. The price set for this silver
was a fraction above 50 cents an ounce.[31] Senator Pittman, in a
public statement, declared:

> It is a process that will hasten the complete absorption of the
> silver surplus in the world. As the surplus is absorbed in the

Treasury of the United States, the price of silver will steadily rise until it reaches $1.29 an ounce.

Then the Governments of the world will be in a position to open their mints for unlimited coinage at the ratio that exists in the United States. This will settle the silver question forever.[32]

That might well have been the senator's dream; the political realities as he and President Roosevelt shaped them were far different. In an impressive feat of political alchemy, Roosevelt had succeeded in stabilizing a highly volatile substance.

NINE

The Agricultural Disparity
and General Economic Recovery

A MAJOR, IF NOT OVERRIDING, impulse in President Roosevelt's use of unorthodox monetary experiments was the compelling sense which he shared with others that something had to be done for agriculture.[1] Ideally, whatever was done had to be both politically dramatic and economically effective—a bold new departure from the ineffectual farm policies of the immediate past, a program that would not only restore farm prosperity but also serve as a reliable catalyst for a general recovery of the economy as a whole. Agriculture was thus a preeminent priority in the Roosevelt administration's agenda for national economic recovery. The rationale for this precedence was a complex intertwining of ideological, economic, and political considerations which provided an effective appeal for public support and plausible argument in support of its economic utility.

Ideologically, Roosevelt was in many ways a latter-day exemplar of what Richard Hofstadter has aptly termed "the agrarian myth."[2] This style of thought—with its powerful, evocative appeal to those who cherish the land, particularly farm folk—rests upon several potent assumptions. A close identification, for example, is assumed here between the work of the farmer and the producing class. Farmers produce *real* things, the tangible resources which provide the essential basis for the nation's wealth. Beyond this, the very nature of intimate contact with the soil is believed to promote personal and social values—self-reliance, resourcefulness, individualism—qualities that are vital, irreplaceable ingredients for nurturing democratic man and sustaining a democratic society and political system.

The political considerations justifying agricultural precedence in New Deal politics were of a more mundane, immediate sort. The agricultural disparity—the broadening gap between what farmers received for their produce and what they paid for their supplies and services—was an undoubted breeding ground for severe political discontent. The Farmers' Holiday Association movement was merely the most evident expression of class instability and a militant forecast of future possibilities.[3] Roosevelt was highly sensitive to these signs and their disruptive potentialities, and he moved, in part, to counteract them by articulating an economic theory of recovery which followed the assumptions of the agrarian myth. In its baldest form, this theory held that general economic recovery depended upon the prior achievement of recovery for agriculture. The farmer's ideological preeminence as producer was here reflected in his economic indispensability as the harbinger of recovery. Recovery, like national wealth and virtue, properly originated with the farmers and in the countryside. Once the farmer recovered his purchasing power through government-induced higher prices for agricultural commodities, the beneficial effects would spread far and wide throughout the economy, culminating in national recovery.[4]

These ideas were widely cultivated by the president and his chief agricultural advisers, such as Henry A. Wallace, M. L. Wilson, and Chester C. Davis.[5] In his last speech of the 1932 campaign, in Boston, Roosevelt made the message explicit for his urban audience:

> We need to give to 50 million people who live directly or indirectly upon agriculture a price for their products in excess of the cost of production. That will give them the buying power to start your mills and mines to work, to supply their needs. They cannot buy your goods because they cannot get a fair price for their products. You are poor because they are poor.

Secretary of Agriculture Wallace, in a statement at the outset of the New Deal, asserted:

> The Administration accepts as a fundamental principle the view that restoration of the farmers' buying power is an essential part of the program to relieve the present economic emergency, not only for agriculture but for all industry and a large portion of our national credit structure.

M. L. Wilson, the chief architect of the revised domestic allotment plan, in defending the proposal at a congressional hearing, argued that "the farmer is incidental. The primary benefit . . . is to the nation as a whole." Increasing the farmers' purchasing power, he insisted, was the quickest way to get the economy off dead center. But perhaps the most cogent statement of this economic theory was that of Chester Davis, successor to George Peek as head of the Agricultural Adjustment Administration. In April 1934, he stated:

> The purpose of the act is to restore the buying power of agriculture as an essential part of general recovery. It is intended that the effects of improved prices of the basic crops will be reflected in better prices for other farm products and in increased employment in the cities as the farmers regain the ability to buy goods of mills and factories.

All of these pronouncements, beyond their obvious function as efforts in political persuasion to win support for New Deal policies, reveal the pervasive agrarian bias that was shared by Roosevelt and some of his most influential advisers. Nor was the preference for country life over city life in policy decision-making confined strictly to agricultural programs. The same bias is evident in such diverse activities as the Civilian Conservation Corps, farm resettlement efforts, the greenbelt towns, and the Tennessee Valley Authority. At a time when there were only 6 million farms and perhaps 9 million farmers among 120 million Americans,[6] the Roosevelt administration's stress upon agriculture in its recovery strategy was eloquent testimony to the persistence and economic elaboration of the agrarian myth.

Overall, Roosevelt's agricultural recovery policies can be fairly comprehended under three broad categories of activity:

direct federal attempts to raise farm commodity prices through primary reliance on curtailing supplies by restricting production; the expansion of federal farm credit agencies and the creation of new ones to protect farmers against foreclosures and inadequate, prohibitively priced credit; and a wide range of monetary experiments to cheapen the dollar, raise farm commodity prices, and relieve the pressure on debtors. Each of these approaches was formally recognized as a separate title of the first Agricultural Adjustment Act: (1) the Agricultural Adjustment Act proper; (2) the Emergency Farm Mortgage Act; (3) the Thomas Amendment.[7]

The credit provisions of this act, together with the administration's subsequent legislative enlargement of agricultural credit facilities, such as the Farm Credit Act of 1933, and the consolidation of these agencies by Henry Morgenthau, Jr., in the Farm Credit Administration, can be regarded as the agricultural counterpart of the administration's initial emergency banking program. In both instances, liberal federal aid was used to rescue seriously endangered business enterprises. In effect, the Roosevelt administration socialized the losses of bankers and farmers with public funds through the successful completion of an extensive reconstruction effort. Two basic free-enterprise institutions—privately owned banks and farms—were stabilized and preserved. It is a curious fact, however, that while historians of the New Deal have pointed out that Roosevelt deliberately allowed an unmatched opportunity to nationalize the banking system to pass by,[8] no one, to my knowledge, has remarked that he showed the same conservative restraint in forgoing an equally possible opportunity to nationalize the nation's farms. Roosevelt was perfectly consistent in his disinterest in both possibilities. New Deal governmental intervention in the economic process was designed to aid and preserve privately owned capitalist institutions, not to supplant them by radical innovations.

While New Deal farm credit policies could and did stabilize land ownership, farm mortgages, country banks, and large insurance companies (which, like the banks, had invested heavily in farm land), these policies had no direct effect on farm income. That is, farm credit could save the farmer his home and land, it could provide him with cheap short-term, intermediate, or long-term credit to meet his varied obligations, and it could supply needed producer's capital, but it could not raise farm prices. In retrospect, agricultural historians are undoubtedly correct in judging New Deal credit policies to be far more significant for the welfare of agriculture than the artificial price-rising expedients which absorbed so much of contemporary attention.[9] Politically, however, this is largely irrelevant, for the simple reason that farmers thought and acted otherwise. For them, the immediate need was for higher farm prices, and they were convinced that the most effective means for securing their goal (other than inflation) was by positive federal intervention in the marketplace. Their attitude was well expressed by farm spokesmen such as John Simpson, whose repeated message in this regard was that farmers did not need more loans—what they badly wanted was more cash income. "The success of all plans," Representative Edward C. Eicher of Iowa wrote to Roosevelt, "is contingent upon the event of rising price levels. More bond issues, further extension of the last administration's policy of lending interest-drawing government credit, will not add to existing gross spending power, will not thaw out frozen spending power, *and will not raise price levels.*"[10]

Roosevelt's monetary experiments, as we have seen, were in the main a direct response to this intense pressure by farm spokesmen and leaders. He undoubtedly hoped that monetary measures would provide some degree of economic relief by way of higher prices, particularly for the producers of basic staple crops. This expectation was disappointed. The positive returns from monetary policies were political, not economic, and here Roosevelt may well have achieved at least as much as he had planned. The political objectives were to dampen farmer militancy, to prevent more drastic inflationary policies, and to gain sufficient time for the more permanent economic resolution of the farm price problem to take effect through the AAA. The AAA, once functioning, was expected to relieve Roosevelt of these combined economic and political pressures, achieve one of the administration's prime recovery objectives, and effectively contain the restless energies of farmers within the safe administrative confines of the Department of Agriculture. The AAA clearly was loaded with exceedingly ambitious goals and extravagant expectations.

The Agricultural Adjustment Act has been very accurately described as an "omnibus measure."[11] This refers to Roosevelt's tactic—by no means confined to agriculture—of incorporating into one legislative act most, if not all, of the competing proposals currently being pushed for enactment. The use of this technique reveals a great deal about such diverse matters as Roosevelt's leadership, the Congress, the farm bloc, the diversity and disunity of American agriculture, the functioning of power politics, and the neutralization of political discontent.

Roosevelt, in the rush of the First Hundred Days, found it expedient to secure the undelayed enactment of his major proposals by combining competing farm plans in one big package. This procedure undoubtedly saved a great deal of time, and it had the added advantage of initially ensuring broad political support from nearly every segment of American agriculture, since practically everyone's pet idea was included. This eclectic approach also facilitated cordial relations with the Congress, especially the farm bloc. For years farm spokesmen, both inside and outside the Congress, had been unable to agree upon one farm program. Each went his unreconstructed way, with the predictable outcome that the major proposals—McNary-Haugenism, the export debenture plan, cost-of-production-plus-a-profit, domestic allotment in its evolving versions—went unrealized in law.[12] Furthermore, for the Congress to choose one proposal against all the others meant, if nothing else, making more enemies among the disappointed than friends among the victors. Contemporary critics called this development "congressional abdication of responsibility," and they also deplored the trend of granting the president what they regarded as vast, even "dictatorial" powers.[13] Both criticisms were exaggerated; it would be more accurate to describe congressional behavior in this instance as politically prudent. Why take the heat when President Roosevelt was willing to accommodate?

The omnibus approach also frankly acknowledged the wide,

complex range of American agriculture. It was surely unrealistic to think that any one program could serve the multiple, conflicting requirements of diverse sections and crops, large and small farms, private and cooperative enterprises—in short, the continental variety of American agriculture. Henry Wallace made this point most persuasively on Capitol Hill:

> Production and marketing conditions for the various basic agricultural commodities vary from one to another. The continuous change in economic situations makes any inflexible solution certain to be found unsuitable or ineffective after a comparatively short time. To deal with the many factors that contribute to the farmers' present situation . . . and to meet the changes in the economic situation, Congress must enact legislation granting broad and flexible powers to the Administration. It must trust for a solution of the present emergency to the exercise of sound discretion by the Chief Executive and those who carry out his program. Nothing less will suffice to meet the realities that now confront us. Congress has granted such authority to meet the banking emergency. It should . . . do likewise in meeting the agricultural emergency, which is so intimately woven with the banking situation and the industrial depression. . . .[14]

The "broad and flexible powers" of the AAA to which Wallace alluded were truly remarkable. Included among the act's sweeping provisions—a synthesis of farm proposals old and new—were the latest version of the domestic allotment plan, ideas from McNary-Haugenism (Marketing agreements, import quotas, export subsidies), government land leasing, federal purchase of surpluses, the processing tax, and the authority to license processors for the purpose of enforcing compliance. In addition, the Thomas Amendment further enlarged the administration's options by permitting the use of such monetary methods as the remonetization of silver, the alteration of the gold content of the dollar, and the resort to issuing greenbacks.[15]

When the original bill was first sent over to Congress, Roosevelt accompanied it with a dramatic statement. "I tell you frankly," he wrote, "that it is a new and untrod path, but I tell you with equal frankness that an unprecedented condition calls for the trial of new means."[16] However improbable, the bill in its amended form reduced the president's words to understatement: the "new means" had multiplied appreciably, and the "untrod path" had become more akin to a virgin forest.

The price of Roosevelt's acquiescence in these inclusive proposals was congressional acceptance of his demand that all of its provisions be made permissive—subject, that is, to the president's discretion. As it turned out, the New Deal was to use all of these options at one time or another during the years 1933–41. In fact even proscribed plans, such as the cost-of-production plan championed by the Farmers' Union, were eventually adopted in practice—although admittedly in a restricted, piecemeal fashion. Cost-of-production was essentially a proposal for governmentally administered farm prices specifically fixed at a level that would guarantee producers a profit. In one of its popular versions, this plan specified that the tabulation of cost of production for a farmer should include such items as "5 per cent on his real estate investment, 7 per cent on his personal property and equipment, and $100 per month for the farmer's own labor and management."[17] Using this formula, specific farm prices could then be calculated to provide the desired income. Secretary of Agriculture Wallace objected to the plan's rigidity, its absence of production controls, and the fact that it involved undisguised price fixing by the government. But even this technique was later adopted selectively when the AAA established fixed loans on cotton and corn. In this instance, as in others, such as the compulsory production control features of the Bankhead Cotton Control, Kerr-Smith Tobacco Control, and Warren Potato Acts of 1934 and 1935, the political pressure of interested farm groups overwhelmed Wallace's dislike of mandated policies.[18]

Nonetheless, despite these occasional political setbacks Wallace's dogged insistence that agriculture must emulate the businessman's tactic of adjusting to economic depression by cutting back production did prevail over the other competing strategies. And this meant, programmatically, that the Roosevelt administration's major emphasis in recovery policies for agriculture would be placed on the voluntary domestic allotment plan.[19]

Domestic allotment gained the inside track during the 1932 presidential campaign. At that time Rexford Tugwell introduced the plan and its sponsor, M. L. Wilson, to Roosevelt as part of his idea-gathering function as a Brain Truster. That lead, once secured, was never surrendered. This was due in large part to Wilson's persuasive talents as a salesman of ideas, and his equally impressive gifts as the organizer of a national campaign to promote public understanding and acceptance of his plan. His success was assured when he converted not only Roosevelt and Tugwell but Wallace and Edward O'Neal, the president of the most powerful of the farm organizations, the American Farm Bureau Federation. The Farm Bureau enjoyed influential connections with Congress as well as intimate links with that organized, interconnected agricultural complex composed of the state agricultural colleges, the Extension Service, and the county agents. In effect, these organizations overlapped in personnel and shared common political and economic objectives. They represented the nation's larger, commercial farmers—particularly those in the Midwest and the South; they accepted the idea, widely shared at the time, that agricultural commodities suffered in price because they were overproduced; and they therefore supported the administration's emphasis upon the restriction of production as an effective method of price support.[20]

The most significant political consequence of the omnibus approach to resolving the programmatic differences within agriculture was that these persistent disagreements were not, in fact, settled at all. What occurred instead was merely a shift in the location of the political battlefield, from the public arena to *within* the AAA itself. As Arthur M. Schlesinger, Jr., has demonstrated, the struggle for ascendancy among the advocates of competing farm programs continued unabated as partisans maneuvered to make their favorite policy the dominant thrust of the AAA. One outcome of this infighting was the successive purges of the extremes at both ends, and the administrative consolidation of the middle position—in this case, the domestic allotment plan supported by Wallace, Wilson, and Chester Davis.[21]

It was predictable that George Peek, the first administrator of the AAA, would attempt to supplant domestic allotment by policies he had long personally championed. As one of the original formulators of McNary-Haugenism, Peek had fought tenaciously throughout the 1920s for the acceptance of this plan, which relied on a two-price system (high, protected domestic prices and lower, prevailing foreign market prices), high protective tariffs, marketing agreements negotiated with the processors, export dumping, and the equalization fee (precursor of parity payments). Peek had seen the successful political realization of his ideas in Congress only to have them thwarted twice by President Calvin Coolidge's vetoes, and thereafter blocked by another consistent opponent, President Herbert Hoover. It is understandable that Peek attempted to transform Roosevelt's support of himself as administrator of AAA into support of his ideas. Peek's efforts to do so, however, involved him in a short and decisive power struggle with Wallace, Wilson, Tugwell, and the general counsel of the AAA, Jerome Frank, and his liberal supporters.[22]

Peek, who utterly disbelieved in the necessity of production controls, sought to circumvent this policy by aggressively pushing his own preferred solutions. This resulted inevitably in a direct conflict with Wallace. At the same time, Peek was bitterly at odds with the liberal faction led by Jerome Frank over issues of social policy. In brief, these disputes involved the conflicting claims of landowners and sharecrop tenants to government benefit payments (that is, the way in which these payments were to be divided between them), as well as related social issues, such as the protection of tenants against displacement from the land, and the advisability of protecting the consumer's interest in pricing policy.[23]

Actually Peek, Wallace, and Davis, as well as prominent agricultural economists, all shared a common view, expressed in their refusal to consider the correction of longstanding social injustice, particularly the deteriorating economic position of tenant farmers, as a proper function of the AAA.[24] Peek's forced retirement in December 1933 was due, consequently, to his policy differences with Wallace over means, not ends. The separate dispute over social policy continued under his successor until it was resolved decisively in Davis's favor when Frank and his adherents were purged from the AAA by Wallace in February 1935.[25]

What emerged from these protracted struggles within the AAA was political vindication of the Wallace-Wilson belief that agricultural recovery was unobtainable without a system of enforceable production controls. This appeared to them as the inescapable lesson of past attempts to raise and stabilize farm prices, notably the signal failure of the Farm Board during the Hoover administration. That costly venture demonstrated that federal stabilization efforts (buying and storing surpluses to keep them off the market), as well as official exhortations aimed at persuading farmers voluntarily to produce less, had proved to be totally inadequate. Government support and subsidies, in other words, would raise and sustain prices only if these benefits were given as a quid pro quo—in return for farmer agreement to limit production by agreed-upon acreage allotments. This signified, of course, that domestic allotment was another thoroughgoing expression of the economics of scarcity and economic nationalism.

The economic objective of domestic allotment was the eventual restoration of the parity ratio that had existed between farm income and outlay during the period August 1909–July 1914. "Up to 1949," as Rainer Schickele has explained, "the computation of parity prices was made as follows, using wheat as an example,

The 1910–1914 average farm price of wheat was   \$ 0.88

The 1910–1914 average index of prices paid by farmers was set at   100

The 1949 index of prices paid by farmers stood at   242

The 1949 parity price of wheat was

$$\frac{0.88 \times 242}{100} \quad = \quad \$ \ 2.13$$

"It simply means," he concludes, "that, if the prices of things farmers buy increased by 142 percent over the base period, the price of wheat would also have to be 142 percent higher if one bushel of wheat is to buy in 1949 the same amount of goods as it did in 1910–1914."[26]

Pre–World War I parity was thus not only the stated goal of New Deal agricultural policy, it also provided a fixed, historical standard for measuring statistically the drastic effect that economic depression had had, and continued to have, on farm prices and farm income. By February 1933, according to Theodore Saloutos and John Hicks, "the general level of farm prices and their exchange value had dropped to the lowest point on record, 49 percent of the prewar average."[27] The effect of this on farm income, Wallace maintained, was to cut the farmers' share of national income from 15 percent prewar to 7 percent in 1932. The farmers' plight was further compounded by the disparity between the rate of fall of farm prices and that of manufactured products. From 1929 to 1932 farm prices declined by 54 percent, while manufactured goods came down by only 25 percent. In 1932 gross farm income was at $5 billion, from $12 billion in 1929.[28] These figures indicate, in part, what farmers had in mind when they protested against the agricultural disparity and insistently demanded equality for agriculture.

Furthermore, farmers, who could compute parity prices as readily as anyone else, were impatient with the explanation that the Agricultural Adjustment Act specifically provided for the realization of parity "gradually" or, at best, as quickly as "feasible."[29] When Roosevelt replied to critics by citing the increase in farm prices, he was not addressing himself to the real issue as his impatient correspondents understood it. Roosevelt compared current prices to their pre–New Deal, all-time depression lows; farmers compared all prices with parity. For example, from mid-March to mid-October 1933 agricultural commodity prices increased by 47 percent, but this constituted only a 22 percent gain in exchange value. That is, farm prices were rising, but so were those of manufactured products under the stimulus of the National Recovery Administration.[30]

Despite the AAA's drastic decision to remove one-fourth of the cotton acreage from production by plowing up ten and a half million acres of standing cotton, and the premature slaughter of six million pigs, the outcome was insufficient in itself to raise prices as high and as fast as farmers were demanding. While supporters of the Agricultural Adjustment Act had found it politically expedient to describe the bill before Congress as a temporary, emergency measure, they actually intended it as a permanent policy.[31] What they had not anticipated was the political fallout which occurred when production control failed to meet the farmers' impatient expectations. The invariable consequence of farmer displeasure with prices was the rapid acceleration of political pressure on Roosevelt, Wallace, and the AAA.

One reason for the farmers' early disaffection with the AAA was that its central policy—the voluntary domestic allotment plan—was the brainchild of agricultural scientists rather than of the farmers themselves. Most dirt farmers preferred the more radical cost-of-production scheme.[32] This preference was undoubtedly fortified by the NRA's virtual adoption of cost-of-production for manufacturers and businessmen through its extensive acquiescence in production-control and price-fixing practices by code authorities. Farmers were not so much critical as they were envious of the success of the trade associations in this regard. And they concluded, quite understandably, that what was good for the manufacturer was good enough for them too.

The assault upon the Roosevelt administration's farm policies took a number of different forms. Milo Reno's Farmers' Holiday supporters were among the severest critics of the AAA, and they demanded anew the adoption of cost-of-production by extending NRA ideas and practices to agriculture. Governor William Langer of North Dakota announced, in October 1933, a state embargo on wheat as a means of putting pressure on Roosevelt and Wallace to fix minimum farm prices. Then in early November, five Midwestern governors met in conference with Roosevelt and Wallace, with a program emphasizing price fixing, inflation, and compulsory controls by licensing farmers, processors, and distributors. The object of these sweeping measures was an immediate leap to parity, which they insisted was 70 percent above current prices.[33] Publicly Roosevelt rejected these demands for cost-of-production and mandatory controls; privately he was already shifting toward a form of price control through the establishment of selective minimum prices, and in 1934–35 he accepted mandatory production controls for cotton, tobacco, and potatoes.

Roosevelt's response to the rising gale winds of the autumn of 1933 from the farm country was to combine a short-term expedient with a long-range policy. Instead of battening down the hatches, Roosevelt chose to set out boldly on an uncertain economic sea by adopting the dubious inflationary theories of Professor George Warren—highly popular among farmers—and meanwhile announcing the creation of the Commodity Credit Corporation by executive order on October 17, 1933.

The CCC, an independent agency closely affiliated with the Reconstruction Finance Corporation, was another, more permanent New Deal mechanism for raising and stabilizing commodity prices. Unlike monetary policies such as the gold experiment, which operated in a circuitous way, the CCC was meant to apply direct leverage on prices by establishing minimum prices on selective farm products. The first beneficiaries of this tactic were cotton and corn producers who were offered, respectively, nonrecourse loans of 10 cents a pound and 45 cents a bushel for the 1933 crop. Participating farmers, who were obliged to cooperate in the production control plans of the AAA, could sell their crops to the CCC at the loan rate, with the option of later reclaiming them if the market prices rose above the loan price. In the meantime, the crops were tagged and stored in warehouses or on the farm, and thereby kept off the market. The CCC functioned, in other words, by setting a government floor under prices, and by attempting to influence supply by a withholding operation reminiscent of the recently defunct Farm Board of the Hoover years. The main difference was that the CCC tied benefits to production control, in an effort to avoid the Farm Board's experience of being overwhelmed by steadily mounting, unmanageable surpluses.[34]

Another consequence of the CCC was that its support prices replaced parity as the actual determinant of prices paid the farmer. While parity continued to be the goal, however distant and elusive, that the administration was committed to achieve, the prices farmers realized in pocket were generally at or near the loan rate. It is necessary, therefore, to look somewhat more closely at CCC operations and their results in the market.

During the years 1933–37, a period which Geoffrey S. Shepherd characterizes as one of "rising demand," the CCC "appeared" to be successful in meeting its most important objective of raising and sustaining prices. Cotton and corn loans were originally set at prices "nearly twice as high as the open market prices previously existing." The loan on cotton was then raised to 12 cents in 1934, and lowered to 10 cents in 1935 and 9 cents in 1937. Corn loans ranged from 45 cents to 57 cents from 1933 through 1939, although market prices after the middle of 1934 were "far above" the support price, due to the effects of drought, especially in 1934 and 1936. Wheat, like corn, was particularly hard hit by drought, and no loans were made on it in the first five years of the CCC, during which the price hovered around $1.00 a bushel. According to Murray Benedict, the drought year reduced the gross physical product of farms by 5 percent or more, and this was largely responsible for the price increases of these years. Shepherd, who is highly critical of the CCC, regards it as a repeat performance of the mistakes made by the Federal Farm Board, particularly the fallacy that prices can be raised in the long run through the withdrawal of crops by storing them. "Whatever is put into storage," he points out, "must eventually come out, and when it comes out it will depress prices about as much as it raised them when it was put in." The "appearance" therefore of the CCC's success was more in the nature of a mirage—the illusion that artifically enhanced prices can be sustained over a period of time without increasing demand or decreasing the supply.[35]

And yet these critical observations are all addressed to an economic condition economically perceived and analyzed. The fact of the matter, as far as President Roosevelt was concerned, was that he found himself sorely beset by a political problem.

It was totally in keeping with his own perceptions that Roosevelt met and deflected the pressures converging upon him in a political manner. The story of cotton, one of the major basic crops, can be used to illustrate the political dynamics which played upon and distorted economic policy.

One of the political functions of Roosevelt's secretary of agriculture was to make economic sense of policies which were essentially political in origin and motivation. In a long memo for Roosevelt's use in answering critics of cotton control policies, Wallace attempted to justify the evolution of the cotton program during 1933–37 in rational, economic terms.[36] A major argument of his defense was his assertion that the Roosevelt administration's agricultural policies represented a sharp departure from those of the Hoover administration—the AAA was the diametric opposite of the Federal Farm Board in conception, execution, and results.

The Farm Board had entered the market actively on October 21, 1929, by making loans on cotton up to 16 cents a pound. It continued its stabilization operation through the 1930–31 season accumulating a total holding of cotton of 3,400,000 bales. By the summer of 1932 the Farm Board was unable to pursue further its withholding program, and it began liquidating its stocks, which, by April 1933, reduced cotton held under loan to 2,500,000 bales. The outcome of the Farm Board's activities was that the government suffered a loss of $129 million, cotton dropped to a 1932 low of 5 cents a pound, and the cotton carryover rose to new heights—13 million bales in August 1932. "The farm value of the 1932 crop," Wallace pointed out in an invidious comparison, "totaled $484,000,000 as compared to more than a billion and a half dollars in 1928."

The legacy, therefore, of the Farm Board was a disastrously low cotton price, a market-depressing surplus, and, most important, the failure to establish an effective production control mechanism to limit supply. The AAA, in addition to this unwelcome inheritance, confronted the certain prospect of a big crop in 1933, already planted and growing on an increased acreage—40,929,000 acres, compared to 35,891,000 acres in 1932. The AAA immediately acted to remove one-fourth of the acreage from production; and on September 18, the CCC announced the 10 cent loan. "From virtually every standpoint," Wallace stated, "the 10-cent loan was a success. It accomplished its primary purpose of enabling farmers to hold their cotton long enough to benefit by price increases." And indeed by February 1934 cotton had climbed to 12 cents a pound.

In 1934 two important policy changes were made. In April the Bankhead Cotton Control Act was passed, abandoning voluntary production control for a mandatory one, and a 12 cent loan was announced. The Bankhead Act provided for the issuance of tax exemption certificates to participating farmers to cover their crop. Excess cotton was taxed at the rate of 50 percent of the market price of a bale of cotton. "By taxing excess production," Wallace explained, "the act made it possible to prevent noncooperators from defeating the efforts of other producers to adjust their output to the demand." In regard to the increased loan rate, which he had unsuccessfully opposed, Wallace was apologetic:

> The 12-cent loan coincided with a sharp drop in American cotton exports. Other factors, among them the trend toward nationalism, accounted for a part of the decrease. But the loan also served to restrict exports by creating an artificial disparity between the price of American cotton and foreign cotton. Because of this many who urged the loan now believe that rate was too high.

American exports of cotton, more specifically, dropped from 7,534,000 bales in 1933 to 4,799,000 in 1934. To counteract this trend, the loan in 1935 was reduced to 10 cents, with a government subsidy "representing the difference between the price at which [farmers] sold their cotton and 12 cents." Furthermore, Congress repealed the Bankhead Act shortly after the United States Supreme Court's Hoosac Mills decision in January 1936, which found the production control mechanism of the AAA unconstitutional. The court's action was a severe setback for the administration, since it put the control of surpluses in jeopardy. To meet this threat, the administration devised a temporary replacement for the AAA—the Soil Conservation and Domestic Allotment Act of 1936. But as Wallace conceded, "From its inception, . . . Administration officials realized that the conservation program, assuming normal weather, would not prevent the accumulation once again of burdensome surpluses." Wallace's warning was buttressed by statistics:

> The 10,638,000 bale crop of 1935 was followed by a 12,399,000 bale crop in 1936. This increased supply sold at a price exceeding 12 cents and still more cotton was planted in 1937. Favorable weather combined with the increased acreage to foreshadow a crop, as of August 1, of nearly 15,600,000 bales. Already declining, prices fell below 11-cent levels.

While Wallace was here clearly appealing for a more effective replacement of the conservation program by Congress—later realized in the Second Agricultural Adjustment Act of 1938— nonetheless he regarded the agricultural program of 1933–36 with some satisfaction. He pointed out, for example, that the farm value of cotton and cottonseed increased from $484 million in 1932 to $1,036 million in 1936, including rental and benefit payments. "The increased cotton income since 1932," he concluded, "alleviated distress and improved living conditions among cotton growers and contributed to a quickening of business and industry throughout the south and the Nation."[37]

What was singularly notable about Wallace's defense of his custodianship of agriculture was the complete omission of the political factors which shaped these events. But since his memo was for President Roosevelt, Wallace hardly needed to recount the politics of agriculture. That essential part of the story, however, must now be added. Without politics, there is little meaning to any New Deal policy.

If one were disposed to invent a political maxim regarding the politics of federal support programs, it might run this way: whatever the existing level of support, it is not enough. Certainly President Roosevelt would have had no difficulty in verifying this as a truism. His correspondence of these years, particularly with members of both houses of Congress, provides ample documentation that the administration was continually being pressured to go further—in the amount of loans and their continuation from year to year, in the scope and stringency of compulsory federal controls, and in the adoption of even more direct and ambitious schemes for support and subsidization.

In agriculture, the closest approximation to the mediating role played by Senator Key Pittman in silver policy was the influence with the Roosevelt administration enjoyed by Senator John H. Bankhead of Jasper, Alabama. But Bankhead, who could quote the statistics on cotton as though he were speaking of intimate friends, used a subtle persuasion far removed from Pittman's strident tone and blunt demands. Bankhead's way was a nice blending of encouragement, congratulation, and gentle prodding toward the next step in the salvation of Southern agriculture. In support of this cause, he kept up an active correspondence with Roosevelt and Wallace over the years.

Late in 1937, Bankhead looked back over the preceding years to assess his partnership with Roosevelt in the fight for the Southern cotton farmer. "From the beginning of your Administration," he wrote to Roosevelt,

> you and I have seen eye to eye on cotton legislation and the record shows that we have been right. The cotton exporters for more than two years have been engaged in a widespread propaganda campaign in an effort to continue the use of cotton farmers for their special benefit as they have done for many long years. They are most diligently at work at this time. Unhappily, the farmers have not been situated so that they could carry on a counter-propaganda campaign.
>
> They are looking to you to protect them. Their faith in you is unbounded. They do not look to their Senators and Representatives, or to Henry Wallace. President Roosevelt is their Moses.[38]

The battle for cotton was a long, arduous, and unresolvable one, but Bankhead's basic position over the years was remarkably consistent.

In a 1934 memorandum, Bankhead posed a fundamental question: "Who," he asked, "is going to buy the cotton?" The problem of effective demand was unavoidable, because the traditional outlets, starting with the foreign markets, were drying up. "The mills," he also pointed out, "are not in the market.

The speculators have discounted the short crop and with a supply of about 20,000,000 bales to meet consumption requirements of about 13,000,000 bales there is likely to be an absence of sufficient buyers to absorb the hedging sales." Bankhead, in short, expected the price for cotton to drop sharply. "The loan plan saved us last year," he insisted, and he proposed the same for 1934—only more of it. A loan of 13 cents, he argued, together with benefit payments, would give the farmer a parity price. And if the administration also announced that it would buy one million bales for relief purposes, that "would greatly help the psychology." A higher loan on a smaller crop would provide farmers almost the same income as in 1933.[39]

Actually, 1934 was a good year for Bankhead and cotton farmers. Besides the 12 cent loan, there was Bankhead's system of compulsory marketing quotas. Thereafter, Bankhead kept up his quiet campaign to perpetuate the high loan rate and compulsory controls by conducting periodic polls and surveys and reporting them to Roosevelt; they all showed overwhelming farmer support for these policies. He was assisted in this effort by like-minded Southern senators as well as more unlikely allies, such as the Cotton Textile Institute and the American Cotton Manufacturers Association.[40] In March 1935 Senator Walter F. George of Georgia, for example, wrote:

> There is not a cotton grower from Georgia to Texas who does not believe that he will get at least twelve cents for his cotton. He believes in this Administration. . . . If he does not get the price all of our efforts will be thrown in the basket. From a political viewpoint ten cents cotton will mean the failure of the whole program to the cotton growing States.[41]

George's appeal was accompanied by a petition from senators representing the cotton states which urged Roosevelt to continue the 12 cent loan and the compulsory program.[42]

The support of cotton textile manufacturers was on different grounds. Their great need, they told the president, was for stability and predictability. Since the administration had adopted the 12 cent loan in 1934, they felt it should be continued in 1935 to dispel one great uncertainty hampering business confidence. The 12 cent loan, according to the attorney for the Cotton Textile Institute, "would remove the shadows of fear that hang like a black cloud over the textile industry," and "it would inspire over a half million textile workers who would be reasonably assured of steady employment." It was not the price of cotton that mattered so much, it was the businessman's fear that he would be caught with high-priced cotton stocks on hand when the new crop of cheaper cotton came on the market.[43] Senator Josiah Bailey of North Carolina, while expressing "some sympathy with the cotton manufacturers who had piled the goods up on their shelves in order to employ their workers and maintain their organizations," nonetheless supported the 1935 policy of a 10 cent loan and a 2 cent subsidy: in the choice of who should win or lose, Bailey preferred to promote the interest of the cotton grower over that of the manufacturer. "I may say to you," he told Roosevelt, "that the value of the cotton crop in North Carolina has increased from $27,000,000 in 1932 and 1933 to $57,000,000 in 1934 and 1935. This is more than 100% and 100% is 100%."[44]

Despite such moments of satisfaction, the more typical cadence of cotton spokesmen mingled the sounds of deep alarm, high dissatisfaction, and sustained pleas for more federal aid. In the fall of 1937, as cotton moved into the market, Senator Bankhead took up a familiar appeal. "Cotton eligible for nine cent loan," he telegramed the President,

> is selling below nine cents. Why should not the government acquire title by purchase. If the federal surplus commodities corporation should enter the market and offer to buy three or four million bales of the present crop at a price not to exceed ten cents a pound I submit that the market price would go up to that level. . . .
>
> This is the principle of the McNary Haugen Equalization fee bill . . . except that the government furnishes the money and removes the constitutional objection to the equalization fee. The plan . . . would save the government many millions of dollars under adjustment payment plan. . . . If the price can be put above ten cents the farmers will not be required to wait an entire year for payment of substantial part of adjust-

ment payments. I earnestly hope you can see your way clear to handle this matter before leaving for the West. It will help the farmers and also the government.[45]

Roosevelt replied that Bankhead's idea had far reaching implications; he would have to consider it carefully.[46]

Important legislation, such as the Bankhead Act, clearly benefited some groups, but invariably at the expense of other interests. So from the outset critics were active in pointing out the losers, in an attempt to modify or, better still, suspend entirely the operation of the Bankhead cotton policy.

Henry Wallace, in assessing group interest reactions, pro and con, for the president's information, wrote Louis Howe that

quite a large number of requests have been received that the Bankhead Act be suspended by the President. . . . A large portion of the opposition . . . have come from cotton ginners and the cotton trade and only a comparatively small number from actual cotton producers. On the other hand, a very large number of communications have been received from cotton producers themselves urging that the Act be enforced.[47]

A repeated argument of opponents was that Providence, in the form of the drought in 1934, had more than realized the original purpose of the Bankhead Act to limit the cotton yield to approximately ten and a half million bales. Beyond the weather, opponents argued that overly restricted crops and high prices would erode further the nation's dwindling foreign trade by encouraging foreign cotton cultivation and the use of substitutes. Wallace shared this concern, and in time it would put the Department of Agriculture and Senator Bankhead at odds over a serious issue not easily covered over by compromise. In addition, those groups who constituted the cotton trade—ginners, processors, brokers, and merchants—were consistent critics of production control, since their profits depended upon volume.[48] Finally, some few spoke of the detrimental effects of the Bankhead Act upon small farmers and tenants.

Oscar Johnston, from his double vantage point as a Mississippi resident and a member of the AAA, warned Wallace of some of the more serious implications of the Bankhead Act for tenant farmers. The president, he felt, needed to be informed of some essential facts:

1. More than seventy percent of the cotton produced in America is grown by tenant labor, farmed on a share system.

2. Less than 15% of the cotton grown in America is grown by farmers who, themselves, plant, cultivate and harvest the cotton.

3. A negligible percentage of the total crop is grown by the land owner, who actually performs the manual labor.

The tax exemption certificates, however, were to be issued to the land owner, "most of them not residing upon the farms." Then, in a remarkably accurate analysis, he predicted that

these landowners will naturally make every effort to obtain the maximum number of exemption certificates. The landowner will then rent his land, as usual, upon a share basis to tenants, and will allocate to each tenant the number of bales that he may gin and market. As a matter of course, the landowner will retain sufficient exemption certificates to enable him to gin his share, a fourth or half, as the case may be, of the cotton produced on the farm. Assume that the allocation or allotment to the tenant is five bales, a normal expectancy on the acreage he plants. Because of favorable weather conditions, he produces eight bales. Two or four of these bales will go to the landlord for rent, according to the system under which the tenant rents. It will probably require the proceeds of three bales for the tenant to pay the debt incurred by him for his operation from March 1st to September 1st. In the case of the fourth share tenant this takes up five bales or the alotted quota for that tenant. He has three bales left over from the proceeds of which he expects to live through until March, but is not allowed to market this cotton without paying a seventy five per cent tax.

"My thought," he concluded, "is [that] nothing short of armed force would prevent these tenants ginning their surplus, and no political organization on earth would be able to withstand the pressure of a million families, each in possession of a bale of cotton, worth on the market between $75.00 and $80.00, themselves hungry and ill clothed, and demanding the privilege of marketing the fruits of their labor." [49]

Johnston's forecast was soon verified in fact. James F. Byrnes of South Carolina, one of Roosevelt's favorite senators, wired late in 1934 urging the president to suspend enforcement. "Many small farmers have made more than amount allotted," he reported. "If permitted to sell what they have made they can pay their rent and debts. If they have to pay prohibitive tax on all over allotment it means we will have additional persons appealing for relief." From Georgia, Representative M. C. Tarver sent Roosevelt a farmers' petition against the injustices of the Bankhead Act and its enforcement and review procedures by owner-dominated county committees. "These farmers," he wrote, ". . . believe in you and in your sense of justice." Like Byrnes, Tarver asked for suspension. Senator Bankhead attempted to meet this objection by urging Roosevelt to increase the benefits for small farmers. "I hope you will direct the AAA to make a reasonable minimum allotment for the small farmer. I think two bales covered by non-transferable exemption certificates would serve the purpose." This was a small concession, quite in keeping with the New Deal's habitual treatment of small farmers and tenants.[50]

In cotton politics, Roosevelt had decided convictions about who his friends and enemies were. Responding to one critical letter in late 1934, Roosevelt instructed Marvin McIntyre how to reply:

> I know he is not connected with them but he is lining up with cotton growers, cotton warehouses and exporters who naturally prefer to play with a fifteen million bale crop than with a ten million bale crop. These people represent less than a tenth of the cotton farmers. I prefer to help the ninety per cent at the expense of the ten per cent rather than the ten per cent at the expense of the ninety per cent.

And to Secretary Wallace, who had passed along a letter of interest to him, Roosevelt replied, "The man is right about the foreign firms but we must remember that the Administration is opposed by the majority of the cotton brokers, warehouse men, railroads and ginners."[51]

There were limits also to Roosevelt's patience and generosity with his friends. This was especially evident in 1937, when he was engaged in a major campaign to cut expenses and to balance the budget. In August 1937 Roosevelt confronted the breakdown of effective production control in cotton, and his usual tolerant attitude towards requests for loans vanished. "Lending money on an unrestricted cotton crop," he told Representative A. I. Ford, "is not the answer."

> I am opposed to setting up any system of loans to cotton farmers representing the difference between the world price and a parity price because, as you and I well know, that means a straight subsidy out of the Treasury and will, if applied to all crops, make a balanced national budget an absolute impossibility. . . . Surplus control is the only answer if the Treasury is not to go broke.

To Senator Walter George he added, "Obviously to loan money on a per pound basis, higher than the existing or prospective market, will cost the Government many millions of dollars out of pocket unless some form of surplus control is established by action of the Congress." In October, Bankhead informed the president of a plan by Senator Ellison Smith to use tariff income to give farmers parity by an "equalization payment." Roosevelt replied in blunt, fighting fashion:

> I guess there is going to be a battle with Senator Smith's cotton-exchange-export-market crowd. The best answer to them is that if they insist on an equalization subsidy to cotton, wheat and corn growers, they have got to find the money to pay it. Any effort to take the money out of tariff taxes merely transfers those funds from the regular running expenses of the Government and creates a deficit. Any diverting of revenue to some specific payment has to be replaced by other taxes. . . .
> Furthermore, I propose to be very definite this fall in saying that if the Congress exceeds my budget estimates, which will provide a balanced budget, the Congress can stay in session or come back once a week in special session throughout the full year until they give me additional taxes to make up the loss.[52]

Thus in cotton, as in other basic crops such as corn, wheat, and tobacco, all roads ran to Washington. Roosevelt and Wallace became the political arbiters of the economic fortunes of all those who planted, bought, processed, manufactured, and sold agricultural products. These diverse groups and trades, in competition with one another, were transformed into government supplicants and clients, pursuing their economic self-interest by political means. Intense competition was clearly not a New Deal invention, but the Roosevelt administration was instrumental in promoting the thoroughly political nature it assumed at this time. Economic self-reliance and political independence are relative concepts, but neither can be said to have been encouraged or sustained by policies oriented to political tutelage and economic dependency.

Nor were these consequences confined to the basic crops. General crops, such as strawberries, watermelons, vegetables, and citrus, as well as other perishable products—particularly dairy, as the most important—fell outside the domestic allotment mechanism. Instead, the AAA attempted to regulate these commodities by marketing agreements and the licensing authority—devices incorporated in the Agricultural Adjustment Act by the effective lobbying of George Peek.

The politics which came to characterize this sector of American agriculture were as intense and complex as those of cotton. In neither case can the conflict be understood as a simple dichotomy between producers and processors. Marketing agreements—or the attempts to negotiate them—generated different alignments on issues of self-interest

> among distributors, processors, and producers; between co-operatives and non-co-operatives, both on the producer and on the distributor side; between large processors and distributors (including co-operatives) and small ones; and between geographical districts within the area covered by an agreement or license.

In addition to the variety of participants, the devices used for realizing higher, stabilized prices were equally diverse. Since these agreements were exempt from the antitrust laws, all the techniques for regulating production, marketing, and price which had been developed by the cooperatives and the trade associations, especially in the 1920s, were tried—including those previously prohibited by law. These attempts to create unity and cooperation where rivalry had long prevailed, even with means that borrowed from monopoly and cartel practices, proved largely unavailing.[53]

New Deal policies represented a distinct watershed in the government's intervention in the nation's agriculture. Nothing so extensive had been tried before, and while some programs turned out to be ephemeral, the overall effect of government intrusion in decision-making, regulation, and control was to alter permanently the conditions under which the farm sector functioned. And the consequences of these policies affected far more than the life and business of farmers; they extended to related trades, country banks and merchants, farm suppliers, and insurance companies. Some of these groups gained and others did not. Geographically, the principal beneficiaries were the South and the Midwest; in crops, it was the producers of tobacco, cotton, wheat, corn, and hogs. Those who gained little or lost included farmers in New England and the Northeast and the raisers of poultry, dairy, and livestock whose costs increased through higher priced grains for feed. New England textile manufacturers, in particular, complained long and hard, and fruitlessly. And while it is seldom mentioned or emphasized, consumers throughout the nation paid in good part for the redistribution of income brought about by these policies.[54]

Lists of winners and losers, however distributed, do not answer the two basic questions with which this inquiry started—to what extent did New Deal farm policies foster recovery within the agricultural sector, and what effect did they have as a stimulus to more general economic recovery? Were the economic results the anticipated ones announced by President Roosevelt and his farm advisers? Perhaps it should be emphasized here that it is the economic and not the political effects of the AAA which are being considered.

In 1937 the Brookings Institution published a careful analysis of the AAA by Edwin G. Nourse, Joseph S. Davis, and John D. Black. Their generalizations and conclusions regarding the recovery performance of the AAA were carefully qualified, since it was extremely difficult to separate qualitatively the results stemming from the AAA alone and those from other sources, including New Deal monetary, credit, relief, or other recovery programs such as the NRA or the PWA, as well as general economic conditions, particularly the drought.

Overall, agricultural income since the inception of the AAA showed "striking increases." In 1933 total cash farm income increased by 24 percent, and thereafter by lesser percentages. For 1935, total cash income from farm production, including AAA payments (which averaged about $500 million per year) came to $7.2 billion. The farmers' enhanced purchasing power obviously improved the economic position of financial institutions which serviced farmers, farm suppliers, mail-order houses, and generally all those who sold goods to farmers (automobiles, cement, etc.). For this group, business confidence was positively affected; the gloomy business outlook of 1932 was counteracted by the renewed ability of people in the countryside to pay their debts and taxes and resume expenditures.[55]

The negative effects of the AAA on general recovery included "some retarding effect" on cotton textiles; "a retarding influence on the export trade in cotton and some other agricultural commodities"; potential pressure on labor for wage demands to meet the increased cost of living; and some loss of business among those, like railroads, whose profits were related to quantity production, processing, and shipment. On balance, the study concluded, the positive stimulus outweighed these negative factors. Yet despite this carefully hedged assessment, two of the authors dissented. Davis explicitly disagreed, and stated that the administration's recovery argument (which the Brookings study was supporting in qualified fashion) was unsound, especially for 1933–34. Black conceded that the AAA's "contribution" to general recovery "was not of great consequence." Murray Benedict, in a later analysis, strongly confirmed the dissenters' judgment. "The record," he concluded, "does not indicate any significant effect from the farm program in serving as a stimulus to recovery in the economy as a whole."[56]

America, by the 1930s, was predominately an industrial-urban society. While the agrarian myth was still very much alive in the hearts of men, it was an unreal basis upon which to construct an economic recovery program for the nation as a whole. The assertion that "industrial prosperity depends upon the farmers' purchasing power," Rainer Schickele remarks,

> is wrong simply because farmers constitute less than 16 per cent of the total consuming public. In the depths of the last depression, the total number of unemployed nonfarm workers alone was larger than the total full-time labor force in agriculture (roughly 12 million as compared to 9 million). During the twenties, agriculture was in a depressed condition while industry prospered; it would be hard to find a period in the last 100 years when agriculture prospered while industry was depressed.[57]

And yet when all is said and done, the political fact of the matter remains: the agrarian myth, or Roosevelt's adaptation of it, was not meant as an accurate statement of economic reality. Ideologically, it spoke to men's feelings by evoking a potent symbol of national mythology—and Roosevelt fully understood this, and successfully made political use of it. Until the congressional election of 1938, he had the farmers in his pocket.

TEN

Industrial Recovery

THE CAPSTONE OF PRESIDENT ROOSEVELT'S RECOVERY PROGRAM was the deliberate attempt to restore industrial prosperity by positive governmental intervention. However resonant in the hearts of Americans the agricultural theory of general recovery might have been, economically it would have made far more sense—and considerably clarified public understanding of New Deal recovery policies—if Roosevelt and his advisers had stood the agrarian myth on its head. Rural America would recover if, when, and to the extent that urban America recovered. This fact of life was certainly well known to economists even if it was not readily acknowledged or publicly affirmed by politicians. Contemporaries often referred to the National Industrial Recovery Act—the initial New Deal program for business-trade-industrial recovery—as the counterpart of the Agricultural Adjustment Act. They might well have added that while the two programs were intended to complement one another economically and politically, objectively they constituted a very unequal friendship. Without the effective demand of the vast urban market, farming was bound for trouble.

In his ceremonial signing of the act, on June 16, 1933, the president stated:

> History probably will record the National Industrial Recovery Act as the most important and far-reaching legislation ever enacted by the American Congress.

It represents a supreme effort to stabilize for all time the many factors which make for the prosperity of the nation and the preservation of American standards.

Its goal is the assurance of a reasonable profit to industry and living wages for labor, with the elimination of the piratical methods and practices which have not only harassed honest business but also contributed to the ills of labor.[1]

Roosevelt's customary hyperbole on such occasions aside, his words nonetheless captured the ambitious sweep of an unprecedented peacetime collaboration between government and business designed to combine recovery, relief, and reform objectives within one program. The administration of this act, a Brookings Institution study observed, "has definitely affected not only every industry but almost every person in the economic life of America." "Washington," it concluded, "has become the industrial as well as the political capital of the nation."[2]

Henry I. Harriman, president of the Chamber of Commerce of the United States and an early advocate of a government-business partnership, watched the legislative progress of the NIRA with undisguised satisfaction. "You know," he wrote Roosevelt, "how deeply interested I am in the industrial bill you are now preparing." Harriman, who preferred Senator Wagner's draft over others because of its "greater use of trade associations," added that he "earnestly" hoped that the bill would be a permanent measure rather than a temporary, emergency one. "The psychology of the country," he explained,

is now ready for self-regulation of industry with government approval of agreements reached either within or without trade conferences. When prosperity has returned, selfishness or self-interest, which ever you prefer to call it, may have again asserted itself to such a degree that a sound law cannot be passed, hence my great desire that the measure be a permanent one. . . .[3]

"I consider this measure," he informed the president on another occasion, "the companion piece to the farm bill. The farm bill, this measure and a reasonable program of public works will, in my judgment, constructively turn the tide towards permanently better times."[4]

Senator Robert F. Wagner (D–N.Y.), one of the important members of the large group who collaborated in devising the bill, quickly assumed the task of explaining its objectives—particularly its anticipated impact upon working people—to the public and to his associates in Congress. In a statement before a congressional committee, he said:

> This bill is essentially an employment measure. Its object is to bring about an increase of employment at a level of wages which will afford a standard of living in decency and comfort. The methods of accomplishing this object are, first through co-operative action within industry itself, and second, by direct government expenditure on public works.
>
> I believe, too, that in addition it is going to improve and strengthen the ethics within industry itself by doing away with the sweatshop, the kind of competition which has been tearing down industry and where in self-defense frequently they have been required to reduce wages below a standard of decency. In that way it is going to have not only a great economic effect by increasing purchasing power, but also a great social effect in giving the worker a wage which will permit him to live in decency. . . .[5]

Actually, the NIRA was all that Roosevelt, Harriman, Wagner, and others said it was, and more. Like the Agricultural Adjustment Act, it was an omnibus measure, with its objectives even more vaguely defined, therefore affording Roosevelt an even broader choice of action. The NIRA was basically "a piece of enabling legislation" which permitted Roosevelt, with a modicum of explicit legislative guidance, to proceed with virtually "a free hand." It was a prime illustration of political eclecticism and experimentalism—inevitably burdened with a more than usual measure of confusion of policies and administrative untidiness.[6]

The act itself came in two titles. The first provided for the creation of the National Recovery Administration, while the second established the Public Works Administration. Title I involved an extraordinary expansion of executive authority over the entire range of business life, particularly the regulation of competitive practices, price and production policies, wages and hours, and relations between business and organized labor. The president was authorized to approve codes of industrial self-government which conformed to certain very general requirements; that is, unfair restrictions to membership were prohibited, and monopolies and other practices harmful to small business were to be avoided. Once a code was approved by the president, violations of its provisions were to be treated as "unfair methods of competition." Enforcement of the new rules of business behavior was assigned in the first instance to the code authorities, backed up by the Federal Trade Commission and the federal courts. The threat of an even more stringent enforcement procedure was provided by the president's power to license business—limited to one year, instead of the full two-year run of the NIRA. As another powerful and enticing means of fostering the act's objectives, the president could also suspend the operation of the antitrust laws, and he was given new tariff authority to protect American businessmen against their foreign competitors. Finally, the president was granted an open-ended authority to modify or abolish the existing codes at any time.[7]

Beyond the elaborate code-making procedure, the act also provided an alternative method of government-business cooperation by authorizing the president to formulate a President's Re-employment Agreement (or a "blanket code") with individual businessmen. This simplified procedure, designed for speed, avoided the involved and time-consuming process of negotiating a code for an entire industry; instead the individual employer merely pledged to abide by certain specified conditions, namely, maximum hour and minimum wage provisions, a guarantee of the workers' right to organize and bargain collectively and to join unions of their own choice, the elimination of child labor, and reaffirmation of the Norris-LaGuardia Act's prohibition against the use of the "yellow dog" contract—an employer tactic which made employment conditional on joining a company union. These labor provisions were also made mandatory for all industrial codes.

Despite the word "recovery" in its title, the NIRA did not in fact contain a precise, articulated theory of recovery. This was largely because its sponsors were preoccupied with developing the different possibilities of this experiment, and thus failed to arrive at any consensus. Nonetheless, some assumptions and expectations were generally entertained, and these suggest at least the broad framework of a recovery theory. One aspect of this theory was that the labor provisions of Section 7(a) would operate to increase employment and hourly wages, thereby expanding the purchasing power of wage earners. Larger payrolls in turn would circulate rapidly through the entire economic system, benefiting retailers, wholesalers, manufacturers, and producers, and induce each to take on more workers, setting up a circular movement of increasing momentum. A second aspect of the theory emphasized the positive economic effects of restricting competitive price cutting and other unfair trade practices which, it was assumed, would lessen risk and uncertainty and encourage expanded operations. It was further anticipated that business confidence would be stimulated as a consequence of the codification of business behavior. Business reform, in other words, would function to encourage economic recovery.[8]

General Hugh Johnson, a principal draftsman of the bill and the first administrator of the NRA, sanctioned these ideas and also made explicit the complementary economic functions of the NRA, PWA, and AAA as the major New Deal components in a coordinated recovery program. "We relied," he recalled in *The Blue Eagle from Egg to Earth*, ". . . on PWA to activate the heavy industries at once and thus increase the total number of available purchasers. We relied on AAA to increase farm purchasing power immediately and thus still further add to the number of purchasers. These added to NRA additions would so far increase volume that we thought (and I still think) the increased labor cost could be absorbed without much increase in price."[9]

Johnson had expected to be chosen head of both the NRA and the PWA; when Roosevelt decided otherwise he was crushed, and threatened to withdraw. His bitter disappointment was in large part due to the fact that he saw the two parts of the NIRA as inseparable pieces of a larger recovery strategy.

The success of the entire plan, in his view, required both speed in execution and a degree of close coordination which, he felt, only one man could manage effectively. Instead he got only one part of the job while the PWA went to the cautious, slow-moving secretary of the interior, Harold Ickes. Johnson therefore began his quest for national recovery in control of one leg of a precariously balanced three-legged stool.[10]

Johnson's immediate task, as far as quick recovery was concerned, was to expand mass purchasing power *before* businessmen raised prices to cover their increased costs.[11] He confronted this problem with his usual vigor and in his colorful, persuasive style. In a speech of June 25, 1933, he explained the crucial necessity of maintaining a "price lag":

> First and foremost among those things is a contract to divide up the existing work in such a way as to put hundreds of thousands of new names on the payroll and then raise the wage scale high enough to give all workers a living wage for the shorter shift. If they do this, buying will move forward on a rapid scale, and that in itself will put many more men back to work. Their own profits will come back and we shall be on our way back to the kind of a country that we knew in happier years.
>
> If that were all there is to it, it would be simple. But there is more to it. In the first place the tendency of higher wages is higher prices. If we do a thing like this and do not also put some control on undue price increases so that prices will not move up one bit faster than is justified by higher costs, the consuming public is going to suffer, the higher wages won't do any good, and the whole bright chance will just turn out to be a ghastly failure and another shattered hope.[12]

Despite Johnson's urgency, what he feared was soon realized: prices were in fact raised in anticipation of the increased cost of operating under the NRA.[13] This was a serious setback to the economic rationale of the NRA as a means to quick recovery. But perhaps an even more serious challenge to the possibility of an NRA-induced recovery was that from the very outset, the reform aspect of the plan was running a race for dominance over its more direct recovery features.

Among the four major groups most directly involved in the NRA—government, business, labor, and consumers—organized business was in the best position by far to seize the initiative, to assume the leadership in the code-making process, and, as a consequence, to define and control what the NRA was to be. And despite General Johnson's disclaimer that his role was merely that of an impartial umpire among clashing group interests, his efforts at mediation invariably gave further support to the more organized segment of the business community.[14]

The great advantage from which businessmen started was that they knew what they wanted and they commanded the means to get it. As economists of the Brookings Institution dryly remarked in explaining business willingness to cooperate, "The positive incentives were (1) relief from the anti-trust laws; (2) the authoritative enforcement of price-control measures; and (3) relief from competitive practices deemed to be ruining the market." The "central motivating force," therefore, was the businessman's hope of raising prices "by collective action among competitors" through "control of the market."[15] And the existence of trade associations and their prior work in developing price and production control devices for their own industries assured organized business the ready means for translating aspiration into actuality.

During the critical first six months of the NRA, it "negotiated and approved codes of fair competition covering the major portion of American industry and trade.".[16] At the end of two years 546 codes had been approved, as well as 185 supplementary codes covering some twenty-two million workers. In addition, there were 2.3 million separate agreements, or blanket codes, involving another sixteen million workers. From beginning to end, the code-making process and the resulting code authorities (which were to administer and enforce the codes) were dominated by the trade associations, aided by the government's deputy administrators, who were recruited from the industries which were to be regulated.[17] As Ellis Hawley has remarked, "Only 51 authorities, less than 10% of the total, ever had labor members, and only 10 had consumer representatives."[18] Most of the conflicts of interest which punctuated the process of code formulation, therefore, occurred among competing businesses within the same industries, among different but competing products, and along regional or sectional lines. These disputes were resolved by a bargaining process which put a premium on size and strength, as well as influence within the all-important trade associations. That is, the larger, better-organized corporations had a marked advantage not only over workers and consumers but also over their smaller competitors.[19]

In such a gigantic undertaking, one that aspired to nothing less than a reconstruction of business ethics and that intruded new methods of control over the daily operations of the larger part of the nation's five million business enterprises, it was inevitable that the reality of the new order would fall far short of the dream. Labor activists, epitomized by the resourceful, dynamic John L. Lewis, seized the opportunity afforded by Section 7(a) to attempt to organize the unorganized. Employers, who believed that AFL intrusion into their shops and factories was not part of the bargain, strongly resisted organized labor's interpretation, and hampered its organizing efforts by such traditional devices as the company union, obstruction, intimidation, and violence.[20] While the hope of labor stability was turning sour, the promise of rationalization, stability, and order within business enterprise itself also turned out to be difficult to realize, for it involved far more than merely outlawing cut-throat competition, defining unfair business practices, or condemning noncooperators with epithets such as "chiselers."

The NRA was surely unrealistic to base its recovery strategy on the expectation that businessmen would increase their labor costs but defer raising prices until they were told to do so. After the burden of three years of depression, neither big nor small business would consent to operate without profit or at a loss. Undoubtedly, some of the larger industrial corporations could absorb temporarily the increased costs, either by using their accumulated reserves or by bank loans. But this was highly unlikely, and did not materialize. For small businessmen, whose situation was already desperate, these alternatives were not even a theoretical possibility. Neither General Johnson's inspirational "jawboning" nor the more systematic use of public pressure by the Blue Eagle campaign with its "We do our part" pledges could alter the fact that business could not be moved without the prospect of profits.[21] It is thus within this prevailing, traditional context of belief and behavior that the success or failure of the NRA as a recovery program must be analyzed.

It should be emphasized that the NRA was not a hostile program imposed on the business community by an antibusiness Roosevelt. The president had told business leaders, in effect, to get together, work out an acceptable plan, and then try it out. In this respect the genesis of the NRA duplicated exactly that of the AAA. Contemporary business comment on the NRA, which was voluminous in the public press, was therefore presented with some awareness that this was an ideological experiment, as Ellis Hawley has described it, in planning and creating "a government-sponsored business commonwealth."[22]

One of the most astute contemporary economic analysts was Colonel Leonard P. Ayres, who provided a running commentary on the NRA as a recovery mechanism in his influential monthly "Business Bulletin." Ayres was one of the first commentators to criticize New Deal recovery policies on the grounds that they sustained only a partial and unstable recovery confined largely to consumer goods industries. Ayres argued forcefully that producers' goods were economically more important for full recovery than services, and that among the producers' goods, producers' durables such as buildings, machinery, bridges, tools, ships, and locomotives were the critical group; yet the NRA neglected producers' durables by concentrating on increasing the purchasing power of consumers. The difficulty was that increased purchasing power failed to spread out and stimulate the production of more producers' durables; these large capital expenditures could be, and were being, postponed.[23]

Ayres pointed out that according to the 1930 census, there were forty-nine million gainfully employed persons, of whom twenty-six million were producers of goods and twenty-three million of services. Unemployment in September 1933, he estimated conservatively, was about ten million—half in each category. "If we could put the producers of goods back to work and keep them employed," he argued, "the providers of services would soon be re-employed also, and the depression would be over."[24]

During the NRA's tumultuous two-year existence, assessments of its performance among spokesmen for the business community varied widely. The two most prominent business organizations of the day, the Chamber of Commerce of the United States and the National Association of Manufacturers, exemplify this divergence.

The Chamber was in the forefront of the defenders of the NRA. It performed the varied roles of principal advocate of the original legislation, energetic propagandist in persuading industry to cooperate in the venture, and chief monitor of its administrative development—guarding its continued adherance in practice to the ideas of industrial self-government of, by, and for business autonomy.[25]

Henry Harriman, for instance, while he agreed with the essentials of Colonel Ayres's economic analysis of the faltering recovery, nonetheless thoroughly rejected the idea of dismantling the NRA. "It cannot be denied," he informed Roosevelt early in November 1933,

> that, from a statistical and a psychological standpoint, there has been a decided recession of business for the last two months, and a substantial loss of confidence in the ultimate effectiveness of the National Recovery Act. . . .
>
> Consumable goods have moved forward with much success, both in volume and in price, and there has been a substantial decrease in unemployment; but we can go little further until there is a decided increase in capital-goods industries, among which private construction occupies an important place. . . .

Harriman insisted that expansion in construction could be fostered by Roosevelt's removing two obstacles—the overly restrictive and punitive provisions of the Securities Act, and the delay in approving a general code for the construction industry. As for the NIRA, he remained "thoroughly convinced of the ultimate gains" which this measure would bring "to all parts of our population."[26]

The NAM, on the other hand, was guarded in its endorsement of the NRA, qualified in its support, and ever ready to sound the alarm, especially against what it regarded as dangerous tendencies toward encroachments into the traditional spheres of business control by organized labor and the federal government. Initially the NAM, like other business organizations, became involved in planning for business reorganization because of its apprehension at the rapid legislative progress of Senator Hugo Black's thirty-hour-week bill. This proposal, which sought to deal with the unemployment problem by strictly limiting industry to a six-hours-a-day, five-days-a-week schedule and thus spreading the existing work among more workers, was endorsed by William Green, president of the AFL, and unanimously condemned by business as a rigid, unrealistic, and unworkable scheme. The NAM attempted to head off Black's bill by recommending its own legislative program for industrial recovery—a tactic which President Roosevelt used with greater success.[27] Roosevelt, who was also concerned with the prospect of congressional action on an enormous public works program—Senator Robert M. LaFollette, Jr., was actively campaigning for a $10 billion appropriation, although he conceded to Roosevelt that $6 billion as a minimum might be effective—moved quickly to regain the initiative. Politically, the NIRA, as an administration-sponsored measure, gave the president and not Congress control over establishing government policies for hours and wages, industrial planning, and public works.

Perhaps the NAM should have been won over by Roosevelt's successful maneuver against congressional alternatives, but it gave no such indication. Instead, James A. Emery, counsel and chief lobbyist for the NAM, suggested strongly that "Congress should look before it leaps, and not make haste to repent at leisure." His basic criticism was that the recovery bill would "tend to retard rather than promote business recovery. It will in fact," he added, "nip in the bud the business recovery already manifesting itself."[28] Recovery would be hampered, he argued, by three adverse consequences which he predicted would result from government's unrestrained leap into industrial affairs:

. . . It will transfer . . . all control and authority over every aspect of business operation and management from its private owners and managers to a Government bureaucracy. . . . Nothing may be done without Government sanction and approval. Anything may be ordered or may be forbidden by Presidential edict.

. . . It will retard business and industrial recovery because with increased prices and without correspondingly import control, the American manufacturer will be under increased competitive handicaps in the home markets and foreign goods will undersell and displace American goods with consequential decline in production at home and added unemployment— less work instead of more, for the American worker.

. . . The bill in effect—and designedly—means the virtually immediate and complete unionization of all labor in all industry and the closed shop.[29]

In addition, the NAM strongly objected to granting the president authority to license business, as a dangerous expansion of federal power that it insisted was unconstitutional. While its stance was undoubtedly mild compared to that of other critics—Senator David Reed commented, "I think the plan is insane," while Representative James W. Wadsworth (R–N.Y.) remarked, "I cannot get out of my mind that government is politics, and if government controls business, politics controls business, and politicians are still looking for votes"—nonetheless the NAM's original position on the NRA could hardly be called an endorsement.[30]

In an effort to adapt the bill more to its own thinking, the NAM organized a meeting in Washington for June 3, 1933, attended by one thousand representatives of industry. Concentrating its attention on the more acceptable Senate bill, the NAM listed a number of amendments whose acceptance, it declared, was necessary if it were to give its wholehearted support. These included the elimination of the licensing authority, modification of the labor provisions "to prevent interference with present relationships between employers and employees," provision for a group to administer the NRA instead of one person, and the addition of new tariff authority to enable the president to protect regulated American industry against cheaper, unregulated foreign imports. With the exception of the last suggestion, which, ironically, increased executive power even more, the demands were not adopted.[31]

Despite this outcome, the NAM joined the Chamber of Commerce in an appeal to industry to give its unanimous support to the NIRA on the day the president signed it into law. Robert L. Lund, president of the NAM, while conceding that only some of the modifications his organization sought had been accepted, expressed gratification at the suspension of the antitrust laws. Industry, he stated, "will now have an opportunity to police itself against ruthless competition in the form of unregulated price cutting." Furthermore, since the meaning of the NRA would be determined by its administration, Lund was clearly reassured by the president's choice of General Johnson. "We have every assurance," he remarked, "that the law will not be so administered as to upset existing satisfactory employment relations." And he concluded:

> In this case, . . . the character of administration is as important as the terms of the statute. With full confidence in the earnestness and fairness of the administrator, I urge that manufacturers give their wholehearted co-operation to him and to the President in increasing employment and speeding up the business recovery which is already clearly under way.[32]

Lund's confidence in Johnson's soundness was repeated by Henry Harriman so that there would be no doubt on this score. "I have been assured," he stated publicly, "by those who will undoubtedly administer the Act that it is their intention to see that the provisions of the law are fairly and impartially administered both for the interests of labor and industry and that the Act will not be used unfairly against any group of employers or employees."[33]

On July 21, 1933, General Johnson, with Roosevelt's approval, began the more controversial and dramatic phase of the NRA—the attempt to enlist all of the nation's business establishments in the recovery program through the alternative device of the blanket codes, supported by the full use of techniques of mass persuasion learned during World War I, such as in the Liberty Bond campaigns. The board of directors of the NAM responded almost immediately by issuing a bulletin warning its members to get certain clarifications in writing before they signed up. They were particularly concerned with the labor provisions of the president's agreement. They insisted that employers should protect themselves against the possibility of having to pay the same weekly wage for reduced weekly hours of work, and that they should also ensure their constitutional right of dealing with their employees in a "mutually agreeable way." Without these guarantees, the contract with the president was "insupportable." [34]

In November the NAM concluded that the NRA required much closer surveillance; for this purpose it created a committee composed of trade association officials "to formulate policies on the problems of industry resulting from the recovery program of the federal government." The problems that were specified nicely summarized emerging business grievances against the New Deal. In the committee's resolution,

> it was pointed out that industrial codes, the uncertainty of monetary policies, the difficulty of securing capital under the National Securities Act, and the disruption of present relations of employees and employers, are creating grave problems and that unified action by American industry is needed to support basicly sound policies of recovery.[35]

While the NAM's caution and guarded criticism about the New Deal in 1933 was premature, at least in regard to general business sentiment, it was an accurate forecast of an attitude which was to become widely expressed during the next year. The evolution of the Chamber of Commerce's position on the New Deal was a case in point.

At the Chamber's annual convention in 1933, President Roosevelt appeared in person to trade compliments with business leaders. In his short speech, Roosevelt touched upon mutually shared ideas which resonated in the longer speeches of business spokesmen—the themes of a government-business alliance and of the necessity of curbing the ruthless minority of overly zealous competitors who were charged with being largely responsible for perpetuating "overproduction," "unfair wages," and "improper working conditions." "I can assure you," he stated, "that you will have the co-operation of your government in bringing these minorities to understand that their unfair practices are contrary to a sound public policy."[36] The president's audience of fifteen hundred businessmen, the *New York Times* reported, responded "with an enthusiasm which can hardly be overemphasized."[37]

Henry Harriman, the Chamber's president, describing the existing economic system as "antiquated," admitted further that "we are aghast at the devastating economic and social results that have come through ruthless and unrestrained competition in times of great human deprivation."[38] Gerard Swope, president of General Electric and, like Harriman, a strong advocate of industrial self-government and business planning, urged his fellow industrialists to grasp the offer of government cooperation for "service to the community," efficiently performed at "a fair and reasonable" profit, and under new rules designed "to coordinate production and consumption to stabilize employment—in this way the great advantages of private enterprise and initiative will be retained to the greatest extent." Their failure to act, he cautioned, would only confront them with consequences beyond their influence and control. "I have said before, and I repeat, that if industry does not see its opportunity and embrace it, it will be done from without. The alternative, therefore, is not should it be done, but by whom it shall be done. . . ."[39]

This gathering, which in a curious way represented both the low water mark of business self-confidence and morale and the high tide of support for New Deal interventionism, heard a good deal of talk about freedom. But ironically, what was meant at this point of crisis was freedom from too much free enterprise, too much individual initiative, and much too much competition. Harriman, in a letter to Roosevelt thanking him for his "splendid address and your note of confidence," added that "business is leaving this Annual Meeting with the firm conviction that you are going to promptly lead us out of the depression."[40]

This unusual harmony was bound to moderate considerably once industrialists recovered from their nervous apprehensions, and once the price exacted for exemption from the antitrust laws became clearer and could be coolly calculated. Then mutual accord changed to bickering, fault-finding, and second thoughts about the value of the NRA, which rapidly became, as the economists of the Brookings Institution put it, a "sprawling Administrative colossus."[41]

When the Chamber gathered for its 1934 meeting, Roosevelt was not present to address its members personally, but he sent a message assuring business leaders that his administration and Congress would continue the good work for national economic recovery. "Private business," he added peremptorily, "can and must help to take up the slack." He went on:

> Your membership largely represents those interests which, from motives of self-interest as well as good citizenship, have a leading role to play. The people as a whole will be impatient of those who complain and of those who hold out false fears. It is time to stop crying "wolf" and to cooperate in working for recovery and for the continued elimination of evil conditions of the past.[42]

If it was the president's intention to command good behavior among businessmen and to forestall complaint, he surely must have been taken aback by the free flow of criticism of much of the New Deal which marked this meeting. While the president of the Chamber, Henry Harriman, sought to create a mood of good will and conciliation by praising the NRA and the AAA, his attempt failed to deter the other speakers from specifying their accumulating discontents.

Individual business leaders singled out for criticism what they regarded as particularly misguided New Deal policies, and urged that the offensive measures be amended, reversed, or abandoned altogether. Among their major targets were the Securities Act of 1933 and the proposed Stock Exchange Control Bill, which "have caused almost complete cessation of private investment"; the Banking Act of 1933, criticized for prohibiting commercial banks from engaging in underwriting capital issues; the heavy tax burden, which was described as becoming "unbearable, if not confiscatory"; the proposed regulation of commodity exchanges; the processing taxes; and the PWA's bureaucratic barriers to a construction revival.[43]

"Until recently," the ultraconservative editor of *The Commercial & Financial Chronicle* observed reproachfully of the past reticence of businessmen, "there has been a general feeling among most businessmen that it was their patriotic duty, or else that it was the better part of valor, to refrain from expressing views they were known privately to hold concerning the course of events in Washington."[44] But now, happily, businessmen were beginning to speak out with a new spirit of candor and criticism.

It was precisely this critical tendency, however, which Harriman attempted to excuse in his correspondence with the president. Shortly after the Chamber adjourned, Harriman sent Roosevelt a copy of the resolutions which had been adopted, while putting the most constructive interpretation possible on both the resolutions and the conference itself:

> As you well know, three thousand business men could not meet at any time and not differ widely in their views, and this is particularly true at the present time, when such vital problems are before the country for its consideration. Neither the right wing nor the left wing, whatever that may mean, was in the ascendency. Parts of your program were not agreed to, but, on the whole, I feel that American business recognizes the magnificent effort you have made to assist recovery, appreciates your absolute sincerity, and agrees with many of the basic principles, if not the details, of your program. Above all, I am sure that while business may be critical of details, it earnestly desires to cooperate with the government to the end that permanent and lasting prosperity may be restored at an early date.[45]

Harriman's effort to appease the president was disingenuous, nor was it likely to convince him. The signs of business criticism were simply too widespread to be explained away. And beneath the specific objections, one could detect a more fundamental suspicion that the New Deal was challenging, if not actually attempting to supplant, the free-enterprise, private profit system by government dictation of the nation's essential economic functions. This fear was most commonly expressed by businessmen in the repeated complaint that the federal government was increasingly competing with private business. The charge of encroachment had been made explicitly at the Chamber's meeting by George H. Houston, president of the Baldwin Locomotive Works.

Throughout the 1920s, Houston asserted, the annual capital investment in private enterprise by businessmen averaged about $3.5 billion. During the previous six months ending in March, this had been reduced to $58 million. He attributed this drastic decline to specific New Deal "obstructions" to capital investment, particularly in durable goods, partly caused by the Securities Act and the threat of stringent Stock Exchange regulation. In addition, the paralysis of the capital market was aggravated "by the lack of confidence among investors in the conditions under which American business must be conducted." The remedy was in the hands of the Roosevelt Administration if it announced its intention,

1. To encourage the profit motive in business.

2. Not to interfere with business through further regulation, and

3. To balance the budget as soon as possible and cease to compete in the capital markets with private enterprise through a constantly expanding public debt. A balanced budget will also end any feeling of uncertainty with respect to monetary stability.[46]

Several months later George Houston was able to present his defense of free enterprise and the profit motive directly to President Roosevelt in his capacity as chairman of the Durable Goods Industries Committee—a committee originally organized at the request of General Johnson. Houston's report was a direct assault on the New Deal, a severe criticism of its economic policies, particularly the attempt at a governmentally initiated recovery, and a strong assertion of the thesis that the only way to achieve a sound recovery was to unfetter private enterprise. "Private enterprise," it announced flatly, "must replace Government expenditure, and the industrial investor must be given confidence that all legitimate business ventures will be encouraged to the end of returning a fair profit." The overriding priority, in short, was to restore confidence, and the essential means to that end was to reverse the government's takeover of rights, prerogatives, and incentives which properly belonged to those who best knew how to exercise them—businessmen.[47]

Shortly after the Chamber members had dispersed, Roosevelt publicized a forecast of his legislative plans for the next Congress, which would meet in 1935—perhaps, as the *New York Times* suspected, to influence the outcome of the 1934 congressional elections, but certainly also as a means of counteracting the growing public appeal of the ideas being broadcast by Senator Long, Father Coughlin, and Doctor Townsend.[48] Roosevelt's proposed program was a sweeping one, including unemployment insurance, old age pensions, selective medical insurance, the establishment of a permanent labor board, a federal housing program, and a permanent system of public relief. While still in rudimentary form, these proposals provided the groundwork for another notable legislative outburst—that of the "Second Hundred Days" in 1935. For conservatives, this projected, dramatic expansion of the New Deal was just as unpalatable as an anticipation in 1934 as it was to be as a reality in 1935 and thereafter.

In August, Roosevelt publicly chided businessmen for continually asking that he make further statements to encourage business confidence. This reminded him too much of President Hoover's overworked exercises in that genre. "There is no lack of confidence," Roosevelt insisted, "on the part of those business men, farmers and workers who clearly read the signs of the times." Confidence had already returned, and, furthermore, businessmen had nothing to fear from the New Deal. "This government," he assured them, "intends no injury to honest business. The processes we follow in seeking social justice do not, in adding to general prosperity, take from one to give to another."[49]

In September, the growing tension between the New Deal and business spokesmen was confirmed by several heated exchanges between Roosevelt and Harriman and the Chamber's board of directors. The immediate cause of this split was a statement adopted by the board and sent to the president by special messenger four days before it was nationally advertised by the press. For eighteen months, the directors claimed, the Chamber had "wholeheartedly supported the President and his administration in the effort toward business recovery." "Today," however, they added,

> the Directors are conscious of a general state of apprehension among the business men of the country. They are confident that recovery cannot be accomplished unless men are put to work and the wheels of industry begin to turn much more generally and rapidly than at present. Continuous employment cannot be furnished by the government. That must be afforded by business and industry and cannot be brought about without a restoration of confidence.[50]

The present crisis in business confidence was put squarely at the feet of Roosevelt and New Deal policies—specifically, "enormous expenditures" resulting in higher taxes and unbalanced budgets; bureaucratic control over private business, which "all history records as destructive of nations"; government competition with business; a more militant, strike-prone labor force; and "utterances by those who assume to speak for the Administration which destroy confidence in the security of property and investments and fill the minds of our citizens with grave apprehension for the stability of our government and its financial integrity."

This was merely the prelude to a more blunt request that the president provide "a definite statement" to six questions. When would he balance the budget? Did he intend to devalue the dollar further? When would he agree to international monetary stabilization? Would he attempt to promote recovery by relying primarily on business initiative rather than by government interference? What were his intentions regarding agriculture? And, did he plan to continue unnecessary public works? A presidential statement on these issues, the directors suggested, would do much to restore confidence and "the general welfare." Roosevelt's reply to Harriman, on September 23, could hardly have been anticipated.

> I know that you personally will understand if I tell you quite frankly that I am very much amazed by the request of the Board of Directors of the Chamber of Commerce of the United States that the President make categorical answer to six short questions propounded by a wholly private organization.[51]

Roosevelt objected to the general nature of the questions, which "cover the whole policy of American government, not only at the present time but for many years to come." He rejected the idea of establishing a precedent of answering questions on demand by every conceivable organization. And he suggested that the Chamber would do "a greater service" by giving him its views, not in "glittering generalities," but in practical terms. Let the directors give their own "definite" answers to their own questions—for his benefit. "Perhaps," he told Harriman, "after my return to Washington you will run in to see me. I should like to propound the questions to you in person."

Harriman responded by denying that the board intended its questions as a questionnaire. It was merely making "a statement of its views as to public matters," which it hoped the president might discuss "at an opportune time."[52] Roosevelt was not appeased, pointing out through Stephen Early, his assistant secretary, that the nation's press universally described the board's statement as a questionnaire; if the press was mistaken, "the Chamber's very excellent publicity department, if called upon to do so," could easily rectify the misunderstanding.[53]

In the midst of this squabble, Harriman attempted to patch up another dispute involving the NRA. He assured Roosevelt that the Chamber had not turned against the NRA, as "garbled and misleading statements" in the press suggested. The board's position was rather one of "constructive criticism." It did not oppose "the basic principles of the N.R.A.," but it did want it amended when the emergency measure came up for renewal as a permanent program. This should confine the jurisdiction of the NRA strictly to interstate businesses, excluding the service trades and others which were primarily intrastate. Then, coming to the central issues, Harriman added that the

> new legislation should permit each industry to formulate rules of fair competition, which will become effective when ap-

proved by the government; that the government should not have the right to impose or modify codes; and that the labor clause should contain provisions against coercion of labor, either by employers or others, and that, with the right of collective bargaining, should go obligations on the part of labor, similar to those imposed in England. There is certainly a right to strike; there is, equally, a right to work.[54]

Harriman, in summarizing for Roosevelt the report of the Chamber's Special Committee on the National Industrial Recovery Act, a copy of which he enclosed, considerably softened its position and recommendations. Yet it was the committee's blunt recommendations, and not Harriman's brief, which were subsequently submitted to a referendum vote by more than nine hundred business organizations polled—and they approved them overwhelmingly.[55]

Roosevelt, faced with conflicting advice from the Chamber and the NAM, urged business leaders to get together in a conference, thrash out their differences, devise a consensus, and tell him what they wanted. This familiar technique, which had worked so well for Roosevelt at the inception of the NRA and the AAA, did not on this occasion run according to rule. It began well and ended badly. Officials of the two business organizations issued invitations to a "Joint Business Conference for Economic Recovery," which met December 17–19, 1934, at White Sulphur Springs in West Virginia. Eighty-four prominent business leaders attended, including officers of the Chamber, the NAM, the Industrial Advisory Board of the NRA, and the Business Planning and Advisory Council of the Department of Commerce, along with an assortment of presidents of prestigious commercial and manufacturing enterprises.[56]

In their survey of steps necessary "to revive industry and accelerate recovery," the participants considered the NRA and its future, but they also turned to a series of policies and issues which they regarded as being directly related to economic recovery. These included federal finance, foreign trade, agriculture, business financing, transportation, government competition, the durable goods industries, relief, and unemployment reserves. In sending Roosevelt their official resolutions, the conferees not only stated their consensus on an alternative recovery program, they also presented him with a severe critique of New Deal recovery policies.

Concerning the NRA, they rejected the idea of permanent legislation in favor of a temporary measure for one year. Industrial codes, confined to enterprises engaged in interstate commerce, were to be formulated solely by representative trade groups and agreed to voluntarily, with the reserved right to withdrawal. Codes would include maximum hour and minimum wage provisions, the prohibition of child labor, and the workers' right "to deal with employers either individually or collectively directly or through representatives of their own free choice without intimidation or coercion" by either management or labor. Code provisions would remain exempt from the antitrust laws. In the case of industries which declined to adopt a code of fair competition, an "appeal" would be made to these employers to conform to code standards "voluntarily" if hour, wage, or child labor abuses existed. The objective for the continuation of an altered NRA remained the same—it would promote recovery by increasing employment, by avoiding destructive competition, and by providing relief from unstable markets.

The industrial leaders were thus proposing a reorganization of the NRA which would consolidate their gains, particularly the freedom of action permitted them by exemption from the antitrust laws, while neutralizing concessions to labor and government. In their view, experience under the NRA demonstrated an alarming tendency by the government to penetrate too deeply into industrial affairs. While the slogan was not yet used, they were demanding "a rollback of the New Deal" and the restoration of their autonomy in industrial management. But to realize this goal fully, they went beyond a reformed NRA; they made other recommendations which were meant as a comprehensive program of business-initiated recovery. The necessary consequence of this was that business control would supplant government control, or what they called government interference.

In the full program, business leaders called upon the Roosevelt administration to commit itself to balancing both the ordinary and emergency budgets "at the earliest possible date" by government retrenchment. Unemployment relief should be cut "to an indispensable minimum," and responsibility for it should revert to local and state authorities. Government spending projects designed to increase purchasing power, including public works, hindered recovery, they argued. On the other hand, a balanced budget "will allay fears of currency inflation, permit more refunding of government debt on a long-term basis, release investment funds for normal enterprise, safeguard the government's credit position, and induce a greater mobility of private resources and energy." Government competition with private business was "wasteful and inefficient," unfair, a breach of tradition, and "leads towards Socialism."

The counterpart of a drastic cutback in federal financing was the restoration of conditions for facilitating business financing, primarily by dismantling the obstacles thrown up by the New Deal. This required the restoration of the international gold standard, and assurances that the banking system would remain in private hands and that the monetary management of reserves would be made "independent of governmental domination and political influence." The channels of long-term capital financing, clogged by reforms, should be cleared by softening the provisions of the Securities and Securities Exchange acts. Further New Deal reforms, particularly in banking and unemployment insurance, should be deferred until competent commissions had thoroughly examined these matters.

These changes would permit private enterprise to turn its full attention to reviving the stagnant durable goods industries. In an analysis similar to that of Colonel Ayres, the business leaders started from the assumption that "the durable goods industries constitute at once the heart of the depression and the road to recovery." They asserted that three-fifths of all industrial unemployment was concentrated here—with more than two million unemployed in construction alone. "Reemployment in the consumers goods and service industries . . . depends upon linking idle capital with idle men in the durable goods industries, thus providing the increase in the real income of the nation which is the only sound basis for national recovery." According to their account, a survey of 2,274 companies in this sector showed that between 1929 and 1933 total assets declined by 28 percent and sales by 67.2 percent. New capital issues dropped from an annual average of near $4 billion in the 1920s to $160 million in 1933—a decline of 96 percent.

The stagnation of durable goods, in this view, was not due to lack of demand. In fact, the conference resolution insisted that "there does exist . . . an almost unlimited deferred demand for the product of the durable goods industries." This was especially true of the crucial construction industry. In 1929, consumer and producers' durable goods made up 42.6 percent "of all values created by industry in the United States," and of this, construction accounted for 21.5 percent. Once confidence was restored in future prospects, capital investment would resume, durable goods would revive, and general recovery would follow. But to restore confidence, the New Deal must first be largely liquidated.

This analysis was hardly new; it represented a restatement of traditional beliefs steeped in orthodox economics. *The Commercial & Financial Chronicle* filled issue after issue with long extracts from speeches, statements, and newsletters by bankers, businessmen, and economists who had been repeating the same argument for some time past. What was significant was that the Joint Business Conference for Economic Recovery now had given these criticisms official sanction as a consensual analysis by a group representing itself as the voice of organized business.

Roosevelt was thoroughly aware of this line of criticism of New Deal policies. It was a staple of the *New York Times,* the *Journal of Commerce;* indeed, it was part and parcel of his personal correspondence with friends on Wall and Broad Streets as well as industrialists, businessmen, and bankers elsewhere who made no pretense of being sympathetic to his policies. But Roosevelt complained that this view told him what not to do without giving him anything in the way of a positive program. Wait patiently for businessmen to bring about recovery—this was hardly acceptable advice for an activist leader. Nor was it likely that Roosevelt would dismantle major components of the New Deal which he so recently had enacted.

The business leaders' recommendations to Roosevelt are more understandable if they are viewed as the initial, maximum demands of one party in a four-way bargaining process—the other players being Roosevelt, organized labor, and the United States Senate. The political maneuvering already evident in 1934 picked up momentum as the date for the expiration of the NRA, June 16, 1935, approached. Organized labor was determined to preserve the gains it had derived from Section 7(a). Beyond that, American Federation of Labor president William Green also wanted the thirty-hour-week bill adopted, as well as the addition of Senator Wagner's Labor Board, an early version of the senator's powerful National Labor Relations Board.[57]

Despite these public signals of dissatisfaction by organized business, Roosevelt nonetheless disregarded their proposed modifications of the NRA and proceeded with his own ideas. Initially, the president attempted to realize his aims through the Senate. Declaring that to abandon the NRA was "unthinkable, for it would spell the return of industrial and labor chaos," he proposed a two-year extension, with changes that aimed at winning support among senators and organized labor. For senatorial skeptics, he announced that "the fundamental principles of the anti-trust laws should be more adequately applied," while for labor he held out the lure of maintaining Section 7(a) intact. The major beneficiary, however, was clearly the executive power of the Roosevelt administration. Government was to have "unquestioned power" to compel industries to abide by codes "of nominal standards of fair competition in commercial practices, and especially adequate standards of labor relations," while the president's authority to amend the codes, at his own initiative, was reaffirmed. The effect of Roosevelt's proposals was to transform an extraordinary grant of presidential power, which many had accepted originally as a temporary expedient, into permanent legislation legitimizing the authority of the government to intervene in the economy to prevent depressions.[58]

Politically, the major flaw in Roosevelt's strategy was in his choice of houses for the adoption of his plan. In the Senate a determined opposition to the NRA had already built up. Senator William Borah, who had opposed suspending the antitrust laws from the very beginning and had welcomed any and all attacks on the NRA, including the Darrow report, now saw his opportunity to strip the NRA of its antitrust immunity. His allies included Senator Glass, who preferred abolishing the NRA entirely, and Senator Pat Harrison (D–Miss.), who occupied the strategic position of chairman of the Finance Committee, which had jurisdiction over revising the NRA.[59]

Members of the Finance Committee were among the most vocal detractors of the NRA. Senator George informed Roosevelt that "there was not enough sentiment in Congress to have a law compelling industries to enact codes." He believed that codes should be voluntary, with the exception of the hours, wages, and child labor provisions, which would continue to apply nationally for all industries involved with natural resources such as coal, oil, and gas. Enforcement of the voluntary fair trade practices codes was to fall under the jurisdiction of the Federal Trade Commission. The administrative entity of the NRA, in other words, was to be abolished. Meanwhile, on the floor of the Senate, Senator Hastings's challenge for "anybody" to defend the NRA provoked total silence. Senator King's opposition followed the more formal procedure of requesting a "thorough investigation." Borah, who was not a committee member, stated the essential argument of the opposition in succinct fashion: "Elimination of price-fixing destroys monopoly, and elimination of the intrastate regulations will protect 80 per cent of the small business of the country."[60]

Faced with the determined opposition of the Senate Finance Committee, Roosevelt called its members, together with other Senate leaders, to a White House meeting in an attempt to devise an acceptable compromise. The maneuver failed to resolve the impasse, and Senator Bennett Clark announced that a majority of the Finance Committee was ready to vote on his joint resolution. This proposed to deprive the NRA of its price-fixing authority, to eliminate all intrastate businesses from its jurisdiction, and to extend the life of the agency only until April 1, 1936.[61]

The anti-NRA temper of the Senate was clearly confirmed

when the Finance Committee reported favorably on the Clark joint resolution. The Senate, in turn, supported this open defiance of the president's wishes by approving, without a record vote, the committee's handiwork. Roosevelt, opposed by organized business and thwarted by the Senate, turned abruptly from one house to the other in the pursuit of his objectives. The administration's proposal was introduced in the House Ways and Means Committee, and the Speaker stated that the House would support the president's wishes despite the action of the Senate. Roosevelt, in a move to strengthen further his bargaining position with the Senate and business leaders, called for "full speed ahead" on the House bill, and announced his support of Senator Wagner's controversial National Labor Relations Bill by designating it part of his "must" legislation.[62]

These political maneuvers and power plays were suddenly ended by the decisive intervention of the United States Supreme Court. In the Schechter decision, the justices "demolished the chief administrative recovery weapon of the New Deal," unanimously deciding that the Congress had overstepped its constitutional bounds by improperly delegating power to the president and by intruding unlawfully into the states' preserve of regulating intrastate commerce.[63] The NRA experiment in fostering economic recovery through industrial self-government was finished. But while the Court effectively disposed of the constitutional question, it did not provide any judgment on the economic and political utility of the NRA as a recovery policy. Roosevelt, however, had not been silent on this score.

Economically, Roosevelt staked out a large claim for the NRA's success. It was responsible, he stated, for employing four million workers; it had eliminated child labor and sweat shops; and it inaugurated a "pattern of a new order of industrial relations."[64] In Hugh Johnson's vindication of himself and the NRA, he claimed both more and less than Roosevelt had. "Whatever may be properly criticized about NRA," he wrote,

> it created 2,785,000 jobs at a desperate time and added about $3,000,000,000 to the annual purchasing power of working people. . . . It abolished child labor. It ran out the sweat shops.

> It established the principle of regulated hours, wages, and
> working conditions. It went far toward removing wages from
> the area of predatory competition. It added to the rights and
> the freedom of human labor.[65]

The economists of the Brookings Institution provided a
more accurate assessment of the economic effects of the NRA
on recovery in *The National Recovery Administration* (1935). Taking issue with Roosevelt's claim, they estimated that only one
and a half million workers were added to the employed work
force, and this was achieved largely by spreading the work: that
is, employed workers had their hours reduced—and received
less pay—in order to provide work for the unemployed. While
the NRA raised hourly wages and living costs by approximately
the same amount—9 to 10 percent above the precode period—
the average loss in real wages was between 5 and 6 percent.
The NRA also had an adverse effect on the durable goods industries. So that if recovery is defined as the achievement of
increased production, consumption, and real wages, the NRA
hindered rather than advanced it. "The NRA on the whole,"
the study concluded, "retarded recovery." [66]

Thus the NRA's utility to Roosevelt and the New Deal cannot be found in its economic performance. But if it is viewed
differently, by the political functions it served, then a very different assessment seems warranted. Two days after the NRA
was declared unconstitutional, the governor of the New York
Federal Reserve Bank stopped by the White House to visit with
Roosevelt. "He seemed," George Harrison recalled, "harassed
and stumped and for once I thought he had no definite plan
and seemed quite hopeless and helpless." "I am sure," he added,
"that at this time he had no definite plan of action in mind and
seemed quite at a loss how to proceed." [67] And indeed Roosevelt had very good cause to be deeply perplexed, for with the
loss of the NRA he had been deprived of a major political lever
for ensuring reasonable behavior and cooperation by business
and labor leaders.

Roosevelt could and did recoup his control on labor by
sanctioning the replacement of Section 7(a) with the more powerful instrumentality created by the National Labor Relations

Act. But Roosevelt found no equivalent substitute for industry *as a whole* to replace the bait taken from him. And while the NRA had only imperfectly dampened business discontent and criticism, nonetheless it had provided him with a degree of management and control which he now no longer possessed. In this regard, as in so many others, the NRA was cut from the same political cloth as the AAA. The significant difference, however, was that Roosevelt had quickly repaired his loss to the Court of the first AAA with the Soil Conservation Act and the second AAA. In his dealings with industrialists and businessmen, however, the Court in effect took away his carrot, leaving him with only the influence he could wield by threatening to renew a stringent enforcement of the antitrust laws. This was a blunt instrument for realizing the delicate objective of maintaining political harmony with the business community.

ELEVEN

The Crisis of the New Deal Program

A CENTRAL ISSUE of the New Deal's recovery program, which contemporaries only gradually perceived, was the decided shift taking place in the relationship between government and business. Businessmen were accustomed to regard themselves as the preeminent proprietors of the economic sphere. The conduct of the nation's economic life was their preserve; they were the decision-makers in commerce, trade, and manufacturing, estimating what the market would take and at what price. If the federal government had a role in the marketplace, it was to act as the helpmate of business, not as its equal, and most decidedly not as its master.

The disruptive events of the Great Depression jolted this sense of self-esteem by exposing the helplessness of business leaders, their inability to restore prosperity on their own initiative, and by subjecting them to public assaults on their honesty, wisdom, and prestige. Then the New Deal assailed the business community with powerful aftershocks. While President Roosevelt repeatedly talked of a government-business partnership, a theme echoed by such widely assorted New Dealers as Hugh Johnson, Raymond Moley, Adolf Berle, Rexford Tugwell, Henry Wallace, and Jesse Jones, the truth of the matter belied their words.[1] Clearly the initiative in the New Deal recovery program rested unequally on the side of the federal government. Roosevelt in particular regarded businessmen as junior partners in the enterprise, and he treated them accordingly. Speaking before the American Bankers Association convention in 1934, Roosevelt defined his conception of the presidential role. "A true function of the head of the Government of the United States," he explained, "is to find among many discordant elements that unity of purpose that is best for the nation as a whole." Then, in a revealing moment, he added, "The old fallacious notion of the bankers on the one side and the Government on the other as more or less equal and independent units has passed away. Government by the necessity of things must be the leader, must be the judge of the conflicting interests of all groups in the community, including bankers." [2]

For those who customarily discounted what Roosevelt said, there was more empirical proof that a sharp tilt was occurring in the balance of power between government and business in the regulation of the economy. The major components of the New Deal recovery policies, including the RFC, monetary management, agricultural and industrial policies, and the techniques used by the PWA, CWA, and WPA "to prime the pump," demonstrated convincingly that the federal government was the new headmaster.

Nonetheless these recovery measures, as important as they undoubtedly were, did not constitute the whole of the New Deal, nor were they necessarily the primary focus of businessmen's apprehensions. Intertwined with recovery policies were the more ominous reform activities of the New Deal, with their emphasis upon structural changes in basic economic institutions. While the details of New Deal reform fall beyond the scope of this study, the impact that reform had upon businessmen's perceptions of what the New Deal was and where it might be going did affect business behavior in ways that were of crucial importance to recovery. [3]

If one differentiates reform from recovery on a functional basis, a rough distinction can be made between those measures which were intended as permanent institutional changes and those intended to promote immediate recovery. The objectives of New Deal reform were varied, extensive, and politically volatile. Among its major thrusts, New Deal reform attempted to eliminate financial and business abuses, to centralize economic authority, to augment the economic power of particular groups, to diminish that of others, to redistribute national income, and to provide new social welfare services on a national scale.

The means to achieve these ambitious goals included the Banking Acts of 1933 and 1935, the Securities Exchange Act of 1934, the National Labor Relations Act of 1935, Roosevelt's tax proposals in 1935 and 1936, the Social Security Act of 1935, and the reform aspects of such other legislation as the National Industrial Recovery Act, the Agricultural Adjustment Acts, and the Tennessee Valley Authority Act.

The great outpouring of New Deal legislation from 1933 through 1935 resulted in developing what Alvin Hansen called the "hybrid economy."[4] This amalgam was neither a totally free economy nor a systematically controlled one. The outcome was an unplanned combination of elements from both, which for the sake of convenience might be called the New Deal's particular version of political economy. This halfway house uneasily sheltered a heavy burden of economic and political liabilities. Above all, if public policy was to function effectively in restoring prosperity, the sustained economic cooperation of both government and business was required. Roosevelt could and indeed did use the resources of government to rescue the banks, build up their reserves and capital, and bring them to the brink of lending. But he could not command the bankers to lend or, for that matter, the businessmen to borrow. In these vital matters Roosevelt could neither dictate compliance and cooperation nor ensure success. He could only attempt to persuade, but here he was handicapped by the growing distrust of the New Deal by important segments of the business community.

Business criticism of the New Deal, muted in 1933, burst out in full voice during the course of 1934. The catalogue of complaints touched upon practically all aspects of Roosevelt's policies, while anticipating more of the same or worse. The New Deal, so the businessmen's reckoning went, was grossly extravagant, wasting the nation's substance by deficit spending, pump priming, and unbalanced budgets, thereby fostering a pervasive "dole psychology." The channels of credit and the capital investment market were disrupted, reducing both to a state of malfunction. The attempt to promote the redistribution of income by tax, agricultural, and labor policies attacked the legitimacy of business profits. Government was directly invading the business realm by actively competing with private enterprise, especially in the field of electrical power, but also by extending its operations to more mundane matters, such as mattress making. Businessmen repeatedly complained that government, by penetrating economic affairs, was creating business uncertainty and a depressing lack of business confidence. In sum, the federal government's ventures in reform served only to discourage recovery; it was time for a "moratorium" on the whole bloody business.[5]

Beneath these complaints against Roosevelt and the New Deal, several general and related themes of protest can be discerned. There was a dawning awareness among business leaders of a basic change in the nation's political economy, involving an erosion of business autonomy and the piecemeal but persistent dismantling of what contemporaries called the traditional American System. In its place, Roosevelt was constructing a new economic order which was variously described as government planning, collectivism, and state capitalism. The major characteristic of the new order was the direct intrusion of the federal government in the economy. The New Deal was preempting central prerogatives of private enterprise by assuming the responsibility of managing the economy, and it was bit by bit taking over the economic instrumentalities necessary to realize its new mission. This perception, which was a strong suspicion in 1934, became by 1937 more akin to a settled conviction.

In retrospect, the conservative business critics were correct. The New Deal years from 1933 through 1938 represented a genuine watershed in the evolution of the political control of the economy. While Roosevelt did not invent government intervention in business and banking, the New Deal was unprecedented for the speed with and the extent to which it developed government dominance in regulation of the economy.

Basic changes of this magnitude inevitably cause tension, protest, and resistance. The opposition to these changes, starting with the uncoordinated expressions of individual discontent, soon broadened into a more coherent, organized group demand that Roosevelt sharply bridle the government's role in managing recovery and turn this function back to private initiative.

Roosevelt attempted to reassure businessmen and refute criticism of the New Deal at the same time that he was proposing a significant elaboration of his reform program. In his special message to Congress, outlining his legislative agenda for 1935, Roosevelt addressed business fears directly:

> Ample scope is left for the exercise of private initiative. In fact, in the process of recovery, I am greatly hoping that repeated promises that private investment and private initiative to relieve the Government in the immediate future of much of the burden it has assumed will be fulfilled. We have not imposed undue restrictions upon business.
>
> We have not opposed the incentive of reasonable and legitimate private profit. We have sought rather to enable certain aspects of business to regain the confidence of the public. We have sought to put forward the rule of fair play in finance and industry.[6]

The response to Roosevelt's call for reconciliation and co-operation revealed a growing cleavage between the officers and the membership of organized business. At the annual convention of the American Bankers Association in 1934, billed as a "ceremony of exchanging olive branches" between the bankers and Roosevelt, both the former and current presidents of the ABA appealed for a "pact of peace." The principal provision of the peace treaty was a "pledge of co-operation" to expand business enterprise. But despite the leaders' injunction to lay aside hostility, the *New York Times* observed that many of the four thousand bankers present remained bitter about Roosevelt and the New Deal, and resentful of their leaders' efforts to arrange a cease-fire.[7]

This outward show of amity was even less evident at the national Chamber of Commerce's convention in November.

Despite the directors' efforts "to pledge the support of organized business to the recovery efforts of the Administration," the reports of its committees showed a more grudging attitude. The Federal Finance Committee, for example, concentrated its attention on the very heart of the New Deal by urging a sharp reduction in government spending, while the Committee on Manufactures strongly opposed the adoption of a mandatory thirty-hour work week nationally. Henry I. Harriman, the Chamber's president, perhaps best expressed the tension between business and government when he remarked, "All we want, all we ask for and all the country needs is a thorough spirit of co-operation. And when I say 'co-operation,' I mean a condition in which Government does not attack business and business does not attack the Government." [8]

Leaders of the National Association of Manufacturers were predictably the most plainspoken in criticizing the government's burgeoning role in the economy. In October the board issued a statement of protest declaring:

> Entrance of the Government into the manufacturing business in competition with its own citizens even to supply relief for the unemployed constitutes an extravagant use of the taxpayers' money in further experimentations. It simply shifts employment from private to public enterprises and serves to retard stable business recovery.[9]

The president of the NAM, C. L. Bardo, followed this up with a speech emphasizing the necessity of restoring a sense of confidence among entrepreneurs. His characterization of the proper milieu for the renewal of confidence made it absolutely clear that he meant a complete withdrawal by the government from the advanced positions it had occupied in directing the economy.[10]

This demand for New Deal retrenchment by businessmen and their national organizations in order to provide space and incentive for a resurgence of private enterprise in leading the nation to economic recovery was soon taken up by other influential voices. From 1935 onwards, publicists, political commentators, and economic analysts called upon Roosevelt insistently for what one editor aptly termed "a breathing spell."[11] The assumption here was that businessmen, buffeted by two years of rapid changes, needed a respite, a season of legislative and administrative quiet, to regain their economic bearings. With a calm sea and with businessmen restored to the helm, the prediction was, private enterprise would summon up the resources for recovery which the government could not achieve. Beyond this argument for confidence, a more philosophical issue was perceived to be involved in the recovery process. This was the contention, rooted in ideological belief, that the preservation of private enterprise and the protection of economic freedoms were inseparable issues: the diminution of the one inevitably diminished the prospects of the other's survival.[12]

Major exponents of this view included such prestigious advocates as the Brookings Institution, the New York Federal Reserve Bank, and President Roosevelt's Hyde Park neighbor and friend Secretary of the Treasury Henry Morgenthau, Jr. By 1935 Morgenthau had traveled far from the early days of the New Deal, when he had arranged for George Warren to meet Roosevelt for a teatime discussion of Warren's unorthodox monetary theories. Now, when Warren was once again urging a renewed application of the gold experiment by a new increase in the dollar price of gold, Morgenthau's ardor had cooled to skepticism and disinterest.[13] His position, in fact, was virtually indistinguishable from that of the internationalist-minded critics of the original attempt to lift commodity prices by bidding up the price of gold. Morgenthau had become, as John M. Blum has remarked, "the most influential spokesman of orthodox economics in Washington."[14] Like his newfound conservative brethren, Morgenthau was now concerned with such matters as international monetary stabilization, balanced budgets, and runaway inflation. "The situation, as I see it, after eight months of Congress," Morgenthau remarked in September 1935, "is this—that it looks to me as though the old nag 'economy' which has been out in the pasture for the last three years has been brought back again and is going to be put into training."[15] In anticipation of the political battles he foresaw for 1936, Morgenthau wrote in December:

My big fight is going to be to keep expenditures for the next fiscal year to a sum which will be less than the expenditures of this fiscal year. If I can accomplish this, any fears that I may have as to inflation and the printing of paper currency will be put to the background for keeps but if we keep on spending more money each year I greatly question if we can keep Congress from forcing us into the printing of paper money with which to pay the deficit.[16]

Morgenthau's fight for economy and fiscal orthodoxy was ultimately with Roosevelt, for it was the president who had to be persuaded to forgo deficit spending. In 1936 this task was decidedly simplified by the political climate generated by a presidential election year. Discussing the political situation with Roosevelt in February 1936, Morgenthau warned the president that he was "vulnerable on spending." When Roosevelt agreed, Morgenthau offered some conservative remedies. He suggested gathering together a select group from within the administration "to see if they can come up with a saving program." He also urged Roosevelt to appoint "a national figure as Director of the Budget" to replace Lewis Douglas, who had resigned in August 1934 and had been temporarily replaced with an acting director, Daniel Bell. Someone was needed, he insisted, who could make a convincing case "that Roosevelt is trying to economize." The last, most immediate item involved the federal budget of $4.8 billion. Both Morgenthau and Roosevelt were determined to keep spending for the fiscal year below this figure.[17]

In thus making a campaign pitch for business support, Roosevelt, while concerned with his standing among businessmen, was also mindful of the immediate needs of other constituencies, particularly the farmers. When Morgenthau pushed him too hard on publicizing the savings program, Roosevelt replied, "I must not talk too quickly or too much about saving, otherwise the impression will go out that I am afraid I am licked." On another occasion, when the troublesome price of cotton was being discussed, Roosevelt repeated several times a political imperative: "Henry, through July, August, September, October and up to the 5th of November I want cotton to sell at 12 cents.

I do not care how you do it. This is your problem. It can't go below 12 cents. Is that clear?"[18]

Roosevelt's handling of the budget problem, as Morgenthau recounted it in his diary, was a further demonstration of a political strategy for campaign effect. Roosevelt was explicit in stating that he was "up against a political situation which makes unpopular any tax bill." Instead of additional tax revenues, savings had to be wrung from the lending and spending agencies. At a conference at the White House on February 6, Morgenthau noted approvingly, Roosevelt "stated that he had instructed Harry Hopkins to reduce the rolls of the Works Progress Administration as fast as it is possible to do so, the employees to be transferred to public works projects under the supervision of the various departments other than Works Progress Administration or absorbed in industry." A day earlier, Morgenthau chaired a meeting which explored the possibility of liquidating the WPA entirely by July 1 (the end of the fiscal year). Discussing the Department of Agriculture's need for $500 million to put the new farm bill into operation, Roosevelt mused that he preferred $490 million because "that seems less than $500 million." All of this was accompanied by a frank juggling of the books to demonstrate publicly that money was saved, then quietly to return it for spending after July 1. And it was all worked out, Roosevelt exulted, "just as he thought—that on July 1, there will be left $1 billion out of the $4.8 billion."[19]

Roosevelt's ventures in fiscal conservatism were augmented by complementary monetary policies executed by officials of the Federal Reserve and the Treasury Department. By 1936 they had become increasingly concerned with the danger of an uncontrolled inflation. Specifically, they worried about the continued growth of excess reserves among member banks, which by the early part of the year amounted to $3 billion. The members of the Federal Open Market Committee determined to reduce this by using the authority granted to the Federal Reserve by the Banking Act of 1935 to increase the required reserves of member banks. The first increase of 50 percent went into effect on August 16, 1936; this was followed by a second, similar increase that came in phased parts on March 1 and May 1, 1937, which raised the reserve requirement to its legal limit.[20]

224

In the course of this operation, the Treasury Department announced its decision to sterilize gold imported into the country, largely from Europe, in an inactive gold account. The aim here was to neutralize the monetary impact of this gold by preventing it from enlarging the monetary base. This was achieved by the technical device of paying for the gold by issuing government securities instead of gold certificates, a technique which averted new deposits (and potential new reserves) at the Federal Reserve.[21] In this way Morgenthau continued and elaborated upon a conservative monetary policy that he was already pursuing in 1934. At that time he had quieted conservatives' fears of the inflationary potential of the government's gold profit of $2.8 billion from devaluation by establishing a $2 billion Exchange Stabilization Fund.[22]

Morgenthau's handling of the Treasury's large silver purchases, a program which began in earnest in 1934, was designed to honor the political commitments made to the silver producers and their congressional supporters while minimizing the inflationary consequences. Silver producers (and speculators) received the enhanced price of 64.5 cents an ounce for newly mined silver, representing half of its official coinage value of $1.29. The remaining half was retained by the Treasury, ostensibly to meet seigniorage costs. However, the Treasury only issued silver certificates in an amount equal to silver's market value, not its official value. This meant, in effect, that the Treasury deliberately refrained from realizing its seigniorage (profit) as a means of avoiding one-half the monetary impact of its silver purchases.[23] This policy effectively split the silver producers, who were relatively content with 64.5 cents, from the silverites, whose ardent inflationary expectations were checkmated. It was an illustration of how congressional intention could be effectively balked by administrative interpretation.

Roosevelt's acceptance of conservative monetary and fiscal policies in 1936 and, continuing beyond his impressive reelection, into 1937, was undoubtedly due to more than one factor. While Morgenthau was tireless in urging orthodox economic policies upon Roosevelt, his advice was fortified by other influences impinging upon the president. Foremost among these was the persisting distrust and the relentless criticism of the New Deal by spokesmen of the business community. Roosevelt was both sensitive to and exasperated by these attacks. Nor did it help matters that Roosevelt shared his critics' attachment to a balanced budget. His most recent testimonial to this belief was his veto of the veterans' bonus, which was promptly overridden by Congress. The resulting payment of $1.4 billion to veterans in 1936 provided a powerful impetus to the economizers, including Morgenthau, who were galvanized into action to bring about a balanced budget to counteract the inflationary impact they anticipated.[24]

Roosevelt's political resolution of these converging pressures, seemingly, was to accede to his business critics by agreeing to test the economic utility of their position. He provided them not only with the moratorium from the New Deal that they demanded, but a retrenchment of government spending as well. With the obstacles to business confidence thus cleared away, businessmen were given the opportunity to prove the validity of their argument by achieving a more substantial economic recovery than the New Deal had been able to manage. In effect, Roosevelt agreed to a public trial of an essentially negative recovery program.

The results of this experiment were swift and devastating. The incomplete New Deal recovery was halted and reversed as the economy plummeted between September 1937 and June 1938, erasing many of the gains made since 1933. As Kenneth Roose has concluded, "The nine-month recession itself was without parallel for its severity in American history: industrial production declined by 33% and durable goods production by over 50%; national income declined by 13%; industrial stock averages declined by over 50%, . . . and manufacturing employment declined by 23%."[25]

This severe slump in New Deal recovery provoked a searching debate both within and without the Roosevelt administration to identify the causes of the collapse. If these were understood, then the appropriate economic policies to counteract the recession might be applied. The central issue in this debate was the highly controversial one of compensatory government spending. This involved far more than the economic choice between two opposed recovery programs with conflicting conceptions of fiscal policy. At stake was the more fundamental issue of the future relationship between government and business and the consequent distribution of power and decision-making. The intensity and significance of the competition between proponents of economic orthodoxy and public spending can thus be comprehended more clearly when it is viewed as a clash of ideologies.

Exponents of the two ideologies understood, with varying degrees of clarity, that compensatory government spending could not be turned on and off like a faucet. One implication of such a policy was that the federal establishment, which in the eyes of contemporaries had already grown enormously, needed to become much bigger still. That is, if public spending was to have sufficient leverage to activate the private sector, then the government's involvement in the economy had to be considerably broadened. This implied, furthermore, that the economic power of the New Deal was not to be a temporary phenomenon which would wither away when the emergency passed. If emergencies involving the tendency of the economy to periodic instability and breakdown were endemic to the system, then the more realistic prospect was that of a permanent New Deal.

The issues of contention thus transcended the current crisis. The components of the two ideologies included sharply diverging appraisals of the functional performance of the American economy in the past, its structural strengths and weaknesses, and disparate forecasts of its future prospects. Obviously these economic issues involved major political and social choices and ramifications. How clearly were they understood by contemporaries?

Among the most prominent members of the little band of Keynesians within the government were Leon Henderson, Marriner Eccles, Lauchlin Currie, and Beardsley Ruml. They were supported by a few others, such as Harry Hopkins, Aubrey Williams, and Harry Dexter White. Henderson, as coauthor of the Merriam-Henderson report, which went to Roosevelt through Hopkins on November 9, 1937, was certainly aware of the political difficulties of carrying out a large spending program.[26] The economic options, as Henderson realistically remarked, while defined by economists, would in fact be selectively chosen and applied by political leaders:

> Whether it is to be the national policy to await further developments before arriving at important conclusions and decisions, or to offer verbal or other olive branches to dissatisfied groups in the community, or to undertake direct and specific action toward breaking the bottle necks and establishing a larger area of profitable enterprise, to balance or unbalance the budget, to tax or untax, to rely upon monetary magic and manipulation; these are matters devolving on those with the power and responsibility of political decision and action.

In making these choices, it was imperative that the objectives of the New Deal be kept firmly in mind. Henderson summarized these briefly:

> This administration is committed to a wide social program, which includes social security, parity of farm prices and farm income, better housing, work for the unemployed; all pointed toward higher living standards and juster distribution of the gains of civilization. Validation of this series of commitments depends upon wider distribution of an immensely enlarged national income.

Some of the economic barriers to the realization of this vision had already been removed by New Deal policies. As Henderson expressed it, "We are passing out of a period in which chief emphasis has been laid upon (a) repair of the weaknesses of the economic system and (b) care for the victims of the depression." The pressing task now was to generate the huge funds needed, which he added, "must come from a level of national income and business activity far higher than that of 1929." This required significantly improved "management methods" than had so far been developed.

It was on this crucial point of managing the economic revival that Henderson frankly acknowledged the limitations of the government's power and, therefore, the necessity for a collaborative program with business. "This government," he cautioned, "even if it thought it wise to attempt their use, does not have the powers, techniques and organization of forces necessary for controlling the national economy within precise bounds." The government did have the resources, however, to manage a more modest role, that of "exerting a directional influence by choices of governmental policies, such as Federal reserve actions, spending, taxation, relations to business, etc."

Prominent among the difficulties Henderson foresaw in managing the economy so that it might meet the New Deal's objectives was that of smoothing out the tangled, conflicting motivations and values associated with advocates of the old and new regimes:

> Many of the future problems may be viewed as clustering about the *relation of government to business*—a relationship which has not yet been clarified, and can not be clarified until a far more momentous question has been settled and the settlement accepted as national policy, viz.: to what extent can *competition be relied upon as the automatic regulator of our economic system,* and to what extent can it be *supplemented* without destroying our industrial morale or our national unity.

On the basis of this analysis, Henderson anticipated the possibility of choosing one of three major ideological alternatives. These were to return to laissez-faire by dismantling most if not all of the New Deal; to proceed ahead to a fully managed economy; or to maintain a middle position between these extremes, characterized by an emphasis on "increasing productivity, encouraging fair profits and broadening the zone of general prosperity." He made his own preference clear when he remarked approvingly, "The National Resources Committee recommended in 1936 the appointment of a Fiscal Advisory Board for the purpose of observing the trends of the business cycle and of recommending from time to time, if and as necessary, governmental expenditure or other appropriate expedient as an aid to preservation of the balance of the national economy." [27]

Days later Henderson mulled over the problem of "What

caused the slump?"[28] He took strong exception to what he termed the "current propaganda" in business-financial circles that new taxes—particularly the undistributed corporate profits tax enacted in 1936, which business leaders had strenuously opposed—were responsible for the slump. He dismissed even more abruptly another business contention which linked the recession to the stagnation of new capital issues. These had "dried up" because large investors were engaged in a "sit-down strike," and not because of overly restrictive government regulation. The real source of trouble, he suspected, was "a lessening of the demand for producers' durable goods."

Subsequently, on June 9, 1938, Henderson reviewed the course of the recession for Harry Hopkins in a somber report.[29] Citing the *New York Times* Weekly Business Index, which showed "that the trend is still down," Henderson felt that "most of the Government guesstimators, . . . expect a 'creeping recovery,' that is, nothing sensational." Ruml, he added, "expects this and says it will be most disastrous because real correctives will be postponed." Henderson's pessimism stemmed from his realization of the uncertain prospect of an energetic government spending program. He was, however, positive that the current "amount of the net governmental contribution to purchasing power is not sufficient to compensate for the lack of private spending." That clearly had to do with the unrecognized importance of Keynesian economics, as Henderson regretfully conceded:

> I agree with Eccles and wish we might be bolder and less apologetic about compensatory fiscal policy, which I regard as a necessary, positive economic policy, deserving and requiring aggressive presentation. I believe that the immediate prospects require considerable concentration of spending in the Summer and early Fall months both to prevent acute situations developing and to help in finishing up the corrective period. Otherwise, we'll hear more from the monetary meddlers when Congress reconvenes.

Henderson was mistaken on one point. Marriner Eccles was hardly reticent in proselytizing the new economic doctrine of systematic public spending. The difficulties in winning public acceptance of Keynes's prescription, however, demanded far more than just persistence. The combined novelty of the Keynesian concept, its radical departure from conventional economic beliefs, and its unproven effectiveness constituted an enormous deadweight that was not easily moved. Some indication of the hostile reception that Eccles's efforts provoked can be gathered from a conversation between Governor George Harrison and Walter W. Stewart in April 1937, one of a series of talks with bankers that Harrison conducted to find out what was bothering them. As Harrison recalled Stewart's remarks,

> . . . he thinks Eccles as a central banker is going pretty far afield into tax and fiscal affairs and is expressing himself so freely about them that ultimately he will be made a goat. . . . The whole trouble is that he fundamentally believes so strongly in a managed economy and realizes that there are so many limitations upon the powers of credit control to accomplish complete management, that logically he has to get into these other matters. He thinks, however, that it is a mistake that will come back to plague him.[30]

Harrison's own familiarity with Eccles's ideas was informed by an extensive correspondence which the two exchanged between November 1937 and May 1938.[31] As articulate advocates of the contending ideologies of economic orthodoxy and government management of the economy, Harrison and Eccles expressed the essential differences involved in one of the most important and inconclusive debates of the New Deal years.

Harrison initiated the correspondence two weeks after attending the president's conference to discuss what should be done about the developing recession. His two major purposes were to establish the clear preeminence of the private over the public sector as the critical factor to consider in devising a new recovery program; and to make a strong case against reverting to a large government spending program. Harrison recognized that the transition from government to business spending had not worked well, but he thought this was due to persisting barriers to business spending and faulty management of the transition. "I think we are all agreed," he stated, "that more government spending is not a feasible way out." This was not only

Harrison's and his directors' conviction; it was also his opinion that "the government and the people have set their faces against continued deficit financing."[32]

After skillfully shifting the onus for the recession from business and invoking public opinion against deficit spending, Harrison moved to what he regarded as the central issue. "The real problem," he explained, "is to get private spending going again and in sufficient amounts to fill the gap left by the sharp decline in the government's net income producing expenditures. There is plenty of private spending that needs to be done and there is plenty of money available." Harrison conceded that the "machinery" for private spending was "partly stalled" at the moment, but this could be corrected by adopting his suggested program "to accelerate business recovery."

Harrison's recovery program warrants close attention since he stated so clearly and in summary fashion the convictions and policy preferences of the economically orthodox. He presented the issues under three broad heads: problems concerning business confidence, the potential areas of new business investment, and the inhibiting effect of federal taxes. In elaboration, he wrote:

> (1) I am sure I do not need to emphasize the fact that the business community is just now extraordinarily sensitive to every wind that blows from Washington. Whatever can be said or done to indicate the awareness of the Administration concerning the problems business now face and to clarify its objectives as they relate to business is likely to be as effective as more specific action. Business is now hesitant about making long term plans partly because it feels it does not know what the rules of the game are going to be. . . .
>
> (2) On the more specific business problems and more specific ways in which spending may be expedited and employment increased, the four fields which appear most promising are: (a) building, (b) public utilities, (c) railroads, and (d) general manufacturing and mining. . . .
>
> (3) Concerning the problems of business financing, perhaps the main point to be emphasized is the widespread belief . . . that certain of our present taxes inhibit the financing of business and promote disorder in security markets. A program

to review and revise the tax system, particularly the undistributed profits tax and the capital gains tax, would be a constructive step, not only by the removal of possible defects in the tax system, but also by encouraging business initiative generally.

In reply, Eccles immediately went to the core difference in their analyses of the recession. "My principal point of departure from your summation," he wrote, "relates to what seems to me to be the importance of sustaining government contributions to general purchasing power while the obstacles to private spending are being cleared away." While acknowledging that his was "a minority view," he nonetheless insisted that the major factor was the "precipitous decline in dollar purchasing power," and that this required corrective government action. "For myself," he concluded, "I cannot be blind to the cumulative effects of deflationary forces after our experience in recent years, nor to the futility of talking again about balancing the budget by reducing Federal outlay at a time when private spending is rapidly diminishing and government revenues correspondingly drying up." This was "the height of folly," and to rely on a quick and sufficient revival of private spending was "a foolish risk to take."[33]

Harrison, while conceding that they differed in their recovery methods, centered his argument on the question of relative risks. Where did the greater danger lie? What was the lesser evil?

The question which is immediately raised in my mind . . . is whether a return to government spending might not renew and accentuate some of the uncertainties that are holding business back, and thus further postpone the time when private spending will supplant government spending. Is not the question really whether obstacles to private spending will be courageously and quickly enough removed to justify running the risk to which you refer? Some temporary recession, even admitting that it might be severe for the time being, might in the long run prove to be the cheaper price to pay. At least it seems to us that it is necessary to weigh against that price the risks inevitably involved in an abandonment of the administration's attitude about the budget and an avowed return to government spending.[34]

But as Harry Hopkins once remarked, "People don't eat in the long run—they eat every day."[35]

The Eccles-Harrison exchange of views revealed the ideological chasm that separated the old and the new economic thought. The one important element missing here was the polemical fervor with which this struggle was usually waged. It was perhaps this very intensity that explained the haphazard bridge that emerged between the two camps, a middle way satisfying neither group, not in its design nor its fitful performance. An effective, working partnership between a powerful government and its business counterpart remained more vision than reality.

On April 14, 1938, President Roosevelt announced his new recovery program in a national broadcast. He discussed the current recession in a way reminiscent of his explanation of the more serious crisis he confronted in March 1933. This was the familiar causative thesis of overproduction and underconsumption, with its emphasis upon the insufficient purchasing power of the people. The "visible setback" that had interrupted the New Deal recovery required action, and he was unambiguous on where he stood on the debate between government versus private spending initiatives. "It is only within the past two months," he asserted, "as we have waited patiently to see whether the forces of business itself would counteract it, that it has become apparent that government itself can no longer safely fail to take aggressive government steps to meet it."[36] The experiment in a business-initiated recovery was over.

Roosevelt's program reversed the policy of the Federal Reserve by reducing reserve requirements so as to increase excess reserves; reversed the Treasury Department's policy by desterilizing gold in the inactive account to broaden the monetary base; reversed RFC lending policy to industry by removing restraints; and resumed government spending for work relief and public works. Programmatically, the beneficiaries of new federal appropriations included the WPA, the Farm Security Administration, the PWA, and the U.S. Housing Authority. The New Deal, in short, was thrown back into forward gear, to the consternation of George Harrison and others of like mind.[37]

Harrison quickly expressed his grave reservations about Roosevelt's return to deficit spending. "Whatever may be the merits or the limitations of the program announced by the President last month," he wrote Eccles, "I think it is increasingly recognized that it must be supplemented by, and must in large measure be dependent for its success upon, a program which will further encourage private initiative and employment." After reiterating the essentials of the recovery program that he had urged upon Eccles earlier, he concluded by stressing again that the government's first priority would be to "encourage the recovery of private investment upon which our economy fundamentally depends."[38]

It is in the nature of ideological debate that neither side is likely to be convinced by the other's arguments. Eccles, like Harrison, ended this correspondence as he had begun it, by restating his Keynesian view: the old economics suited an older world; it did not meet the tasks of the world they now faced. The agreement of these two distinguished spokesmen to continue to disagree accurately reflected, albeit in an uncharacteristically civil manner, the same debate that continued within the Roosevelt administration as well as in the larger public arena.[39]

In March 1939 Henry Morgenthau wrote to George Harrison asking him for any material he had on economic recovery. Harrison sent him copies of the letters and memoranda that he had exchanged with Marriner Eccles. That Morgenthau savored only one side of this correspondence can be established by a close look at his leadership of the Treasury Department during and after the recession of 1937–38.[40]

Morgenthau's diaries make clear that one of his preoccupations from 1935 onwards was with the recurring specter of inflation. From a later vantage point it may seem paradoxical that Morgenthau, and conservatives generally, were so apprehensive about inflation during the years of the Great Depression. This curious phenomenon may be explained, in part at least, by citing some of the more apparent factors in its occurrence. There was, for example, nothing imaginary about the extensive appeal and support that deliberate inflationists enjoyed throughout the 1930s, particularly during the early years of the New Deal. The conservatives' intense early fear of monetary inflation shifted later to fear of fiscal inflation when the Roosevelt administration took up, however imperfectly, the idea of compensatory government spending, which obviously necessitated budgetary deficits.

When Roosevelt announced his new spending program, Morgenthau's close friend and adviser Jacob Viner resigned his position at the Treasury in protest. "I believe that heavy deficit spending," he wrote, "if unaccompanied by genuine and courageous effort to eliminate the factors which made our recovery only a halting and incomplete one, and which now have forced us into a renewal of severe depression, . . . will involve serious dangers for the political as well as the economic health of our democracy."[41] For Viner, the debate with the spenders seemed lost. In retrospect, however, there were no decisive victories for either side in the battle to win Roosevelt's mind on this issue. What occurred was more akin to a series of protracted skirmishes, resulting in a seesaw movement.

Within the Treasury itself, the span of the first phase of the debate was roughly from November 1937 to April 1938, when Roosevelt adopted his spending program. On the evening of November 3, Morgenthau telephoned Roosevelt to state, "I have had to come to the conclusion that we are headed right into another depression."[42] He followed this up the next day with a query: "The question is, Mr. President, what are we going to do to stop it?" Morgenthau got his answer at a cabinet meeting when Roosevelt burst out angrily, "I am sick and tired of being told by the Cabinet, by Henry and by everybody else for the last two weeks what's the matter with the country and nobody suggests what I should do."[43]

Morgenthau's preferences at this time were "to retrace the steps that we have taken" in monetary policy by reducing reserve requirements and desterilizing gold. He also suggested that the government concentrate on facilitating private investment in such prostrated areas as public utilities, railroads, and housing. When Morgenthau went on to urge Roosevelt to give fresh reassurances to businessmen in a speech planned for November 15, a revealing dialogue ensued.

MORGENTHAU: What business wants to know is are we headed towards State Socialism or are we going to continue on a Capitalistic basis?

ROOSEVELT: I have told them that again and again.

MORGENTHAU: All right, Mr. President, tell them for the fifteenth time on November 15, because . . . that's what they want to know.

ROOSEVELT: I will turn on the old record.[44]

The president's resigned agreement to play it again, despite his awareness of the futility of the gesture, suggested that he was deeply troubled by the unsettled political relations between his administration and business, which the recession further aggravated. Perhaps it was this deterioration that set off Roosevelt's soliloquy, several days later, that so puzzled Morgenthau:

> I want to put a flea in your ear. Have you ever stopped to consider that Fascism is winning out in this world and that Democracies are gradually becoming weaker? . . . Take the situation in our own country. Four or five people may get together and they'll talk this thing over and they'll simply say we have simply got to get our own man in Washington but there is no use in trying to make them understand. Washington every so often says that they want business to make a profit and they believe in property rights but we don't believe them. Now I don't say that 2,000 men have all got together and agreed to block us but I do say that 2,000 men have come to about the same conclusion.[45]

Morgenthau's reaction was to speculate that Roosevelt seemed like a lion at bay who "does not want to be tamed"; yet "he does not know where he can put his strength at this particular juncture to bring about recovery."

Morgenthau's own disquiet did not concern the political potential of an American fascism; it was concentrated instead on the economic consequences that he thought were inseparable from a heavy resort to deficit spending. His conviction was fortified by detailed reports on this issue by his more orthodox advisers. It was Wayne Taylor's opinion, for example, that "the business community and the new capital market are in a state of stagnation, if not panic." This was due to businessmen's unhappiness about the administration's labor and tax policies, but above all to their fear of new monetary and fiscal experiments. "Either move," he warned, "could mean the beginning of the end in their minds, and the printing press would be just around the corner." The first priority, therefore, was to rehabilitate business confidence.[46]

As the recession lengthened, a sense of urgency began to pervade the daily meetings which Morgenthau held with his staff. Morgenthau's two major purposes were to devise an effective refutation of spending theories, and to prepare a more orthodox alternative which he hoped to persuade the president to accept.[47] These involved the familiar arguments of economic orthodoxy. On April 10, 1938, four days before Roosevelt's national broadcast, Morgenthau presented his recovery program to the president. It was too little and too late. The next day Morgenthau complained bitterly to his staff that all the talk was about spending and Hopkins. He reported that Henry Wallace "said the President's raring to go, and they have just stampeded him. . . . They stampeded him like cattle—they trampled the grass underfoot."[48]

Roosevelt's decision in favor of the spenders did not still the controversy; if anything, Morgenthau intensified his efforts during the remainder of 1938 and 1939 to discredit the idea and reverse the policy. He consistently opposed those urging additional expenditures, and he made it clear to his staff economists that what he wanted from them was a critical refutation of Eccles's theories and policy recommendations. He firmly rejected suggestions that he meet with Ruml or even read his work. "It's not worth it," he told Aubrey Williams; and to Harry White he remarked curtly, "I don't want to get in on the theoretical side. I don't want my thinking clouded."[49]

Despite the Treasury's extended exercise in economic criticism, Roosevelt remained unconvinced. He told Morgenthau plainly, in January 1939, that he "felt the recession in 1937 was largely due to the decline in deficit spending and that he was going to hold to that belief until someone convinced him otherwise."[50] Morgenthau seemed to have forgotten that Roosevelt was always unreceptive to advice which told him what not to do. But perhaps he was reminded of this, for five days later he asked Roosevelt "how he could be of the most help to the President during the next two years." "The President replied that there were two major problems confronting the country— (1) reduction of unemployment, and (2) more equitable distribution of income." He asked Morgenthau to turn his attention to these. After carefully thinking it over for a day, Morgenthau decided that he would quietly gather together a small group of experts to develop plans to reduce unemployment.[51]

These were gloomy times for economic forecasters. Government experts serving on the Fiscal and Monetary Advisory Board, which Roosevelt had authorized "for a season," calculated that "an income of $90 billion or more is attainable through full utilization of our manpower, plant and equipment, technology and natural resources." If this is taken as a measure of full employment, then the shortfall of New Deal recovery was still marked. National income for 1938 was estimated at $62 billion and for 1939 between $65 and $68 billion. In a report by the Division of Monetary Research of the Treasury Department, circulated on May 25, 1939, there was "no expectation of sustaining an $80 billion income," which was termed a "modest" objective. The group concluded that "it is almost the unanimous opinion among Administration officials and technicians in Washington who are on, or are cooperating with the Fiscal and Monetary Board, that there is little if any prospect for marked recovery during the next two years."[52]

It was this dark future that kept Morgenthau running his race against the spenders. "Rather than have a spending program sneak up on me in the dark," he wrote in June, "I thought I'd get out a recovery program of my own to give the President." His program featured an orange and blue food ticket plan, based upon a pilot experiment in Rochester, New York, and a self-help cooperative plan to train and find work for the unemployed. It contained no provision for pump priming. A happy Morgenthau reported to his staff that the president "liked it enormously." "He kept saying," Morgenthau explained, " 'Where is the white rabbit and where is the cabbage to feed the white rabbit!' He said, 'This is a good come-on!' " [53] Such was the affection of Roosevelt for his good and loyal friend Henry Morgenthau.

The long-sought *full* recovery from the Great Depression was not to come to America as a result of this or any other plan. In this regard, John Maynard Keynes proved himself as great a prophet as he was an economist. Writing in 1932, he observed:

> In the past, we have not infrequently had to wait for a war to terminate a major depression. I hope that in the future we shall not adhere to this purist financial attitude, and that we shall be ready to spend on the enterprises of peace what the financial maxims of the past would only allow us to spend on the devastations of war. [54]

During the "Depression Decade" of the 1930s, a powerful group of Americans was transfixed by the elusive search for that orthodox entity "business confidence." No organized constituency existed to provide the political push that was essential if the new idea of compensatory government spending was to displace the older established ones. Proponents of deficit spending, like the supporters of tenant farmers, suffered the disadvantage of being politically frail.

TWELVE

The Political Achievements of FDR

THE 1930S WERE YEARS of recurrent crisis, a decade of world-wide depression epitomized by economic confusion and political experimentation. Like the Great War of 1914–18, and its even greater successor of 1939–45, the Great Depression was a major event in world history. Its withering impact on the world economy was felt everywhere, yet it failed to provoke a corresponding world response, if that means a sustained, concerted international effort to reconstruct a functional world economy. The attempts governments made to this purpose were disjointed and feeble, seriously distracted by a rival vision of seeming simplicity: the lure of economic nationalism. Thus while the Great Depression was economically a complex, intertwined world occurrence, its political expression was that of a host of uncoordinated national preoccupations. Economic nationalism, the drive to achieve an internal national economic recovery independent of other nations, was not far removed from autarky, the ambition to create national economic self-sufficiency. Practitioners of both these inward movements erected the economic barriers that set nations apart, establishing a political climate with a corrosive effect on international amity and accord.

Within the United States, these currents of self-centered preoccupation were manifest in the resurgence of political isolationism in the 1920s, a sentiment which became "rampant" by the 1930s. Among the more notable expressions of isolationism were the American rejection of membership in the League of Nations, which Franklin D. Roosevelt, an erstwhile advocate of American entry, was disinclined to pursue as president; and the legislative adoption of the Neutrality Act of 1935, a voluntary abandonment of the traditional rights of neutral nations, which was led and then perpetuated, however reluctantly, by President Roosevelt, until the onset of World War II in 1939.[1]

The ascendant nature of isolationist thought in American foreign policy had its counterpart in the domestic policies of President Roosevelt, particularly during the early years of the New Deal. This aspect of isolationism has not received the equal recognition it deserves as the other face of America's withdrawal from involvement with Europe. Americans were unwilling to suffer the anticipated consequences of the political rivalry and hostility of the European nations; they were also casting aside the limitations upon their freedom of action which some perceived as an unavoidable corollary to adhering to economic internationalism. Taken together, these complementary components of isolationist thought provide a measure of its formidable influence on policymaking during the New Deal.

In retrospect, Roosevelt's behavior during the London Economic Conference was the opening act in his acceptance of economic nationalism as an expedient means to a quick economic recovery at home. Viewed from this perspective, much of Roosevelt's leadership and the direction taken by major New Deal recovery policies become parts of a comprehensible pattern. The advocates of orthodox internationalism among Roosevelt's close advisers were routed; and with their eclipse, the emphasis upon an internationally coordinated recovery program and its preoccupation with such traditional matters as balanced national budgets, the gold standard, and the unobstructed flow of world trade were temporarily disregarded in Washington.

The displacement of the internationalists brought their adversaries, the spokesmen of economic nationalism, close to the ear of power. Roosevelt, no longer hedged about by the naysayers, was now freed to experiment with unorthodox monetary policies. The new options dramatically shifted Roosevelt's attention and efforts from abroad to home, where the economic nationalists insisted they properly belonged. The acknowledged priorities were now domestic matters: devaluation of the dollar, adjustment of the price and debt levels, an induced rise in agricultural commodity prices, and a stabilized commodity dollar of unchanging value. Economic recovery, in short, was to be managed first at home, where the field of action was unencumbered by the tedious delays of international negotiation, compromise, and constraint. Once American recovery was achieved, there would be time enough to rejoin the larger world abroad.

Roosevelt's adoption of economic nationalism implied little, if any, ideological commitment on his part to that doctrine. Its purpose was to be found in the pragmatic opportunities it afforded him. These included not only undistracted attention to home affairs; he gained also a greater freedom to choose from an eclectic storehouse of tools whatever seemed of use for attacking the puzzle of economic recovery. Roosevelt's dexterous use of these options, which took the outward form of economic policies, perplexed at first and then gradually outraged conventionally minded men, among them bankers, businessmen, and public officials whose perceptions were shaped by their allegiance to orthodox internationalism, as well as economists, academics, and others who sought to understand economic policies in terms of their economic rationale. A major purpose of this study has been to demonstrate that such an enterprise is both fruitless and misleading. There was neither unity nor meaning to Roosevelt's economic eclecticism in his improvisation of the New Deal, if these policies are analyzed and judged from an economic standpoint. His objectives, from first to last, were political, and Roosevelt's performance in pursuit of his political purposes was nothing less than masterful.

It is also essential at this point to recall the state of the nation when Roosevelt assumed power in March 1933. It takes no acute imagination to understand that the economic crisis that the nation had endured for nearly three years might well transform itself into a severe political crisis of similar magnitude. When Roosevelt in his inaugural address warned against fear-ing fear itself, why did he go on to call this a "nameless terror"? If he meant to suggest that the nation stood on the edge of a political abyss, he surely did not exaggerate a conceivable possibility. Among all nations, the Great Depression had its most severe impact upon the economy of the United States; and while neither Roosevelt nor those who listened to his call for action could know it, the depression was to persist here longer than in any other country.[2] The question of why the United States did not emulate one of the totalitarian models prominent during the 1930s, or devise its own, is conjecture, since Americans got the New Deal instead. And whatever else might be said about Roosevelt's New Deal, it was neither an "American revolution" nor an "American dictatorship."

Under the acceptable symbol of an economic recovery program, Roosevelt concocted a splendid melange of public gifts which were then distributed to those groups with the political leadership and the organized constituencies capable of making effective demands upon the government. The first beneficiaries of the New Deal's cornucopia included bankers of all sorts, commercial farmers of staple crops, large businessmen, home owners, states, and cities. Others who benefited less from this first outpouring, such as industrial workers and the unemployed, or gained nothing, like the overlooked elderly and the tenant farmers, sharecroppers, and migrants, were later added to the public list of recipients in what is generally termed the Second New Deal of 1935 and thereafter. What is evident in this roll call of those who received public assistance is that it proceeded by a rough order of political preference. It exposes, therefore, Roosevelt's priorities as well as his perception of relative political visibility.

The unprecedented scale of this public largesse provided Roosevelt with potent levers of influence and control. In this respect, Roosevelt and the executive office ranked first among beneficiaries. Roosevelt possessed not only the power to give, but the power to withhold. He used the latter to deny or to blunt, as circumstances permitted, what he regarded as unacceptable demands. Thus the nationalists' hoped-for inflation became "reflation" or "controlled inflation," the mandated thirty-hour work week and the huge public works program that had been demanded were considerably moderated, requests for fixed farm prices and a guaranteed cost of production plus a profit were neutralized by the promise of parity, the ideal of centralized government planning shrank to a regional experiment in the Tennessee Valley. The listing might go on, but the inevitable question remains: what does it all signify?

If one adopts, for the moment's purpose, Lord Acton's dictum that the proper function of the historian is that of "a hanging judge," then an inescapable obligation here is to ask: what is the verdict to be rendered on Roosevelt's leadership and the New Deal recovery policies?[3] The economic part of that verdict is unambiguous, and it was foretold by John Maynard Keynes when he urged in vain a public compensatory spending program commensurate in size and duration with that only willingly given in the past to wage great wars.[4] Unhappily, it was not in fact until World War II, or more precisely 1941, that the American economy approximated full recovery.[5] Nazi Germany and Imperial Japan provided Americans with a more potent impetus to a unified national undertaking of mammoth proportions than the experience of the Great Depression.

Nonetheless, the Great Depression was a sufficient common enemy for Roosevelt's domestic political purposes. These were to devise a recovery and reform movement of unprecedented scope which functioned like a huge reservoir absorbing the nation's energies. The consequences of Roosevelt's leadership were a dramatic growth in the size, power, and reach of the federal government and the executive office, a decided tilt toward the government in its competitive relationship with business as the chief custodian of the national economy, a successful defense of the nation's traditional political and economic systems, with their attendant institutions and inequalities, and the retention of a level of stability and order that was uncharacteristic of an uncertain, tumultuous time.

This was accomplished essentially through the exercise of a politics of conflict and not by consensus, despite the talk of a "grand coalition" of interests.[6] Conflict was not transcended by the New Deal at any time; it was internalized, by being brought into the bowels of the government itself. In a nation of continental sweep and geographic diversity, with a heterogeneous people, a complex industrial system, competitive groups, and a normal complement of classes, surely conflict is the normal order of affairs. And if, as John Higham has asserted, conflict is the essential midwife of progress, then the healthy perpetuation of conflict during the New Deal should be recorded in the historical register to Roosevelt's credit.[7]

But then what about progress? What is the reckoning on this central issue that is so vital to any reform movement? Progress clearly is a big subject, so a few preliminary comments seem in order. Progress implies change, and change affects people in differing ways, some gaining, others losing. Progress must therefore be specified as progress in what and for whom. The New Deal transformed the nation's political terrain, most notably by the vast augmentation of federal authority and power; it also collaborated in fostering the emerging power of organized farmers and organized workers, thereby diminishing the solitary eminence which the business community had previously enjoyed as a power wielder. And in the process of accepting and dealing with pressure group politics, the Roosevelt administration provided a remarkably ready access to the federal government to all who possessed the will and organization to seek assistance. This brought Washington close to the people and it familiarized the national government to its citizens as the last resort of appeal whenever all else failed.

These political changes obviously involved negative as well as positive consequences. Government aid is not disinterested; it comes with strings attached. The personal autonomy of all who succeed in gaining government favors is diminished by varying degrees. A patron-client relationship is created, with all its connotations of dependent status. Whether a corresponding dependence upon state and local government, in place of that which devolved upon the federal government, differs in degree or kind seems highly improbable in actuality if not in theory. The trend in American political history, particularly notable in the twentieth century, has been for greater numbers of people and their institutions to become beholden to government as a result of factors operating during crises in a modern industrial society. If that is indeed the case, Roosevelt's New Deal was perhaps as much willing victim as villain in this inevitable but troublesome outcome.

How then does political leadership reconcile the tension in values that exists between maintaining national unity and preserving traditional personal liberties? In his classic study on this theme, Herbert Agar provided one answer to the uses and limits of power:

> . . . by diplomacy and compromise, never by force, the government must water down the selfish demands of regions, races, classes, business associations, into a national policy which will alienate no major group and which will contain at least a small plum for everybody. This is the price of unity in a continent-wide federation. Decisions will therefore be slow, methods will be cumbersome, political parties will be illogical and inconsistent; but the people remain free, reasonably united, and as lightly burdened by the state as is consistent with safety.[8]

This is a hard wisdom to accept, especially for a generation nurtured by the extravagant expectations of our immediate past.[9] Yet if Roosevelt's use of economic policies for political ends was more than masterful, if it is to be judged socially wise as well, then clearly the anticipation of progress needs considerable scaling down. We live with the consequences of Roosevelt's achievements, however short these may fall of one or another's dream of the perfect society. Who, in the long days of the Great Depression, might have achieved more? No one comes readily to mind.

Notes

Abbreviations of frequently cited sources:

C&FC   *The Commercial & Financial Chronicle*
CU   Columbia University, Butler Library, New York City
FDR   Franklin D. Roosevelt
FDRL   Franklin D. Roosevelt Library, Hyde Park, New York
GLH   George L. Harrison
HF   Herbert Feis
HM   Henry Morgenthau, Jr.
JHJ   Jesse H. Jones
LC   Library of Congress, Washington, D. C.
OF   Official File
PPF   President's Personal File

I. THE POLITICAL FACE OF FDR

1. Harold F. Gosnell, *Champion Campaigner: Franklin D. Roosevelt* (New York: Macmillan, 1952); James M. Burns, *Roosevelt: The Lion and the Fox* (New York: Harcourt, Brace, 1956), ix; Jesse H. Jones with Edward Angly, *Fifty Billion Dollars* (New York: Macmillan, 1951), p. 260.
2. Frances Perkins, *The Roosevelt I Knew* (New York: Viking Press, 1946), p. 330.
3. Arthur M. Schlesinger, Jr., *The Coming of the New Deal* (Boston:

Houghton Mifflin, 1959), p. 14; Perkins, *The Roosevelt I Knew,* p. 3; Robert E. Sherwood, *Roosevelt and Hopkins* (New York: Bantam Books, 1950) 1: 10–12; Raymond Moley, *After Seven Years* (New York: Harper & Brothers, 1939), pp. 10–12; Edgar E. Robinson, *The Roosevelt Leadership* (Philadelphia: J. B. Lippincott, 1955).

4. Walter Lippmann, "The Candidacy of Franklin D. Roosevelt," *New York Herald Tribune,* January 8, 1932, p. 9.

5. Schlesinger, *Coming of the New Deal,* pp. 18–19.

6. Basil Rauch, *The History of the New Deal* (New York: Creative Age Press, 1944), first made the distinction between the First and the Second New Deal, a conception implicit, however, in Raymond Moley's 1939 *After Seven Years.* This categorization was widely adopted and elaborated upon subsequently by Roosevelt specialists until James M. Burns, in *Roosevelt: The Lion and the Fox,* and William E. Leuchtenburg, in *Franklin D. Roosevelt and the New Deal* (New York: Harper & Row, 1963), took issue with this interpretation, writing instead of the First and Second Hundred Days. The idea of distinct First and Second New Deals is notable for its absence in most monographic studies.

7. Among the most useful are Moley, *After Seven Years;* Rexford G. Tugwell, *The Democratic Roosevelt* (Garden City, N.Y.: Doubleday, 1957); Eleanor Roosevelt, *This I Remember* (New York: Harper & Brothers, 1949); Perkins, *The Roosevelt I Knew;* and James P. Warburg, *The Long Road Home* (New York: Doubleday, 1964).

8. Frank Freidel, *Franklin D. Roosevelt,* vol. 4, *Launching the New Deal* (Boston: Little, Brown, 1973), pp. 47–58; Jordan A. Schwarz, *The Interregnum of Despair* (Urbana: University of Illinois Press, 1970), pp. 205–29.

9. See Chapter Seven for Roosevelt's concern about the prospect of social disorder among "marching farmers"; see also Chapter Eleven for his speculations regarding the potential consequences of political discontent among the business elite. For examples of contemporary comment on dictatorial powers granted to FDR, see the *Journal of Commerce,* March 10, 1933, pp. 1, 4; *New York Herald Tribune,* March 10, 1933, p. 2; *New York Times,* March 21, 1933, pp. 1–2; March 22, 1933, p. 2; and columns by Arthur Krock in the *New York Times* for March 12, 1933, sec. 4, p. 1; March 16, 1933, p. 2; June 17, 1934, sec. 4, p. 1.

10. See Chapter IX.

11. Irving Bernstein, *The Lean Years* (Boston: Houghton Mifflin, 1972), pp. 83–90; Milton Derber, "Growth and Expansion," in Milton

Derber and Edwin Young, eds., *Labor and the New Deal* (Madison: University of Wisconsin Press, 1961), pp. 3–8.

12. James Farley, *Behind the Ballots* (New York: Harcourt, Brace, 1938), pp. 249–52.

13. See Paul K. Conkin, *The New Deal* (New York: Crowell, 1967); Barton J. Bernstein, "The New Deal: The Conservative Achievements of Liberal Reform," in Barton J. Bernstein, ed., *Towards a New Past* (New York: Pantheon Books, 1968), pp. 263–78; Howard Zinn, ed., Introduction, *New Deal Thought* (Indianapolis: Bobbs-Merrill, 1966).

14. Harold D. Lasswell, *Politics* (New York: McGraw-Hill, 1936).

15. Frances Piven and Richard Cloward, *Regulating the Poor* (New York: Vintage, 1972).

16. See David E. Lilienthal, *TVA: Democracy on the March* (New York: Harper & Brothers, 1944), pp. 75ff.

II. ANTICIPATIONS OF THE NEW DEAL

1. Statement of E. T. Weir of National Steel Corporation, *New York Times,* February 27, 1933, excerpted in *C&FC,* March 4, 1933, pp. 1477–78; "The Guaranty Survey," February 27, 1933, excerpted in *C&FC,* March 4, 1933, pp. 1443–44; testimony of Winthrop W. Aldrich, chairman, Chase National Bank, February 22, 1933, before the Senate Finance Committee, reprinted in *C&FC,* March 4, 1933, p. 1435.

2. Samuel I. Rosenman, *Working with Roosevelt* (New York: Harper & Brothers, 1952), pp. 29–30.

3. Rosenman, *Working with Roosevelt,* pp. 31–32; Raymond Moley, *After Seven Years* (New York: Harper & Brothers, 1939), pp. 62–63; see also Elliot A. Rosen, *Hoover, Roosevelt, and the Brains Trust* (New York: Columbia University Press, 1977) for an extended statement and defense of this thesis. For a balanced treatment of Roosevelt's ideas and speeches and their relation to subsequent legislation during the New Deal, see Frank Freidel, *Franklin D. Roosevelt,* vol. 3, *The Triumph* (Boston: Little, Brown, 1956), pp. 368–69.

4. Frank R. Kent, "No Hero in Sight," *Scribner's* 91 (June 1932): 321–22; "Democratic Light Horses," *New Republic,* February 17, 1932, p. 6; Clinton W. Gilbert, "The Roosevelt Convention," *Collier's,* June 4, 1932, p. 24; Oswald G. Villard, "An Open Letter to Governor Roosevelt," *The Nation,* May 11, 1932, p. 532; "Another Hoover," *Outlook,* February 3, 1932, p. 127; *New York Times,* April

20, 1932, p. 22; "Franklin D. Roosevelt's Strength and Weakness," *Literary Digest*, July 9, 1932, pp. 2–3; William Allen White, *New York Times*, May 1, 1932, p. 6.

5. Ogden Mills to Owen Young, December 16, 1932, in CU, GLH MSS., box 12.

6. Moley, *After Seven Years*, pp. 119–21.

7. *C&FC*, April 15, 1933, p. 2540; May 13, 1933, p. 3256.

8. Ibid., May 20, 1933, p. 3445.

9. Ibid., May 13, 1933, pp. 3255–56.

10. *New York Times*, April 29, 1933, p. 4.

11. *C&FC*, May 6, 1933, p. 3084.

12. Benjamin Anderson, speech, June 8, 1933, reprinted in *C&FC*, June 17, 1933, p. 3084.

13. Ibid.

14. Fred I. Kent, speech before The American Institute of Banking, reprinted in *C&FC*, July 8, 1933, pp. 241–42.

15. *C&FC*, August 19, 1933, p. 1341.

16. *C&FC*, June 6, 1933, p. 4354.

17. *C&FC*, July 1, 1933, pp. 25–26.

III. THE POLITICS OF MANEUVER

1. Arthur M. Schlesinger, Jr., *The Coming of the New Deal* (Boston: Houghton Mifflin, 1959), pp. 20–21.

2. Raymond Moley with Elliot A. Rosen, *The First New Deal* (New York: Harcourt, Brace & World, 1966), pp. 215–17; Frank Freidel, *Franklin D. Roosevelt*, vol. 4, *Launching the New Deal* (Boston: Little Brown, 1973), p. 216.

3. John A. Simpson to FDR, May 6, 1933, FDRL, FDR MSS., PPF 471.

4. FDR to John A. Simpson, May 20, 1933, FDRL, FDR MSS., PPF 471.

5. Henry Wallace to FDR, May 16, 1933, FDRL, FDR MSS., PPF 471.

6. Schlesinger, *Coming of the New Deal*, pp. 7–8.

7. Raymond Moley, *After Seven Years* (New York: Harper & Brothers, 1939), pp. 44–45.

8. James M. Burns, *Roosevelt: The Lion and the Fox* (New York: Harcourt, Brace, 1956), p. 144.

9. Elmer Thomas to Louis Howe, December 31, 1932, FDRL, FDR MSS., PPF 6148.

10. Ibid.
11. John A. Simpson to FDR, April 3, 1933, FDRL, FDR MSS., OF 229, box 1.
12. John A. Simpson to FDR, June 5, 1933, FDRL, FDR MSS., PPF 471.
13. *New York Times,* March 23, 1933, p. 3.
14. Ibid.
15. Ibid., April 18, 1933, p. 1.
16. *Journal of Commerce,* April 18, 1933, p. 3.
17. Ibid., April 19, 1933, p. 3.
18. *New York Times,* April 18, 1933, p. 1.
19. Ibid., April 20, 1933, p. 3.
20. Ibid., April 15, 1933, p. 2.
21. Ibid., April 16, 1933, p. 2.
22. *Journal of Commerce,* April 19, 1933, p. 3.
23. Copy of resolution in Edward Pou to FDR, March 16, 1933, FDRL, FDR MSS., OF 229, box 1.
24. Ibid.
25. *New York Times,* April 16, 1933, p. 2.
26. Ibid.
27. Ibid.
28. Ibid., April 15, 1933, p. 2.
29. *Journal of Commerce,* April 18, 1933, p. 3.
30. *New York Times,* April 18, 1933, p. 1.
31. T. W. Lamont to FDR, April 19, 1933, with copy of Morgan statement, FDRL, FDR MSS., OF 229, box 1.
32. *New York Times,* April 20, 1933, p. 2.
33. Melvin Traylor to FDR, April 20, 1933, FDRL, FDR MSS., OF 229, box 1.
34. *New York Times,* April 20, 1933, p. 2.
35. *Journal of Commerce,* April 20, 1933, pp. 1, 3, 4.
36. Moley, *After Seven Years,* pp. 158–61; Herbert Feis, *1933: Characters in Crisis* (Boston: Little, Brown, 1966), pp. 127–28.
37. *New York Times,* April 20, 1933.
38. Ibid., April 21, 1933, p. 2.
39. Ibid., April 25, 1933, p. 2.
40. *Journal of Commerce,* April 20, 1933, p. 3.
41. *New York Times,* April 22, 1933, p. 2.
42. Ibid., April 26, 1933, p. 3.
43. Ibid., April 28, 1933, p. 3.
44. Reprinted in full ibid., April 22, 1933, pp. 2–3.
45. Ibid., April 23, 1933, p. 1.

IV. RELIEF AS RECOVERY

1. See U.S., Congress, House, Committee on Banking and Currency, *Hearings on H.R. 4606, Unemployment Relief,* 73rd Cong., 1st sess., 1933.
2. Robert E. Sherwood, *Roosevelt and Hopkins* (New York: Bantam Books, 1950) 1:67, 73–74.
3. Broadus Mitchell, *Depression Decade* (New York: Holt, Rinehart and Winston, 1947), p. 89.
4. Alvin H. Hansen, *Fiscal Policy and Business Cycles* (New York: W. W. Norton, 1941), pp. 81–85.
5. Jones, speech, New York Southern Society, December 3, 1937, in LC, JHJ MSS., box 220.
6. Bascom N. Timmons, *Jesse H. Jones* (New York: Harry Holt, 1956), p. 259.
7. Jesse H. Jones with Edward Angly, *Fifty Billion Dollars* (New York: Macmillan, 1951), p. 3.
8. Jones, speech, American Society of Newspaper Editors, April 28, 1933, in LC, JHJ MSS., box 212.
9. FDR to Jesse Jones, August 31, 1933, in LC, JHJ MSS., box 29.
10. Jones, speech, NBC, August 1, 1933, in LC, JHJ MSS., box 213.
11. Jones to John N. Garner, November 6, 1934, in LC, JHJ MSS., box 10; Jones to FDR, August 2, 1935, in LC, JHJ MSS., box 198.
12. Jones, *Fifty Billion,* p. 35.
13. Jones, speech, West Virginia Bankers Association, June 8, 1934, in LC, JHJ MSS., box 214.
14. Jones, speech, March 27, 1940, in LC, JHJ MSS., box 223.
15. Jones to John N. Garner, November 6, 1934, in LC, JHJ MSS., box 10.
16. Jones, speech, National Association of Supervisors of State Banks, October 8, 1937, in LC, JHJ MSS., box 219.
17. Jones, speech, ABA, November 15, 1938, in LC, JHJ MSS., box 222.
18. Jones, *Fifty Billion,* pp. 30–46.
19. *New York Herald Tribune,* March 3, 1933, p. 2; *Journal of Commerce,* March 16, 1933, p. 4; *C&FC,* May 20, 1933, p. 3457.
20. Jones, speech, West Virginia Bankers Association, June 8, 1934, in LC, JHJ MSS., box 214.
21. *C&FC,* May 27, 1933, p. 3635; June 17, 1933, p. 4133.
22. Timmons, *Jones,* pp. 177–78; Jones, *Fifty Billion,* pp. 45–46.
23. Jones, *Fifty Billion,* pp. 27–30; Timmons, *Jones,* p. 190.

24. Jones, *Fifty Billion*, pp. 6, 32, 40.
25. Quoted in *C&FC*, September 9, 1933, p. 1879.
26. Quoted ibid., October 27, 1934, pp. 2603–4.
27. Jones, speech, N.Y. State Bankers Association, February 5, 1934, in LC, JHJ MSS., box 214.
28. Ibid.
29. Jones, speech, Reserve City Bankers Meeting, October 14, 1938, in LC, JHJ MSS., box 221.
30. Ibid.
31. Jones, speech, ABA, October 24, 1934, in LC, JHJ MSS., box 215.
32. Ibid.
33. Jones, *Fifty Billion*, p. 146.
34. Jones, speech, December 12, 1934, in LC, JHJ MSS., box 215.
35. Jones, *Fifty Billion*, pp. 147–49.
36. Marriner S. Eccles to Jones, September 29, 1939, in LC, JHJ MSS., box 198; *C&FC*, June 6, 1934, p. 4225; June 30, 1934, pp. 4385–86; August 8, 1934, pp. 1015–17.
37. Jones, *Fifty Billion*, pp. 4, 6–7, 106, 199, 201, 206.
38. Jones, speech, North Carolina State Bankers Association, May 10, 1935, in LC, JHJ MSS., box 216.
39. William E. Leuchtenburg, *Franklin D. Roosevelt and the New Deal* (New York: Harper & Row, 1963), p. 53.
40. Sherwood, *Roosevelt and Hopkins*, I, 64–69.
41. Leuchtenburg, *Roosevelt and the New Deal*, pp. 124–30.
42. Sherwood, *Roosevelt and Hopkins*, 1: 85.

V. ECONOMIC NATIONALISM

1. FDR to Colonel Edward M. House, April 5, 1933, FDRL, FDR MSS., PPF 222.
2. FDR to John Simpson, April 6, 1933, FDRL, FDR MSS., OF 229, box 1.
3. *C&FC*, April 1, 1933, p. 2124.
4. Ibid., p. 2126.
5. Excerpted ibid., April 8, 1933, p. 2309.
6. *Journal of Commerce*, April 21, 1933, p. 4.
7. FDR to Colonel Edward M. House, November 21, 1933, FDRL, FDR MSS., PPF 222.
8. "Business Bulletin," September 15, 1933, reprinted in *C&FC*, September 16, 1933, pp. 1966–67.
9. Text printed in *C&FC*, April 15, 1933, p. 2538.

10. Ibid.
11. Symposium on "The State of the Nation," excerpted in *C&FC*, April 22, 1933, pp. 2725–26.
12. Frank Freidel, *Franklin D. Roosevelt*, vol. 4, *Launching the New Deal* (Boston: Little, Brown, 1973), p. 461.
13. Raymond Moley, *After Seven Years* (New York: Harper & Brothers, 1939), pp. 207–9.
14. Freidel, *Launching the New Deal*, p. 466.
15. Printed in full in *C&FC*, May 13, 1933, pp. 3268–69.
16. Ibid.
17. James Harvey Rogers to Raymond Moley, April 23, 1933, in LC, HF MSS., box 25.
18. James Warburg, memorandum, April 3, 1933, 10 pp., FDRL, FDR MSS., OF 17.
19. Ibid.
20. *C&FC*, May 20, 1933, p. 3396.
21. Ibid., July 15, 1933, p. 366.
22. Text printed in *C&FC*, June 17, 1933, pp. 4173–74.
23. Alvin Hansen, *America's Role in the World Economy* (New York: W. W. Norton, 1945), p. 137.
24. George Harrison to Governor Eugene Black, July 8, 1933, in CU, GLH MSS., box 12.
25. Will Woodin, June 16, 1933, in FDRL, FDR MSS., OF 17.
26. FDR telegram to Cordell Hull, June 17, 1933, in CU, GLH MSS., box 7.
27. Sprague et al. to FDR, June 18, 1933, ibid.
28. Text printed in *C&FC*, June 24, 1933, p. 4315.
29. FDR to Cordell Hull, June 28, 1933, in CU, GLH MSS., box 7.
30. Raymond Moley to FDR, June 30, 1933, ibid.
31. FDR to Cordell Hull, July 1, 1933, ibid.
32. Ibid.
33. Text printed in *C&FC*, July 8, 1933, p. 222.
34. Ibid.

VI. THE BATTLE OF THE MONETARISTS

1. James P. Warburg, *The Money Muddle* (New York: Knopf, 1934), p. 133.
2. James P. Warburg, *The Long Road Home* (New York: Doubleday, 1964), pp. 142–43.

3. Warburg, memorandum, August 2, 1933, 6 pp., FDRL, FDR MSS., OF 229, box 2A.

4. Ibid.

5. J. H. Williams, memorandum to George Harrison, August 3, 1933, in CU, GLH MSS., box 3.

6. Ibid.

7. Will Woodin to FDR, August 29, 1933, with "Interim Report on Monetary Policy," 14 pp., FDRL, FDR MSS., OF 229, box 2A.

8. Ibid.

9. FDR to Nicholas M. Butler, August 14, 1933, in FDRL, FDR MSS., PPF 445.

10. FDR to J. David Stern, August 22, 1933, in FDRL, FDR MSS., OF 229, box 2A.

11. James Warburg to FDR, September 20, 1933, 3 pp., in FDRL, FDR MSS., OF 229.

12. Warburg, *Long Road Home*, p. 147.

13. Will Woodin to FDR, September 28, 1933, in FDRL, FDR MSS., PPF 258.

14. FDR to Will Woodin, September 30, 1933, in FDRL, FDR MSS., PPF 258.

15. James Warburg to Dean Acheson, October 12, 1933, 5 pp., in CU, GLH MSS., box 3.

16. Ibid.

17. Dean Acheson to FDR, October 21, 1933, with memorandum, "How to Raise Prices," 13 pp., in FDRL, FDR MSS., OF 229, box 3.

18. Ibid.

19. Warburg, *Money Muddle*, p. 133.

20. *C&FC*, August 19, 1933, pp. 1308–9.

21. Ibid., January 6, 1934, p. 25.

22. Ibid., November 4, 1933, p. 3204.

23. John Bankhead to FDR, July 20, 1933, in FDRL, FDR MSS., PPF 1362.

24. Ibid., August 21, 1933, in FDRL, FDR MSS., OF 258.

25. Ibid., October 20, 1933, in FDRL, FDR MSS., OF 229.

26. Hugo Black to FDR, September 14, 1933, in FDRL, FDR MSS., OF 229.

27. Elmer Thomas to FDR, August 12, 1933, in FDRL, FDR MSS., OF 230.

28. Printed in *C&FC*, August 26, 1933, pp. 1500–1501.

29. Ibid.

30. John D. Clarke to FDR, September 18, 1933, in FDRL, FDR MSS., OF 229, box 3.
31. John Rankin to Morris Sheppard, September 13, 1933; Sheppard to FDR, September 15, 1933, in FDRL, FDR MSS., OF 229.
32. FDR to Morgan G. Sanders, September 14, 1933, in FDRL, FDR MSS., OF 229.
33. FDR to Joseph Byrns, September 18, 1933, in FDRL, FDR MSS., PPF 835.
34. John McSwain to FDR, September 11, 1933, in FDRL, FDR MSS., PPF 3351.
35. Edward O'Neal et al. to FDR, September 25, 1933, in FDRL, FDR MSS., OF 227-XYZ.
36. Ibid.
37. C. Rogers to FDR, September 6, 1933, in FDRL, FDR MSS.
38. John Simpson to FDR, October 24, 1933, in FDRL, FDR MSS., PPF 471.
39. *New York Herald Tribune,* March 6, 1933, p. 6.
40. *C&FC,* April 4, 1933, pp. 2525–26.
41. Copy of committee's letter to its National Advisory and Auxiliary Committees sent to FDR, May 17, 1933, in FDRL, FDR MSS., OF 229, box 2.
42. Ibid.
43. Committee for the Nation to FDR, October 21, 1933, in FDRL, FDR MSS., OF 229, box 3.

VII. THE POLITICIZATION OF GOLD

1. Text of speech printed in *C&FC,* October 28, 1933, pp. 3033–34.
2. George F. Warren and Frank A. Pearson, *Prices* (New York: John Wiley, 1933), p. 123.
3. George F. Warren, "Causes of the Depression and Remedies for It," paper read before the National Industrial Conference Board, January 26, 1933, New York City, pp. 1–5; Warren and Pearson, *Prices,* pp. 123–25.
4. Warren, "Causes of the Depression," pp. 5–6; Warren and Pearson, *Prices,* p. 69.
5. Warren, "Causes of the Depression," pp. 2–3.
6. Interview with George Warren, October 23, 1933, in "The Country Home," reprinted in *New York Times,* October 24, 1933.
7. Ibid.
8. Warren, "Causes of the Depression," pp. 6, 10.

9. Ibid., p. 9.

10. Warren, interview, *New York Times,* October 24, 1933.

11. Warren, "Causes of the Depression," p. 6.

12. Warren, interview, *New York Times,* October 24, 1933. ·

13. Warren and Pearson, *Prices,* p. 163; see also Warren's address on gold and prices at the Academy of Political Science, printed in *New York Times,* March 22, 1934, p. 16.

14. Warren and Pearson, *Prices,* p. 164.

15. George Warren to FDR, October 16, 1933, in FDRL, FDR MSS.

16. Arthur M. Schlesinger, Jr., *The Coming of the New Deal* (Boston: Houghton Mifflin, 1959), p. 241.

17. *C&FC,* November 4, 1933, pp. 3183–84.

18. J. E. Crane, memorandum, "Roosevelt and Revolution," 6 pp., October 30, 1933, in CU, GLH MSS., binder 46.

19. J. E. Crane, report on the November 12, 1933 meeting, November 13, 1933, in CU, GLH MSS., binder 46.

20. Ibid.

21. Walter Lippmann, "Danger Signal," *New York Herald Tribune,* October 31, 1933.

22. Ibid.

23. *C&FC,* October 28, 1933, p. 3056; December 30, 1933, p. 4625.

24. Anderson, "The Practical Impossibility of a Commodity Dollar," reprinted in *C&FC,* December 16, 1933, pp. 4289–91; National City Bank of New York, "Monthly Letter," November 2, 1933, in *C&FC,* November 4, 1933, pp. 3229–30; *C&FC,* December 23, 1933, p. 4460.

25. "Moody's Investors Service," October 30, 1933, in *C&FC,* November 4, 1933, p. 3231.

26. Recorded by J. E. Crane, November 2, 1933, in CU, GLH MSS., binder 46.

27. *C&FC,* November 11, 1933, p. 3402.

28. Ibid., pp. 3402–3.

29. Ibid., November 4, 1933, p. 3228; November 18, 1933, p. 3593; November 25, 1933, pp. 3778–79.

30. Ibid., November 25, 1933, pp. 3779–80.

31. Ibid., p. 3778.

32. Ibid., December 16, 1933, pp. 4286–87.

33. Ibid., p. 4288.

34. James P. Warburg, *The Money Muddle* (New York: Knopf, 1934); *It's Up to Us* (New York: Knopf, 1934).

35. Sprague's resignation letter is printed in *C&FC,* November 25, 1933, p. 3776.

36. FDR to Robert Bingham, November 13, 1933, in FDRL, FDR MSS., PPF 716.

37. FDR to James H. Rand, Jr., November 21, 1933; FDR to Key Pittman, November 27, 1933, both in FDRL, FDR MSS., OF 229, box 4.

38. FDR to Will Woodin, December 12, 1933, in FDRL, FDR MSS., PPF 258.

39. *C&FC*, November 25, 1933, p. 3772.

40. James Byrnes to Louis Howe, December 2, 1933, in FDRL, FDR MSS., OF 229; Howe's penciled comment was "Agree with this 100%," followed by "So do I. FDR."

41. Telephone conversation between FDR and George Harrison, November 21, 1933, summarized by Harrison, November 22, 1933, in CU, GLH MSS., binder 46.

42. Harrison's report of the December 2, 1933 meeting ibid.

43. Ibid.

44. George F. Warren and Frank A. Pearson, *Gold and Prices* (New York: John Wiley and Sons, 1935), p. 193.

VIII. ROOSEVELT PARLAYS THE SILVERITES

1. "Is Franklin Roosevelt the Bryan of 1932?", *Literary Digest,* June 4, 1932, p. 3.

2. Y. S. Leong, *Silver* (Washington: Brookings Institution, 1933), pp. 61, 68, 70–71, 83–84, 94.

3. Joseph Reeve, *Monetary Reform Movements* (Washington: American Council of Public Affairs, 1943), p. 246.

4. John A. Brennan, *Silver and the First New Deal* (Reno: University of Nevada Press, 1969), pp. 3–5.

5. Key Pittman to Henry Morgenthau, December 11, 1933, in FDRL, FDR MSS., OF 229, box 5.

6. *C&FC,* December 23, 1933, text of proclamation, p. 4441.

7. Reprinted Ibid., December 30, 1933, p. 4623.

8. Key Pittman to FDR, November 23, 1933, in FDRL, FDR MSS., OF 229, box 4.

9. Ibid.

10. *New York Times,* January 8, 1934, p. 2.

11. Ibid., February 11, 1934, p. 3.

12. *C&FC,* March 24, 1934, pp. 2001–2002.

13. *New York Times,* March 18, 1934, p. 3.

14. Ibid., March 20, 1934, p. 1.

15. Ibid., March 25, 1934, p. 12.

16. FDR to Joseph Robinson, January 25, 1934, in FDRL, FDR MSS., OF 229, box 5; summary of the president's conference with members of the House of Representatives, April 15, 1934, in FDRL, FDR MSS., OF 419.

17. *New York Times*, March 2, 1934, p. 1.

18. *C&FC*, April 21, 1934, p. 2678.

19. *New York Times*, April 22, 1934, p. 1.

20. Ibid., May 6, 1934, p. 1.

21. Ibid., May 7, 1934, p. 1; May 10, 1934.

22. Key Pittman to Louis Howe, February 28, 1934, in FDRL, FDR MSS., OF 229, box 5.

23. Key Pittman to Henry Morgenthau, February 16, 1934, in FDRL, FDR MSS., OF 229, box 5.

24. Key Pittman to FDR, April 25, 1934, with enclosure, "Memorandum of Senator Henrik Shipstead," April 23, 1934, in FDRL, FDR MSS., OF 229, box 6.

25. Ibid.

26. Key Pittman to Henry Morgenthau, May 17, 1934, ibid.

27. *New York Times*, June 1, 1934, p. 5.

28. Ibid., June 12, 1934, pp. 1, 4.

29. Ibid., June 1, 1934, p. 5.

30. Key Pittman to FDR, October 3, 1934, in FDRL, FDR MSS., OF 229, box 6; Key Pittman to FDR, April 10, 1935, ibid., OF 229, box 8; Key Pittman to FDR, April 23, 1935, ibid.; Elmer Thomas to FDR, January 18, 1935, with resolutions of the National Monetary Conference meeting, January 16, 1935, ibid.; Elmer Thomas to FDR, March 8, 1935, ibid.; Elmer Thomas to FDR, August 26, 1935, ibid., OF 229, box 9; Edward A. O'Neal to FDR, March 23, 1935, ibid., OF 229, box 8, with statement of the American Farm Bureau Federation on monetary matters; A. P. Lamneck to FDR, December 12, 1935, ibid., OF 229, box 9; see also Allen S. Everest, *Morgenthau, the New Deal and Silver* (New York: Columbia University Press, 1950), ch. 4, pp. 51–78.

31. *C&FC*, August 11, 1934, p. 858.

32. Ibid., p. 866.

IX. THE AGRICULTURAL DISPARITY AND GENERAL ECONOMIC RECOVERY

1. Edwin G. Nourse, Joseph S. Davis, and John D. Black, *Three Years of the Agricultural Adjustment Administration* (Washington: Brookings Institution, 1937), p. 21.

NOTES

2. Richard Hofstadter, *The Age of Reform* (New York: Vintage, 1955), pp. 23–36.
3. For a detailed account of the Farmers' Holiday Association, see John L. Shover, *Cornbelt Rebellion* (Urbana: University of Illinois, 1965).
4. Nourse et al., *Three Years*, p. 420.
5. The following statements by FDR, Wallace, Wilson, and Davis are quoted ibid., pp. 421–26.
6. Ibid., p. 478; Rainer Schickele, *Agricultural Policy* (Lincoln: University of Nebraska Press, 1954), p. 155.
7. Murray R. Benedict, *Farm Policies of the United States, 1790–1950* (New York: Twentieth Century Fund, 1953), p. 281.
8. Barton J. Bernstein, "The New Deal: The Conservative Achievements of Liberal Reform," in Bernstein, ed., *Towards A New Past* (New York: Pantheon Books, 1968), pp. 267–68.
9. Benedict, *Farm Policies*, pp. 280–82.
10. Edward C. Eicher to FDR, April 1, 1933, in FDRL, FDR MSS., OF 327.
11. Nourse et al., *Three Years*, p. 4.
12. Albert U. Romasco, *The Poverty of Abundance* (New York: Oxford University Press, 1965), pp. 121–22.
13. *New York Times*, March 13, 1933, p. 11; March 21, 1933, pp. 1–2; March 22, 1933, p. 2; March 26, 1933, sec. 4, p. 1.
14. Quoted in Nourse et al., *Three Years*, p. 33.
15. Benedict, *Farm Policies*, pp. 283–84; Theodore Saloutos and John D. Hicks, *Agricultural Discontent in the Middle West, 1900–1939* (Madison: University of Wisconsin Press, 1951), p. 470.
16. Quoted in Nourse et al., *Three Years*, p. 18.
17. Saloutos and Hicks, *Agricultural Discontent*, p. 443.
18. Nourse et al., *Three Years*, pp. 84–85.
19. For the role of W. S. Spellman, John D. Black, Beardsley Ruml, H. C. Taylor, and M. L. Wilson in formulating domestic allotment, see William D. Rowley, *M. L. Wilson and the Campaign for Domestic Allotment* (Lincoln: University of Nebraska Press, 1970), pp. 36–59.
20. On the influential role of M. L. Wilson, see ibid.; on the American Farm Bureau Federation, see Christiana M. Campbell, *The Farm Bureau and the New Deal* (Urbana: University of Illinois Press, 1962).
21. Arthur M. Schlesinger, Jr., *The Coming of the New Deal* (Boston: Houghton Mifflin, 1959), pp. 27–84.

22. Gilbert C. Fite, *George N. Peek and the Fight for Farm Parity* (Norman: University of Oklahoma Press, 1954), pp. 35ff.

23. Schlesinger, *Coming of the New Deal*, pp. 43–58.

24. Nourse et al., *Three Years*, p. 349; David E. Conrad, *The Forgotten Farmers* (Urbana: University of Illinois Press, 1965), p. 36; Richard S. Kirkendall, *Social Scientists and Farm Policies in the Age of Roosevelt* (Columbia: University of Missouri Press, 1966), p. 101.

25. Schlesinger, *Coming of the New Deal*, pp. 74–80.

26. Schickele, *Agricultural Policy*, p. 172.

27. Saloutos and Hicks, *Agricultural Discontent*, p. 479.

28. Henry Wallace, *New Frontiers* (New York: Reynal & Hickcock, 1934); idem, *Democracy Reborn* (New York: Reynal & Hickcock, 1944).

29. John D. Black, *Parity, Parity, Parity* (Cambridge: Harvard Committee on Research in the Social Sciences, 1942), p. 54.

30. Saloutos and Hicks, *Agricultural Discontent*, p. 479.

31. Nourse et al., *Three Years*, p. 19.

32. Kirkendall, *Social Scientists*, pp. 51, 58–59.

33. Saloutos and Hicks, *Agricultural Discontent*, pp. 482–85.

34. Geoffrey S. Shepherd, *Agricultural Price Policy* (Ames: Iowa State College Press, 1947), 2nd. ed., pp. 41–42.

35. Ibid., pp. 42, 51, 73; Benedict, *Farm Policies*, p. 314.

36. [Wallace memo to FDR] n.d. [August 1937], 9 pp. in FDRL, FDR MSS., OF 258.

37. Ibid.; the preceding six paragraphs summarize Wallace's memo.

38. John H. Bankhead to FDR, October 13, 1937, in FDRL, FDR MSS., PPF 1362.

39. Memorandum by John H. Bankhead, September 10, 1934, in FDRL, FDR MSS., OF 258.

40. John H. Bankhead to FDR, November 5, 1934, in FDRL, FDR MSS., OF 258; ibid., May 30, 1935, OF 258; ibid., October 13, 1937, PPF 1362.

41. Walter F. George to Marvin H. McIntyre, March 20, 1935, in FDRL, FDR MSS., OF 258.

42. Petition, March 19, 1935, ibid.

43. O. Max Gardner to FDR, March 22, 1935, ibid.; Gardner to Marvin McIntyre, June 8, 1935, ibid.; American Cotton Association, April 17, 1935, enclosure in L. W. Robert, Jr., assistant secretary of the treasury, to Marvin McIntyre, ibid.

44. Josiah Bailey to FDR, September 2, 1935, ibid.

45. John Bankhead to FDR, September 18, 1937, ibid.

46. FDR to John Bankhead, October 1, 1937, ibid.
47. Henry Wallace to Louis Howe, August 28, 1934, ibid.
48. John Bankhead to FDR, November 5, 1934, ibid.; Henry Wallace to John Bankhead, ibid.
49. Oscar Johnston to Henry Wallace, February 19, 1934, ibid.
50. James Byrnes to FDR, September 17, 1934, ibid.; M. Tarver to Roosevelt, November 1, 1934, ibid.; John Bankhead to FDR, November 5, 1934, ibid.
51. FDR memo to Marvin McIntyre, December 17, 1934, ibid.; FDR to Henry Wallace, February 15, 1935, ibid.
52. FDR to A. Ford, August 4, 1937, ibid.; FDR to Walter George, August 6, 1937, ibid.; John Bankhead to FDR, October 13, 1937, ibid., PPF 1362; FDR to John Bankhead, October 16, 1937, ibid., PPF 1362.
53. Edwin G. Nourse, *Marketing Agreements Under the AAA* (Washington: Brookings Institution, 1935), pp. 13, 249, 315, 358.
54. Nourse et al., *Three Years,* pp. 444–46.
55. Ibid., pp. 442–43.
56. Ibid., pp. 444–45, 448, 507; Benedict, *Farm Policies,* p. 315.
57. Schickele, *Agricultural Policy,* p. 155.

X. INDUSTRIAL RECOVERY

1. Quoted in Charles L. Dearing, Paul T. Homan, Lewis Lorwin, and Leverett S. Lyon, *The ABC of the NRA* (Washington: Brookings Institution, 1934), p. 1.
2. Ibid., pp. ix, 91.
3. Henry Harriman to FDR, May 11, 1933, in FDRL, FDR MSS., OF 466.
4. Henry Harriman to FDR, May 1, 1933, ibid., OF 105.
5. Quoted in Dearing et al., *ABC of the NRA,* pp. 12–13, n. 4.
6. Ibid., p. 23.
7. For a detailed description of the act's provisions, see ibid., pp. 16–24.
8. Ibid., pp. 30–32.
9. Hugh Johnson, *The Blue Eagle from Egg to Earth* (New York: Greenwood Press, 1935), p. 164.
10. Ibid., p. 203; Frances Perkins, *The Roosevelt I Knew* (New York: Viking Press, 1946), pp. 202ff.
11. Johnson, *Blue Eagle,* pp. 163–64.

12. Quoted in Dearing et al., *ABC of the NRA,* p. 32, n. 32.
13. Leverett S. Lyon, Paul T. Homan, Lewis Lorwin, George Terborgh, Charles L. Dearing, and Leon C. Marshall, *The National Recovery Administration* (Washington: Brookings Institution, 1935), pp. 92.
14. Johnson, *Blue Eagle,* p. 242; Ellis W. Hawley, *The New Deal and the Problem of Monopoly* (Princeton: Princeton University Press, 1966), pp. 56–57.
15. Lyon et al., *National Recovery Administration,* p. 760.
16. Ibid., p. 48.
17. Ibid., pp. 30–31.
18. Hawley, *New Deal and Monopoly,* p. 61.
19. Dearing et al., *ABC of the NRA,* pp. 82–91.
20. Lyon et al., *National Recovery Administration,* pp. 465–87; Richard C. Wilcock, "Industrial Management's Policies Toward Unionism," in Milton Derber and Edwin Young, eds., *Labor and the New Deal* (Madison: University of Wisconsin Press, 1961), pp. 279–93.
21. Lyon et al., *National Recovery Administration,* pp. 768–69.
22. Hawley, *New Deal and Monopoly,* pp. 35–36.
23. "Business Bulletin," November 15, 1933, reprinted in part in *C&FC,* November 18, 1933, pp. 3558–59.
24. Ayres's analysis can be followed in the long extracts from his speeches and his "Business Bulletin" reprinted in the *C&FC,* July 16, 1933, p. 342; December 16, 1933, pp. 4249–51; June 1934, p. 4018; December 15, 1934, pp. 3707–8; December 29, 1934, p. 4026; January 5, 1935, pp. 59–60.
25. *New York Times,* June 18, 1933, p. 2.
26. Henry Harriman to FDR, November 6, 1933, in FDRL, FDR MSS., OF 446-B.
27. *New York Times,* April 29, 1933, p. 5.
28. *C&FC,* June 6, 1933, p. 3830.
29. Ibid.
30. Ibid., June 10, 1933, p. 4011; *New York Times,* June 18, 1933, p. 4.
31. *C&FC,* June 10, 1933, p. 4013.
32. Ibid., June 17, 1933, p. 4199.
33. Ibid.
34. Ibid., August 8, 1933, p. 974.
35. Ibid., November 11, 1933, p. 3419.
36. Ibid., May 5, 1933, pp. 3086–87.
37. *New York Times,* May 5, 1933, p. 1.

38. Ibid., May 4, 1933, pp. 1, 3.
39. Ibid.
40. Henry Harriman to FDR, May 6, 1933, in FDRL, FDR MSS., OF 105.
41. Lyon et al., *National Recovery Administration*, p. 29.
42. *C&FC*, May 5, 1934, p. 3032 for text of the president's message; *New York Times*, May 5, 1934, p. 1.
43. *C&FC*, May 5, 1934, p. 3031.
44. Ibid., p. 2975.
45. Henry Harriman to FDR, May 10, 1934, in FDRL, FDR MSS., OF 105.
46. *C&FC*, May 5, 1934, p. 3032.
47. Ibid., June 2, 1934, pp. 3713–14.
48. *New York Times*, May 18, 1934, pp. 1–2; June 9, 1934, p. 1.
49. *C&FC*, August 11, 1934, pp. 863–64.
50. "Statement Adopted by The Board of Directors of the Chamber of Commerce of the United States," September 21, 1934, 3 pp., in FDRL, FDR MSS., OF 105.
51. FDR to Henry Harriman, September 23, 1934, ibid.
52. Henry Harriman to FDR, September 28, 1934, ibid.
53. Stephen Early to Henry Harriman, September 28, 1934, ibid.
54. Henry Harriman to FDR, September 24, 1934, with enclosures, "Report of The Special Committee on the National Recovery Act," September 21–22, 1934, William L. Sweet, chairman, ibid.
55. Henry Harriman to FDR, December 28, 1934, gives a breakdown of the poll, ibid.
56. This account of the conference is derived from "Resolutions adopted by Conference of Business Men to Accelerate Business Recovery," 14 pp., ibid., OF 172.
57. *New York Times*, March 30, 1935, pp. 1, 4.
58. Ibid., February 2, 1935, pp. 1–2.
59. Ibid., May 1, 1935, p. 2; May 25, 1935, p. 1.
60. Ibid., March 7, 1935, pp. 1, 6; March 12, 1935, pp. 1, 11.
61. Ibid., May 1, 1935, p. 2.
62. Ibid., May 3, 1935, p. 1; May 15, 1935, p. 1; May 17, 1935, p. 35; May 25, 1935, p. 1.
63. Ibid., May 28, 1935, p. 1.
64. Ibid., February 21, 1935, p. 2.
65. Johnson, *Blue Eagle*, pp. ix–x.
66. Lyon et al., *National Recovery Administration*, pp. 745, 788, 828, 851–53, 873; see also Hawley, *New Deal and Monopoly*, who concludes

that as a recovery measure, the NRA was "one of the New Deal's greatest failures," p. 131.

67. George Harrison, June 3, 1935, in CU, GLH MSS., binder 46.

XI. THE CRISIS OF THE NEW DEAL PROGRAM

1. Raymond Moley, *After Seven Years* (New York: Harper & Brothers, 1939), pp. 184, 189; Hugh Johnson, *The Blue Eagle from Egg to Earth* (New York: Greenwood Press, 1935), pp. 156, 169; Henry Wallace, *New Frontiers* (New York: Reynal & Hickcock, 1934), pp. 29, 38; Rexford Tugwell, *The Democratic Roosevelt* (Garden City, N.Y.: Doubleday, 1957), pp. 284, 325.

2. Quoted in *C&FC*, October 27, 1934, p. 2603.

3. For a thorough study of New Deal reform, its implications and consequences, see Ellis Hawley, *The New Deal and the Problem of Monopoly* (Princeton: Princeton University Press, 1966).

4. Alvin H. Hansen, *Full Recovery or Stagnation?* (New York: W. W. Norton, 1938), p. 285.

5. The *C&FC* regularly published, in full or in part, speeches by business and banking leaders, monthly letters issued by banks and investment houses, and reports of business association meetings. For a representative sample of business criticisms of the New Deal, see statements by Guaranty Survey, February 3, 1934; National City Bank of N.Y., February 10, 1934; Mark Sullivan, February 17, 1934; Edward B. Smith & Co., February 24, 1934; National Association of Credit Men, February 24, 1934; Moody's Investors Survey, March 31, 1934; Merchants Association of N.Y., April 21, 1934; Girard Letter, April 28, 1934; partner in Kuhn, Loeb & Co., May 19, 1934; N.Y. State Bankers Association, June 16, 1934; Paine, Webber & Co., September 15, 1934; New England Council, September 29, 1934; Republic Steel Corporation, October 13, 1934.

6. Quoted in *C&FC,* June 9, 1934, p. 3880.

7. *New York Times,* quoted in *C&FC,* October 27, 1934, pp. 2616–17.

8. *C&FC,* December 1, 1934, pp. 3417–18.

9. Ibid., October 13, 1934, p. 2306.

10. Ibid., October 27, p. 2613.

11. For details on Roy Howard's "breathing spell" letter of August 26, 1935, Moley and FDR's discussion of it, and FDR's reply, see Moley, *After Seven Years,* pp. 317–18.

12. Leverett S. Lyon, Myron W. Watkins, and Victor Abramson, *Gov-*

ernment and Economic Life (Washington: Brookings Institution, 1939) 1:488.

13. John M. Blum, *From the Morgenthau Diaries* (Boston: Houghton Mifflin, 1959) 1:126.
14. Ibid., p. 387.
15. In FDRL, HM MSS., September 6, 1935, box 10, p. 9.
16. Ibid., December 21, 1935, box 14, p. 177.
17. Ibid., February 2, 1936, box 17, pp. 1–3.
18. Ibid., February 6, 1936, box 17, p. 98; February 5, 1936, box 17, p. 83.
19. Ibid., February 4, 1936, pp. 27–37; February 6, 1936, pp. 100, 109–13, in box 17.
20. Lester V. Chandler, *American Monetary Policy, 1928–1941* (New York: Harper & Row, 1971), pp. 297, 310.
21. Ibid., p. 314.
22. Ibid., p. 307.
23. Ibid., pp. 291–95.
24. Kenneth D. Roose, *The Economics of Recession and Revival, An Interpretation of 1937–38* (New Haven: Yale University Press, 1954), p. 22.
25. Ibid., p. 55.
26. Merriam-Henderson report, "Emerging Industro-Governmental Problems," November 9, 1937, 37 pp., in FDRL, FDR MSS., OF 444C. This was drawn up at the president's request in July 1937.
27. Ibid. See also Larry Selzer, memorandum to Henry Morgenthau, December 30, 1938, in FDRL, HM MSS., box 158, pp. 189–91, under the title, "Limitations upon theory that the maintenance of a high level of deficit spending is essential to the continuance of business recovery." For a recent assessment of deficit spending as a recovery policy during the New Deal, see Lester V. Chandler, *America's Greatest Depression* (New York: Harper & Row, 1970), pp. 133, 135, 244.
28. Leon Henderson, memorandum, "What caused the slump?" November 13, 1937, 6 pp., in FDRL, FDR MSS., OF 444C.
29. Leon Henderson to Harry Hopkins, June 9, 1938, 7 pp., in FDRL, FDR MSS., OF 444C.
30. Conversation between Walter W. Stewart and George Harrison, April 27, 1937, in CU, GLH MSS., binder 47.
31. The complete correspondence, with accompanying staff memoranda, is located in CU, GLH MSS., box 4.
32. George Harrison to Marriner Eccles, November 3, 1937, 5 pp.,

with memorandum by John H. Williams, same date, "Comments on the Present Recession," 9 pp., in CU, GLH MSS., box 4.

33. Marriner Eccles to George Harrison, November 15, 1937, ibid.
34. George Harrison to Marriner Eccles, November 17, 1937, ibid.
35. Robert E. Sherwood, *Roosevelt and Hopkins* (New York: Bantam, 1950) 1:65.
36. Speech printed in FDRL, HM MSS., box 119.
37. Ibid., George Harrison to Marriner Eccles, May 20, 1938, in CU, GLH MSS., box 4.
38. George Harrison to Marriner Eccles, May 20, 1938, in CU, GLH MSS., box 4.
39. Marriner Eccles to George Harrison, May 26, 1948, ibid.
40. George Harrison to Henry Morgenthau, March 23, 1939, ibid., box 12.
41. Jacob Viner's letter of resignation, April 14, 1938, in FDRL, HM MSS., box 121.
42. Henry Morgenthau to FDR, November 4, 1937, ibid., box 94, p. 48.
43. Ibid., p. 52.
44. Ibid.
45. Ibid., pp. 152–54.
46. Ibid., November 5, Box 94, pp. 128–29.
47. Wayne Taylor to Henry Morgenthau, April 6, 1938, box 118, p. 182; George Haas to Henry Morgenthau, April 8, 1938, pp. 225–29, ibid.
48. Ibid., April 11, 1938, box 118, pp. 282–84.
49. Ibid., Eccles's Recovery Plan, April 27, 1938, box 121, pp. 149ff.; October 11, 1938, box 145, pp. 239–43; December 19, 1938, box 157, p. 40; December 30, 1939, box 158, p. 168; June 5, 1939, box 194, p. 63.
50. Ibid., George Haas to Henry Morgenthau, January 1, 1939, box 160, p. 1.
51. Ibid., "For the Record," box 160, p. 84.
52. Ibid., "Meeting of Fiscal and Monetary Advisory Board," December 19, 1938, box 157, pp. 17–18; Report of the Division of Monetary Research, May 25, 1939, box 192, pp. 14–18.
53. Ibid., June 6, 1939, box 194, pp. 88, 238.
54. John M. Keynes, *Atlantic* 149 (May 1932): 525.

XII. THE POLITICAL ACHIEVEMENTS OF FDR

1. The assessment of American political isolationism as rampant is found in William L. Langer and S. Everett Gleason, *The Challenge to Isolation* (New York: Harper & Brothers, 1952) 1:13. Roosevelt abandoned his support for American membership in the League of Nations during the 1932 campaign, stating that the existing League was no longer Wilson's League; on Roosevelt and the neutrality legislation, see Robert Divine, *The Reluctant Belligerent* (New York: Wiley, 1965), pp. 22ff.

2. Lester V. Chandler, *America's Greatest Depression, 1929–1941* (New York: Harper & Row, 1970), pp. 1, 11. For a comparative analysis of the varied progress in achieving recovery by different nations, see Charles P. Kindleberger, *The World in Depression, 1929–1939* (Berkeley: University of California Press, 1973), pp. 232ff.

3. Lord Acton, *Essays on Freedom and Power* (New York: Meridian Books, 1957), pp. 41, 48.

4. See Chapter Eleven, note 54.

5. According to Lester Chandler, "Although real GNP rose and remained above its low level of 1933, it did not again reach its 1929 level until 1937, and then it fell in 1938. . . . Only in 1939 and later years did it remain above the level achieved in 1929. Real output remained far below its potential levels until 1941, and even in that year it was at least 8 percent below its potential." See Chandler, *America's Greatest Depression*, pp. 128–29.

6. For an exposition of this concept, see James M. Burns, *Roosevelt: The Lion and the Fox* (New York: Harcourt, Brace & World, 1956), ch. 14.

7. John Higham, "The Cult of the 'American Consensus': Homogenizing Our History," *Commentary*, February 1959, reprinted in Richard M. Abrams and Lawrence W. Levine, *The Shaping of Twentieth Century America* (Boston: Little, Brown, 1971), 2nd ed., pp. 699–709.

8. Herbert Agar, *The Price of Union* (Boston: Houghton Mifflin, 1950), p. xiv.

9. On the development of extravagant expectations among Americans, particularly in the 1960s and 1970s, see Henry Fairlie, *The Kennedy Promise: The Politics of Expectation* (Garden City, N.Y.: Doubleday, 1973); and Godfrey Hodgson, *America in Our Time* (Garden City, N.Y.: Doubleday, 1976). For an example of high expectation projected back to Roosevelt and the New Deal, see Howard Zinn, ed., Introduction, *New Deal Thought* (Indianapolis: Bobbs-Merrill, 1966), pp. xvi–xvii.

Index